MW00772557

BONE
by
BONE

a memoir of trauma and healing

Geralyn S. Ritter

Bone by Bone
A Memoir of Trauma and Healing
www.bonebybonebook.com

Copyright © 2022 by Geralyn S. Ritter

Published by The Core Media Group, Inc., www.thecoremediagroup.com.
The authors are represented by WordServe Literary Group, Ltd., www.wordserveliterary.com.

Cover & Interior Design: Nadia Guy

ISBN 978-1-950465-55-2

Scriptures are taken from the Holy Bible, New International Version®, NIV®. Copyright © 1973, 1978, 1984, 2011 by Biblica, Inc.™ Used by permission of Zondervan. All rights reserved worldwide. www.zondervan.com The "NIV" and "New International Version" are trademarks registered in the United States Patent and Trademark Office by Biblica, Inc.™

Printed in the United States of America.

Contents

For my family.
I am forever grateful.

Prologue

"I'm okay?" These were the first words I tried to whisper when I woke up in the hospital—a statement posed as a question. In the years that followed, those uncertain words continued to ring in my mind: *I'm okay?* I had endured a dozen surgeries and counting; I had graduated from a hospital gurney to a wheelchair to a walker to crutches to standing on my own two feet; and I had weaned myself from the heaviest pain medications and pulled out of my depression, only to have new setbacks steal my progress. I'm okay. Period. Or question mark?

I was a passenger on Amtrak 188 on May 12, 2015, the day that train derailed outside Philadelphia in a massive accident that killed eight passengers and wounded more than 150. My chance of survival was slim. I was thrown from the train at such speed that my abdominal organs were rammed up into my chest, rupturing my diaphragm. Nearly all the ribs on my left side were crushed, my pelvis was broken in half, and multiple vertebrae in my neck and back were fractured. An object had penetrated my left hip, crushing my hip bone, and the wound was open and dirty. My spleen was destroyed, intestines badly lacerated, bladder ruptured, and my lungs collapsed. Later, my orthopedic surgeon said if someone had told him about a patient coming to the ER with my injuries, his next question would have been, "When did they die?" Given the force my body must have absorbed to produce those injuries, the doctors were stunned I was not paralyzed and did not sustain a major brain injury. Nearly every system in my body was severely affected, but over the course of the next few years, I recovered.

I recovered, but I'll never be the same. My body is different, and I am different. Physically and emotionally, I have scars that won't go away. But I *am* okay.

From the moment I returned to consciousness and found myself in the ICU, I had no idea what to expect—I had no idea what the process of healing would involve. Each time I was faced with a new hurdle or setback, I wished someone could have warned me and that I'd been better prepared.

At first, I assumed my bones would mend in a few weeks and I'd be back to normal with an incredible story to tell about how I'd spent my summer. As my pain and recovery wore on month after month, and my expectations were revealed to be wildly unrealistic, I searched for a book to help me understand the aftermath of what doctors call "polytrauma" and make sense of what I was experiencing. Most of the resources I found were dry accounts by doctors and psychiatrists. They didn't tell me what it was actually like to try to get my life back. They didn't describe how it felt to wake up every morning frozen in pain or to endure the suspicious glance of a pharmacist when I went to pick up my fentanyl prescription. They didn't help me understand why my husband, Jonathan, and I were having the worst fights of our marriage. Albert Schweitzer, a famous German physician and philosopher, writes of "the brotherhood of those who bear the marks of pain." I needed to connect to members of that brotherhood—people who had been there—who could help me deal with the present and the path ahead.

Recovery was like hiking a steep and tortuous mountain path, with little guidance on the distance to the top—a lot of effort for minor progress, a lot of doubts about the route chosen, but occasionally, a glimpse of a wondrous view over a valley that helps bring perspective. There were tremendously low moments, but the highs were equally high. I had so many laughs and intensely meaningful conversations with family and friends over those two years, and I have learned much about life I wouldn't have learned otherwise.

To this day, I am frequently saddened by the senselessness of the accident. The names and faces of my fellow passengers who lost their lives are burned into my memory, and I have wept with some of their families. Against this background, it feels heartless to suggest that any kind of silver lining came as a bonus with survival. But it would also be wrong to avoid drawing something positive from the years of pain. There is a Tibetan saying: "Wisdom is like rainwater—both gather in the low places."[1] Psychiatrists call the process "post-traumatic growth." I am a stronger person after what I've been through. The experience has made me more aware of the joy in my life and the freedom and power to frame my own perspective.

During my recovery, I tried to learn as much as I could about how the body reacts to trauma and pain. Developing this understanding helped me control the self-loathing and hopelessness I felt when I simply couldn't get out of bed in the mornings, and it helped me better understand the interdependence of the body and mind. Physical injury to the body can have a profound biochemical effect on our psychological well-being. Conversely, our state of mind can affect sensations of pain and the pace of physical recovery. Understanding this connection gave me back at least some sense of control over a body that I simultaneously hated and revered.

Trauma is a whole-body experience, regardless of which bones are broken. Recovery is similarly all-encompassing. One trauma expert describes three ways of dealing with trauma: top-down, bottom-up, and medication.[2] I used them all. Some of the tools that helped me, I never thought I'd consider—like yoga and breathing exercises. Others came easily, like making jokes and drinking wine with friends.

In the years since the accident, I've met a number of other "miraculous" trauma survivors. Everyone's journey is different, but we all now identify as people with a "before" and an "after" in our lives. There is power in sharing our stories. My hope in writing this book is to offer a resource for fellow survivors, their caregivers, and anyone else who wants to understand the recovery experience and hear the story of someone who has been there—healing moment by moment, bone by bone.

One

I hate that I don't remember. It is one of the most significant moments of my life, profoundly affecting my family and friends, yet I must rely on newspapers and other people's stories. I hate that I don't know who found me and can't thank them for saving my life. People invariably tell me it's probably better that way, but I'm not sure. One thing I know for certain, though, is that life can change in an instant—one perfectly ordinary instant on a perfectly ordinary day.

On the night of May 12, 2015, I rushed to 30th Street Station in Philadelphia. It was close to 9:00 p.m., and I was anxious that I might miss my train home. When I entered the main concourse, the station was nearly empty, making the sprawling marble floor seem even more expansive than usual. I hitched my briefcase over my shoulder and clutched my purse, racing toward my track. Within a few feet of it, I slowed my pace. I could see the long, winding line of passengers still waiting to board. I breathed a sigh of relief. I took my place in line and sensed someone joining behind me. I glanced back to see a confident-looking professional woman with shoulder-length dark, wavy hair.

My ticket was for the first car, business class. As I made my way onto the dimly lit train, I noticed it was rather empty. There were only a dozen or so other passengers spread throughout the car, including the dark-haired woman who took a seat near the back. I chose a pair of empty seats and slid my briefcase into the overhead rack. I settled in by the aisle since I'd be getting off at the first stop. I was heading home to New Jersey, where Jonathan and our three sons, Austin, Bradley, and Steven, were waiting for me. I traced the familiar route in my mind. Just a half-hour train ride to Trenton and then a forty-five-minute car ride home.

It had been a long day. When I got up at 4:30 that morning, I put on one of my favorite spring suits—light beige with clean lines. A zipper that went all the way up the back of the skirt made it more stylish than my usual conservative attire. I had caught the 6:30 a.m. train to Washington, DC, where I'd attended a board meeting of the US Global Leadership Coalition, a group of businesses and nonprofits that support the US government's humanitarian programs around the world.

I loved this side of my job. I had been at Merck for seven years, primarily focusing on public policy, social responsibility, and charitable giving. My interest in politics and public policy had been sparked in college—so much was at stake, and shaping government policy seemed like one of the best ways to have a positive impact on the world. Early in my career, I had been an international trade lawyer working for the White House. I felt that the work we were doing to open new markets for US companies and improve access to American products for other countries really mattered in terms of making people's lives better. Now at Merck, I once again felt that the health-care discoveries we were bringing to patients around the world truly made a difference.

The other plus was that my work allowed me (my husband would say "required" me) to travel often. A typical year would have me on the road every few weeks, and the destination was just as likely to be Uganda, India, or Ethiopia as the major capitals of Tokyo, Brussels, London, or Beijing. When giving career-day talks for my sons' elementary school classes, I would play a geography game with the kids: whoever could name a country where I had *not* been would win a prize.

After the board meeting in Washington, I'd taken the train to Philadelphia. That evening, I spoke on a panel at a Duke University alumni forum for women in leadership. We talked about the central question that each of our careers was designed to answer. The question that had guided my work was, "How can I have the biggest positive impact?" I told the women assembled about one of my favorite projects: Merck for Mothers. I had led the creation of this $500 million program, which sought to make childbirth safer for women around the world. After the panel discussion, I stayed to chat with the other alums. I always find it interesting to hear other women's insights on the defining choices they made in their careers.

As the train left the platform in Philadelphia, I pulled out my phone. I read a text Jonathan had sent earlier from our youngest son's baseball game: "Stevie led off the game with a legitimate base hit."

"Awesome!" I wrote back. Steven was eight, and let's just say baseball didn't come naturally for him. I wanted to congratulate him with a big hug and kiss when I got home, but I was sure he would already be fast asleep. I hoped I'd be home in time to say good night to my older sons—Brad who was twelve, and Austin, who was fifteen. Jonathan got to spend more time with the kids than I did since he'd left his job as a corporate lawyer a few years earlier to start his own business from home.

I texted Jonathan my ETA: 10:25 p.m.

"See you then!" he replied. I put my phone in my purse and got up to grab something to read from my briefcase.

It was then that I noticed the train seemed to be moving faster than usual. For a fleeting moment, I was pleased. *Maybe we'll arrive early.* Those thirty minutes to my stop always seemed to take forever. The train began to sway, and I grew annoyed because I couldn't let go of the luggage rack to reach into my briefcase. The rocking got more violent; now I was clutching the rail with both hands to keep from falling. Then the train tilted. I braced myself, both arms straining to hold onto the bar above my head. "What the—?" I yelled. I remember the overwhelming force pulling my body. I remember my confusion, trying to make sense of it. *The whole train can't actually be tipping over.* In a flash, I realized it was true—we were crashing. The sound of my own scream is the last thing I remember.

Instead of slowing down at Frankford Junction, the sharpest curve on the Northeast Corridor, the engineer had sped up. It was later revealed that he was going more than twice the speed limit—106 miles per hour—on a curve designed for a maximum of 50 mph. When the engineer realized his mistake, he pulled the emergency brake. It was too late. Within seconds, the train broke free from the rails.

I don't recall the feeling of the train hitting the ground sideways, twisting, splitting open, and filling with rocks and clouds of dirt. I don't recall being thrown from the train as the car broke apart.

Other passengers later described the same sensation of the train moving too fast around the curve. Assistant conductor Thomas O'Brien was working in the back of the train and put it simply: "Somewhere between Philly and Trenton, everything was fine—until it wasn't... There was, like, two seconds of shake and two major impacts...then we hit, and I went flying."[3] A man named Daniel Armyn, who was also seated in car one, said he grabbed his laptop and paperwork as they slid to the right. Then the car filled with angry, metallic screeching, and everything was shaking uncontrollably. He knew the train was going off the rails.[4]

At first, Michael Walsh had the uncomfortable feeling of being on a roller coaster—the force of speeding around the curve pressing him toward the windows. The train was turning so far out, he knew it was going to fall. As we hit the ground, Michael saw the front of the car bucking up and down, like it was tumbling down a staircase. Within seconds, he made the decision to get away from the window—he wanted to be in the aisle. He tried to rise and, as the car bucked upward, he was pushed to standing. His quick instinct may have saved his life. The fact that I was standing in the aisle with my hands above my head during the crash might have been what saved me as well. As the trailing cars plowed into car one, Michael went flying forward. In the back of the train, first, objects flew from the left side of the train to the right—laptops, purses, suitcases, shoes—followed by people being tossed through the air. Janna D'Ambrisi was thrown against the woman who was seated next to her, by the window. As the train tipped further, other passengers from across the aisle fell on top of them, one landing in the luggage rack above their heads.[5]

Eli Kulp, a thirty-seven-year-old chef whose wife and toddler were waiting at home, was thrown headfirst into the luggage rack. Buried beneath suitcases when the train came to a halt, he realized he couldn't move. His single injury was simple, cruel, and devastating. He'd broken his C7 vertebra and was instantly paralyzed from the chest down.[6]

In the moments after the crash, passengers in car three who were able climbed out the emergency windows, which were now above them. One woman who made her way out the window was Seyward Darby, an editor at *Foreign Policy* magazine who was getting married the following month. She sustained minor injuries, while the twenty-year-old seated beside her, a naval midshipman in his dress whites named Justin Zemser, was thrown from the train and killed.[7]

One of the first responders, James Morace, a sergeant from the highway patrol, spoke to reporters about the way his group was briefed before arriving at the scene. They were told that if they'd been in combat before, what they would see might be familiar. Otherwise, they were instructed to steady themselves.[8] The most prevalent word used to describe the accident, by first responders and passengers alike, was "chaos."

Back in car seven, assistant conductor O'Brien pulled himself out from under the seat back he had crashed into and later described the scene to investigators:

> As soon as I got up, I'm looking around and there's immediately more blood than made sense for me to be able to see so fast. I just thought, 'How are we all bleeding so much already?' And I'm looking at the walls and I'm looking at the floor and there's just blood and there's stuff everywhere. The seats are all either disconnected and off or rotated out of place. And now people are like yelling about being trapped because they're pinned with these seats. People are screaming that they think that the train's on fire…

When Michael Walsh came to, he knew he was lying on his back in a confined place—an overhead bin? The lavatory? A doorway? It seemed strangely quiet. A uniformed police officer found him.

"Are you in pain?" the officer asked.

"No," Michael replied.

The officer's expression became more intense, and he asked about Michael's shoulder, chest, and leg. "No," Michael repeated.

Placing a hand on Michael's shoulder, the officer tried to comfort him: "You're going to be okay."

Michael's heart sank. He had heard this line before—as a retired New York City policeman, he'd uttered it himself many times as he'd watched injured victims slip away. He knew what it meant. The only response he could think of was, "I don't want to die." That's when he blacked out. The policeman put a tourniquet on his leg before loading him and an injured woman into the back of a police wagon and rushing them to Temple Hospital.

Blair Berman, a woman in her mid-twenties, had moved up to the first car from farther back in the train. During the accident, she was knocked unconscious. Blair woke up in the woods with other passengers collapsed on top of her legs. She stood up, barefoot, and leaned against a tree, screaming in terror. Blair saw a man talking on a cell phone and asked to use it. "No," he refused. It turned out he was Brandon Bostian, the train engineer. She badgered him until he gave in, and she called her father.[9]

Brandon Bostian walked away from the accident with a concussion and says he doesn't remember why he pushed the throttle to speed up, when he should have been slowing down. The National Transportation Safety Board called it a "loss of situational awareness."[10] I think most people would call it distracted driving (of a 1,000-ton passenger train). It seems he got confused and thought he was on the straightaway after the curve. He may have been distracted by radio reports that were coming in of an emergency with another train. But the bottom line is that the deadliest crash in the Northeast Corridor since 1987 was a matter of human error.[11] Worst of all, it was completely preventable.

A technology called Positive Train Control (PTC) has been around for decades. It automatically slows a train that is moving too fast. Amtrak had installed PTC along most of the Northeast Corridor, but not at Frankford Junction, the sharpest curve on the route.[12]

In photographs of the aftermath, viewing the train from a great distance above, it is striking how haphazardly the cars are scattered. Car five, near the end, is perpendicular to the track. Cars two, three, and four are turned on their sides in an arc. The locomotive is many yards away, spun around, but still upright. Car one, where I was sitting, is a pile of crumpled metal surrounded by scattered debris and no longer resembles a section of train. I don't know where I was found or who rescued me. From what I can tell, I was among the first to be saved.[13]

Two

It was around 9:30 p.m., and Jonathan was sitting in his usual chair in the corner of the living room, looking at his phone. He sent a few texts and then began to scroll through the news. He was scanning the headlines absently when a CNN news alert popped up on his screen: "Amtrak 188 Derailed in Philadelphia."

Jonathan's first thought was, *That's Geralyn's train*. He had no idea of my train number, but a gut feeling told him something was very wrong. The news report was brief—there wasn't much information available. Jonathan called my cell. As the phone rang, he tried to reassure himself. Maybe the accident wasn't serious. Maybe it wasn't my train. Most likely, I'd be stuck in a frustrating delay. Maybe he'd have to come pick me up.

Meanwhile, my ringing phone, along with all my identification, was inside my purse, buried in the wreckage. I was lying on the ground unconscious, barely alive, nameless, and unknown.

When my voicemail picked up, Jonathan tried calling again. Nothing. He continued to weigh the possibilities—maybe I was on a different train and couldn't hear the phone ring beneath the hum of the engine. Maybe I would walk through the front door in the next hour and everything would be fine.

Jonathan decided to contact my administrative assistant, Lisa. She would know what train I'd taken. He sent a terse email: "Was Geralyn on that train?"

Jonathan stared at the phone intensely. He needed to know where I was, and he needed to know immediately. He sent a desperate text to my phone: "Are you all right?!!" And another: "Please call me." Then he thought to check Find My iPhone, an application that tracks the location of your phone when it's lost or stolen. An image appeared. It was an icon of my phone over an aerial photo from Google Earth. The photo showed train tracks. Jonathan stared at the image, hit refresh, waited for the location to change. The image didn't budge. A phone icon with an arrow pointed to a spot about twenty feet off the track.

That's when Austin, our fifteen-year-old, arrived home. "Hey, Dad, Duke game, fifteen minutes." Austin started toward the basement. Jonathan didn't answer. He stayed hunched over the phone, anxiously running his fingers through his dark salt-and-pepper hair. Austin stopped at the top of the steps and frowned. "You hear me?"

Jonathan clicked refresh a few more times, but the location of the phone icon didn't change. Panic seized him. Staring at the image of the tracks, new possibilities started to race through his mind. He tried to calm himself. He still didn't know whether the accident was serious. Maybe no one was hurt. Maybe I'd only been separated from my phone. But he knew what he had to do next.

In his state of shock, he didn't pause to think about what to tell Austin or how to break the news gently. "Train crashed in Philly. I think Mom is on it. Stay here—you're in charge." Jonathan called Mercia, the boys' nanny who had been caring for them for the past six years. Mercia is family to us. Deeply spiritual and a native of the tiny Caribbean island of Tobago, she's a lay pastor and was studying at a local seminary at the time. When Jonathan called, Mercia was in the middle of writing a paper due at midnight. She slapped the laptop computer closed, grabbed her purse, and ran to her car, rushing to make the ten-minute drive to our house.

Jonathan snatched his car keys. "Mercia is on her way," he said, moving quickly. Austin stood frozen in the empty living room. Goose bumps raised on his skin as if the temperature had suddenly dropped ten degrees. His heart was racing. He shook himself and, with a look of determination, ran up to his bedroom to get his laptop.

Upstairs, Brad, our twelve-year-old, had just turned on the shower. While the water warmed up, he had taken his phone and sat perched on the edge of the bed, watching YouTube videos. He heard the thumping of Austin running up the stairs, and then his brother burst into the room, hunting frantically for his computer.

"Did you hear what happened?" Austin shouted. He was picking things up and throwing them down, searching the room without really looking.

"No, what?" Brad asked.

Austin stopped what he was doing and looked at Brad. "Mom's train crashed," he said.

"No," Brad said, studying his brother's face. Austin's eyes were serious behind his glasses, but he had to be kidding. It couldn't be true. "That's not possible," Brad murmured. Brad opened his mouth to say something else, but no words came.

"Get off YouTube for two fucking seconds!" Austin exploded.

"No, I…" Brad protested.

Austin snatched the phone out of his hands. "I'll show you," he said, Googling "Amtrak crash." The CNN article came up first. The boys scanned the article. When they reached the end, they sat in silence, staring blankly at the screen. Austin picked up his phone. "I'm going to try calling Mom." He listened to the phone ring until my voicemail picked up.

"Call again," Brad said. Austin called five more times.

They checked the news again. One article linked to a list of local hospitals where injured passengers were being taken. They decided to start making calls. Brad looked up the hospital phone numbers, and Austin dialed. He asked about patients who had been in the train accident. "I'm looking for my mom. Her name is Geralyn Ritter."

When our neighbor, Glenn, heard the doorbell ring at 9:50 p.m., he assumed it was the guy who mowed his lawn. The landscaper tended to show up late at night to collect his check. Glenn opened the door with a huff. He was surprised when Jonathan walked inside, his face buried in his phone. Jonathan didn't say hello or even look up. He started walking in circles around the rug in the foyer.

"There's been a train accident," he said, still staring at the phone. Glenn, who had been watching the news, knew instantly. "I found her phone nearby," Jonathan said, "and I've been pinging it, but she won't pick up." Jonathan's face was uncharacteristically drained of color, and he blinked furiously. He continued to circle around the foyer as he muttered, "I should be there. I need to get there. I just need to get there."

"Let me take you. You're not going to make it out of the neighborhood," Glenn said.

"You'll go with me?" Jonathan asked, finally pausing to look at Glenn.

"I'm driving," Glenn said. "Let's go."

Glenn ran upstairs to tell his wife, Tracy, he was leaving. Tracy is one of my closest friends; we've known each other for years. When Glenn mentioned the accident, she gasped, her eyes opened wide. Glenn couldn't waste time offering comforting words. "I have no idea when I'll be back," he said. He gave her a quick kiss and ran downstairs.

Glenn was probably the best person to help Jonathan in his search. He knows every hospital in Philadelphia because he works with surgeons for a living. Glenn later said he felt a strange sense of certainty that night—somehow, he knew they would find me.

Meanwhile, my assistant, Lisa, had read Jonathan's email: "Was Geralyn on that train?" She was at her mother's house. They turned on the news and saw the live coverage of the accident. There were a few shots of people being loaded onto buses. On impulse, Lisa scanned the screen for a glimpse of me. The reporter said the passengers were being bused to shelters. When Lisa called Jonathan, he told her he was on his way to Philly.

Mercia arrived while Austin and Brad were making calls. She peeked into Steven's room. Jonathan had put our youngest to bed before the news of the accident came, and Steven was still fast asleep on his bottom bunk, clutching his favorite stuffed tiger, his blond hair peeking out of the twisted covers. She stepped inside Brad's doorway. He looked at her with pleading eyes and asked, "Are they going to find her?" His voice broke as he uttered the question and tears welled up in his eyes.

Austin pushed him away. "You're not helping!" So far, their search had been fruitless—the hospitals didn't have any information.

"Stop," Mercia told Austin. She hugged Brad, and he began to sob. "Let's go pray," she said, in her warm, soothing island accent. Then she added, "Your mom is going to be okay."

"How do you know?" Brad asked.

"I already prayed," she reassured him.

"When? How did you know?"

"I don't know if it was a premonition," she said. She explained that the night before, she couldn't sleep. She was lying in bed at 2:00 a.m., and something didn't feel right. She asked herself if it was something with the boys. Then she began to pray for all of us. She prayed until 5:00 a.m., when I was starting my day.

Glenn barreled down the highway with Jonathan in the passenger seat. He was right—Jonathan was in no condition to drive. He was in such a state of shock that he had only liminal awareness of what was going on around him. He noticed a Porsche maneuver between cars and speed past them. "Glenn, can you pick up the damn pace?" he snapped.

"I'm going eighty," Glenn replied. "That guy has got to be going a hundred and five." They laughed nervously, the tension pushing them toward hysterics.

Austin texted again, asking if there were any updates. The hospitals he and Brad had called didn't have anyone by the name of Geralyn Ritter, and they couldn't give out details about unidentified patients over the phone. Jonathan texted back, saying he hadn't heard anything yet, but they were on their way. "Try to get some sleep," he wrote. "I love you."

"I'm not going to bed," Austin replied. "Call me as soon as you hear anything."

Unsure of where to go when they arrived, Jonathan dialed the Philly police. The police said a family assistance center had been set up near the scene of the accident. While Jonathan was on the phone, another string of texts came in from Austin, each more desperate than the last. The latest news reports did not look good.

"Dad, there are at least five dead…"

"Dad, hurry up."

"Six."

"Do something."

"Find Mom."

Jonathan called back and tried to reassure Austin. He said he was figuring out where to go when he got to Philadelphia, but it might take an hour and a half to get there. He didn't know what else to say. Austin told him he didn't care if he was being annoying; he wanted his dad to keep him updated. While they were on the phone, Jonathan held it together, but as soon as he hung up, he broke down. He sobbed as he pictured his kids at home, monitoring the increasingly grim news reports and waiting to find out what happened to their mother.

"We're going to find her," Glenn said. Jonathan gathered himself and refocused on the task.

Jonathan received a text from Lisa, who was also hoping for an update. She was conducting her own search. She had notified Merck security, and they had contacted my boss. Then she started calling hospitals as well. Each hospital said that patients were still arriving, so she should continue to call. Lisa had scribbled the list of hospitals on the back of a tissue box. She went down her list, checking names off after each call, and when she reached the bottom of the list, she started at the top again. Lisa stayed up all night trying to track me down.

Jonathan and Glenn stepped from the car into a maze of police cruisers, ambulances, and fire trucks. Red and blue lights flashed across faces in the crowd; glaring searchlights from the helicopters circling overhead swept across the pavement. The air was thick with a sickening stench—the smell of burning metal and electricity. Glenn recognized the odor—the same one hung over Ground Zero in the days after 9/11. It smelled like tragedy.

The train wasn't visible from where they stood. It was blocks away, behind the blockade of caution tape and orange cones the police had set up. Jonathan and Glenn wandered through the chaos for twenty minutes, trying to find the family assistance center. They walked through a police barricade. "Walk like you belong here," one told the other. Jonathan saw a group of firefighters. It had been only two hours since the accident, but already the first responders were breathing heavily, their faces smudged with dirt and gleaming with sweat.

The men continued walking toward another police barrier fifteen yards away. Behind it, the mayor was giving a press conference. A police officer stopped them. "I'm looking for my wife," Jonathan explained. "She was on the train."

"You're in the wrong place," the cop said. He directed them to a church six blocks in the opposite direction. Putting their heads down, Jonathan and Glenn strode away. After a while, they noticed that the distance between the blocks was random. One block might be 400 feet and the next a quarter mile. Six blocks didn't sound far, but by the time they reached the other church, they felt like they had been walking for an hour.

At the police barricade around the church, the officer told them, "You want Saint Mark's Church. It's six blocks the other way."

Jonathan had no choice but to turn around. By now they were near their car, so they drove back the way they came.

Inside, the quiet, dim church was a stark contrast. The lone policeman by the door said that everyone who was released from the hospital would be coming to that church. Glenn spoke to a man dressed head to toe in Pittsburgh Pirates gear: hat, sweatshirt, and sweatpants. He was a parishioner who lived in the neighborhood. He said he didn't know anything, but he offered what he had. "If you're hungry, I can make you a peanut-butter-and-jelly sandwich. If you need a shower, you can use the one in my apartment."

Groups of people sat in the pews and the men joined them. As they bowed their heads to pray, Jonathan and Glenn noticed the others talking and laughing, as if they had no idea how serious the situation was. Later, they realized these were uninjured passengers who had walked there after climbing out of the derailed train. The church had been opened to assist them as they figured out how to make their way home.

After forty-five minutes, workers from NTSB (the National Transportation Safety Board) arrived. When Jonathan asked about passengers who were supposed to be sent there from the hospital, a worker said, "They're not coming here" and directed them to an elementary school in the direction they had just come. By now it was after 1:00 a.m.

After walking another mile up Frankford Avenue, they reached John Webster Elementary School, where lines of people were exiting idling buses—a man with his arm in a sling, a woman with a blood-soaked bandage wrapped around her head, another wearing a neck brace. Jonathan scanned their faces, searching for mine, before entering the school.

With all the wounded people gathered under the harsh fluorescent light of the cafeteria, the place looked like bedlam. Jonathan wondered who was in charge. Who was making sure people were safe and accounted for?

Again, he asked for a list of the people who had arrived from the hospital. Someone handed him a pile of papers, and he scanned the names—no Geralyn Ritter. Jonathan and Glenn waited among the crowd, praying I would show up on the next bus. It was too much, seeing the dozens of people bandaged, bleeding, and bruised, covered in dirt and soot, scared and tearful.

Jonathan stared down at his feet as his body started shivering. Glenn grabbed hold of him. Jonathan was shaking so hard he thought was going to pass out. Glenn helped him to the floor, where Jonathan rested his head between bent knees. "It's okay, just breathe," Glenn whispered.

When the room stopped spinning, Jonathan stood slowly and walked into a dim hallway. A plastic chair had been left there, beside a case of dusty trophies. Jonathan sat down, put his head in his hands, and started to cry.

"I don't think she made it," Jonathan whispered. It was after 2:00 a.m. He should have gotten a call by now.

Glenn rattled the keys in his pocket. "We're spinning our wheels here. I'll get the car, and we'll go to every hospital in order. If we have to drive to all the hospitals in Philadelphia and Delaware, we're going to do it." Austin and Lisa had been calling hospitals, but there was only so much they could do over the phone. You had to be there in person to identify a patient.

"Okay," Jonathan murmured. Up until this point, Jonathan had pushed through, not letting his mind slip into dark thoughts. He'd held open the hope that any minute, his cell phone would ring and I'd be on the other end, complaining about losing my purse. Now, sitting alone in the hallway of a random school after hours of wandering from one false lead to another, Jonathan realized I was either hurt—too hurt to borrow a phone or tell anyone my name—or I was gone. *Please, just let her be hurt*, he prayed. *God, let her be hurt.* A man wearing a Red Cross uniform came over and crouched down on the linoleum floor beside Jonathan. Without saying a word, he put his hand on Jonathan's knee, offering silent reassurance.

When Glenn got to Frankford Avenue, a cop wouldn't let him go back the way he came. He had to walk a longer route that took him past the wreckage. Glenn could see the last cars of the train, tipped on their sides, and a row of electrical poles toppled on the ground, the wires snapped and tangled. The same metallic, burning smell still hung in the air.

It took Glenn forty-five minutes to return to the school. As soon as Jonathan got in the car, he plugged his phone into the charger. He was ready to keep looking. He searched online for a portrait of me, knowing professional photos had been posted for speaking engagements. He wanted a clear, recognizable picture to show hospital staff.

At home, Austin was lying in bed, wide awake, checking his phone every few minutes, waiting for a text from his dad. Mercia had stayed with Brad, holding him while he cried and praying with him until he fell asleep around 2:00. Luckily, Steven was still sleeping deeply. Now it was after 4:00 a.m., and she was holding vigil, waiting for news from Jonathan.

At Frankford Aria, the closest hospital, staff told Jonathan all their patients had been identified. At the next two hospitals, they were in and out in ten minutes.

As Glenn drove down the deserted streets, he started treating the red lights like stop signs, pausing to check whether anyone was coming and then rolling through the intersections. The red-light cameras caught him, and that's how a stack of traffic tickets ended up in his mailbox. As Jonathan and Glenn made their way to Temple Hospital, they passed a basketball court. Twenty-five men were playing a full-court game at 4:00 in the morning. It was like a strange dreamscape. "Can you believe this shit?" Jonathan said. "Who plays basketball in the middle of the night?"

"Those dudes." Glenn said with a grin.

At Temple, a two-block perimeter had been cordoned off to allow ambulances to get in and out quickly, so Glenn parked on the street, and they walked the rest of the way. In the waiting room of the ER, a group of FBI agents stood at the desk. The cause of the accident was still unknown, so an FBI investigation was under way to rule out the possibility of terrorism. Jonathan overheard a nurse's conversation with the agents; she was giving them the names of passengers who had been killed. Jonathan asked the nurse to show him the list.

"I can't give you that information, sir," the nurse replied.

"I just want to know whether my wife is one of the five. Why can't you tell me that?"

"We don't have that information, sir," the nurse said.

"I just heard there was a fucking list!" he snapped. "I want to see it so I can find my wife. I don't know if she is alive or dead."

The FBI agents went silent. All eyes were on Jonathan. He was rocking back and forth, every muscle tensed. An agent took Jonathan aside and asked, "What's your wife's name?"

Jonathan and Glenn drove to two more emergency rooms. The FBI agent had assured Jonathan that my name wasn't on the list of deceased passengers who had been identified, but that gave him only a modicum of relief. The list was incomplete, and I was still missing almost seven hours after the accident. At the first few hospitals, Jonathan gave the polite speech he had prepared. He would say, "I'm looking for my wife, Geralyn Ritter. She was a passenger on the train that derailed, and she's missing," and then he would show my photo. By the time he reached the last hospitals, he cut to the chase: "Do you have an unidentified female passenger?" he asked, showing the photo.

At Thomas Jefferson Hospital, the ER waiting room was quiet. Jonathan leaned on the front desk with both arms—like he might collapse if it weren't there to hold him. His forehead was creased with worry, and there were heavy bags under his eyes. "You look like someone who could use some help," the receptionist said.

The genuine care in her voice was like a revelation after encountering so much indifference and what sometimes felt like intentional efforts to hinder his search.

The receptionist's name was Jackie. She took Jonathan into a tiny office behind the desk and showed him a list of all the hospitals in the area that had received injured passengers. "They'll talk to me," she assured him, and she started making calls. As Jackie worked her way down the list, she told Jonathan that there were some guys in the waiting room who worked for Amtrak. "Go ask them if they can find out anything," she said.

The two men in Amtrak uniforms were sitting in chairs. It wasn't clear what they were doing there in the ER.

"My name is Jonathan," he said. "My wife was on the train." The men didn't move to stand up. "Do you know if there is a list of passengers who were rescued?" he asked. "I need help finding my wife."

"Naw," one of the men replied. "We don't know anything about that." Then he looked away. He said it so casually. Jonathan spun around and walked off.

That's when Jonathan had the idea to call our neighbor, Jim T, a senior agent in the FBI. Jim's wife, Jen, answered the phone. She had clearly been asleep.

"I'm looking for Geralyn!" he said urgently.

Jen responded groggily, "I don't have her." Jen is a good friend, and we have passed many a pleasant evening enjoying a bottle of wine.

"I can't find Geralyn," Jonathan repeated intensely.

"But I don't have her," Jen repeated defensively, still not understanding. It would have been funny in other circumstances.

Jonathan took a deep breath and backed up. "I'm really sorry for calling so early. There's been a train accident, and I can't find Geralyn. It's been more than seven hours. Can I talk to Jim?" Jim got on the phone and immediately sprang into action. He contacted the FBI at the scene of the accident and began conducting his own search.

When Jonathan came back to the cramped office, Jackie was dialing the last hospital on the list—Penn Presbyterian. Jonathan thought, *If she's not there, it's a nightmare.* He listened intently while Jackie questioned the nurse. She was quiet as she listened to the response. "Yes? You have someone?" Jackie nodded at Jonathan.

Before handing Jonathan the phone, Jackie explained that the patient, Jane Doe, had been airlifted from Frankford Aria to Penn earlier that night—the last injured passenger in a Philadelphia hospital who was still unidentified.

When Jonathan got on the phone, the nurse at Penn said, "She looks like she's thirty or forty years old."

Through his daze, the first thought that popped into Jonathan's mind was, *Geralyn will love hearing that.* (I was forty-six at the time.) Jonathan asked if the patient was between five feet eight and five feet ten.

"We can't give a patient's height," she replied. "It's a violation of privacy laws."

Ridiculous, Jonathan thought. Was that really the law—you could give a person's age and gender, but couldn't say whether they were between five feet eight and five feet ten for the sake of identifying them? Even when it was a matter of knowing whether your wife was alive or dead? He told the nurse he was on his way to the hospital.

As Jonathan and Glenn headed to Penn, reality set in. They knew this was the end of the search—either they had found me, or I was gone.

"I think she's dead," Jonathan muttered.

"Jon, it's her," Glenn insisted. "In my heart of hearts, I have the strange sensation that it's going to be her. I don't know how I know, but I do."

By the time they reached Penn, Jonathan had swung from despair to optimism again. *It's her, it's gotta be her,* he thought. *She's alive.*

At 6:30 a.m. Austin's alarm blared in his ear. He'd drifted off for almost an hour with the phone pressed against his cheek, leaving a rectangular imprint. Austin scanned the screen, expecting updates from his dad. Nothing. No new texts, no voicemails, no missed calls—nothing. Now it was real. *If they haven't found her by now,* he thought, *she's dead.* He wasn't sure what to do. He started going through his familiar routine, slowly getting ready for school, telling himself he had to catch the bus. He tried not to think. If he got on the bus and went to school like everything was normal, he wouldn't have to admit the other possibility.

At Penn, Jonathan approached the front desk and explained why he was there. The receptionist typed a few keystrokes, studied her computer screen, looked up with kind eyes and said, "Sir, you need to meet with the chaplain." Jonathan slumped over on the reception desk. There was only one reason the receptionist would call for the chaplain.

"She didn't make it?" Jonathan mumbled. His throat constricted as he choked down tears before they could reach his eyes. What was he going to tell the kids?

"Hospital protocol," the receptionist replied in a sympathetic but unconvincing tone.

A few minutes later, at a conference room table, the chaplain assured Jonathan that Jane Doe was still alive, and the meeting really was hospital protocol. Jonathan discerned that the man's job was twofold. He was there to screen visitors before sending them in to identify patients. He was also there to comfort them if the patient wasn't their missing relative. The chaplain asked Jonathan, "Does your wife have any identifying characteristics?"

After staring back blankly for a moment, Jonathan blurted out, "She has a mole somewhere on her head." Quickly realizing that a mole somewhere on the head was not exactly useful information, he added, "She's five feet eight with light brown hair." He pulled out his phone with the picture. The chaplain asked to borrow it and left the room.

He turned to Glenn and said, "I've been married close to twenty years. Why can't I come up with anything significant to identify Geralyn?"

"You should talk to Tracy," Glenn said. "They went to that spa on Mother's Day. I bet she would know whether Geralyn got a Brazilian or whatever," he blurted. They burst out in punchy, nervous laughter but quickly hushed themselves when the chaplain returned to the room with another man.

The second man was dressed all in black, like a mortician. Jonathan felt the sinking feeling return. The chaplain introduced the other man as "Jesper" pronounced with a "Y." Jesper greeted them with a thick, eastern European accent. The first chaplain explained that his shift was ending and Jesper was taking over. "He will take you to see the patient. She just came out of surgery."

At the house, Mercia was pouring cereal into a bowl for Steven. He had slept through everything the night before, and Mercia hadn't told him about the accident yet. He was sitting at the kitchen island, munching on Cheerios when Brad came downstairs.

Brad kept his head down, not responding to Mercia's and Steven's greetings, as he took out a bowl and began pouring cereal and milk. He took a few bites before pushing the bowl away and asking with a tremor in his voice, "Is there any news on Mom?"

Mercia shook her head.

"News about what?" Steven said.

Mercia turned and reached out to smooth Steven's rumpled blond hair. "The train that Mom was coming home on got sick," she said slowly. "It vomited up the folks in it." It sounded absurd, but Steven was only eight years old.

"The train got sick? Is she okay?" Steven asked.

"Honey, she's going to be okay," Mercia said. Then she turned back around to face the sink. She looked up at the ceiling and thought, *Please Lord, let the words I told this child be true.*

In the intensive care unit, Glenn sat in the waiting room while Jonathan went into the post-op recovery room. As Jonathan walked through the door, he exclaimed, "Geralyn!" But as soon as the name left his lips, he started to doubt again.

A group of doctors surrounded an unconscious woman. A ventilation mask concealed most of her face, a cervical collar of hard plastic covered her neck and collarbone, and below that, she was hidden under layers of surgical drapes. Her arms were wrapped in bandages and casts. She was entwined in tubes and wires. The drone of the ventilator and the beeping of the monitors muffled any other noise in the room.

Jonathan studied her swollen face and closed eyes, which were taped shut and already bruised black and blue. Her forehead and hair were smudged with dirt and blood. The tips of her right-hand fingers peeked out of a cast. Her nails were painted with pale pink nail polish. *Did she get her nails done on Mother's Day?* he struggled to recall. When Jonathan walked in and said, "Geralyn!" had her eyes moved in response? Maybe. He didn't trust himself. Everything felt strange and unreal. He knew he couldn't admit to being hesitant. If he did, the doctors would make him leave. So he pretended he was certain, and he asked to get Glenn from the waiting room.

"Glenn," he whispered, pulling him aside. "Is it her?"

"It's her," Glenn said. "Those are her eyebrows."

"How do you know what my wife's eyebrows look like?" Jonathan asked incredulously.

"I don't know, Jon," Glenn replied. "I swear, I'm the least observant guy, but when we all went out for dinner on Mother's Day, I noticed her eyebrows."

"I don't know," Jonathan whispered. "I don't think it's her." It was all so unreal; he wasn't sure of anything. Jonathan asked a nurse if the woman had come in with any belongings. The nurse brought him a plastic bag. Jonathan pulled out a tattered suit, soaked through with blood and covered in soot. He tried to remember what I had been wearing that morning. He recalled a light-colored suit. Maybe this suit had once been beige, but it was hard to tell. Jonathan put his hand in the pocket. He pulled out a nickel and more track dust.

Glenn said with odd confidence, "I've seen Geralyn wear that suit before."

Jonathan still wasn't convinced. The nurse pulled out a small plastic bag of jewelry. It had a sticker that read "Jane Doe" and a biohazard symbol. He looked at the diamond solitaire engagement ring and the wedding band that had been cut off the woman's finger. They looked familiar, but many women had rings like these. Then Jonathan saw a white- and yellow-gold watch and a braided bracelet—he knew these objects—they were gifts he had bought for his wife. He looked at Glenn with wild excitement in his eyes. "It's her!" he shouted. "It's Geralyn!" Jonathan pulled Glenn into a bear hug that toppled them both to the ground. Jonathan is six feet two and not the lean and lanky type. Glenn is even taller. The commotion drew sympathetic stares and smiles as the two big men sat on the floor smiling and crying tears of relief. After nine hours, their search was over. They had found me.

Austin was trudging across the front lawn, making his way to the bus stop. He'd gotten ready for school on autopilot. Mercia was sending Brad and Steven to school as well, trying to keep things as normal as possible. Austin glanced down at his phone just as a short text message arrived. The words on the screen seemed to appear in a shout: "We found her. She's alive." Austin crumpled to the ground in the dewy grass. He screamed as tears streamed down his face.

Three

I had been asleep for a long time, dipping in and out of strange dreams. I was a child. I was a teenager on the diving board. I was watching my boys wrestle on the living room rug. But one dream kept recurring—a dream that I was in the hospital. Bright lights glared overhead, and masked people were hovering above. They were talking to me, but they couldn't seem to hear me. Or maybe I wasn't speaking. Gradually, all the dreams began to fade away, except for one. The hospital dream kept coming back and stretched on longer. It became more detailed. Very slowly, I began to think this might not be a dream.

I started to show signs of responsiveness within a few hours of the accident, but I didn't fully realize where I was for a few days, after undergoing two marathon surgeries. The first time I remember opening my eyes, my brother, Scott, was leaning over my bed. I was lying on my back and couldn't turn my head or move my arms or legs. I didn't feel any pain.

"Sis?" Scott said. Sis has been my family's nickname for me since I was a kid, in part because my mom is also named Geralyn (though we've called her Nana and my dad Pop Pop from the time my own kids were little). "Sis, are you awake? Can you hear me?"

I tried to say something, but a hard, plastic tube filled my mouth.

"You can't talk right now. Just blink once for 'yes' and twice for 'no.' Do you understand?" Scott said.

I blinked once, but I didn't understand. Everything still felt fuzzy and dreamlike. Jonathan was there, at the edge of my vision. I sensed they had spoken to me before, but I couldn't remember what they'd said. "Do you want to know what happened?" Scott asked.

I blinked once.

"You're in the hospital. The train you were on crashed."

It seemed like I might be able to close my groggy eyes and let his words dissolve back into my dream. I tried to say something to Scott, but no sound came out of my mouth.

"Don't try to speak. You're intubated, on a ventilator. Just try to relax," Scott said. I gave up, shut my eyes, and drifted back into the darkness.

The next time I remember waking up, I felt someone kissing my head and realized it was my mother. Then my father came into view, and my sister, Wendy, and my brother, Kent. Now it really seemed like a dream. I am very close to my family, but seeing them all together, standing over me, didn't make sense. We are spread out all over the country. Scott lives in the Pacific Northwest; Kent is in Fort Worth, Texas; and Wendy is down in Houston. They are all married and have kids of their own. My parents live on a mountaintop in Colorado. If you want to get all six of us in a room together, it usually takes at least a year of advance planning. The fact that they were all standing beside me in that moment meant I really was dreaming—or something was very wrong.

Scott said, "You were in an accident. You are in the hospital."

"We are here with you, Sis," Kent added in a low voice.

Someone was stroking my hair and asking if I was in pain. I couldn't move or answer, but I wasn't sure I knew the answer. I was floating.

Scott spoke again and reminded me that I could answer by blinking. "Do you want to know about your injuries?"

I blinked once.

"The good news is that you're not paralyzed. You were seriously hurt, though. The crash caused the organs in your abdomen to be thrown up into your chest," Scott said. "There was a lot of damage. Your diaphragm was ruptured, they had to remove your spleen, and they are still working on repairing your intestines. You've had a lot of surgery." He paused, and then, like the internal medicine doctor he is, continued his report. "You have broken bones. Your ribs are basically crushed and your lungs collapsed, so that's why you can't breathe on your own right now. Your leg is in traction because your pelvis is broken. They put some screws in your lower back, but the right side of your pelvis isn't really connected to the left. They'll do more surgery in another day or so."

I couldn't take it all in. I tried to say, "I'm okay?" I was looking for confirmation.

Scott went on, explaining more about the specifics of my injuries. "You've fractured several vertebrae, so you need to stay in this neck collar for a while." I stopped listening and looked for Jonathan. When my eyes found him, I struggled against the ventilator and tried to mouth my question again, "I'm okay?"

"It's a miracle," Jonathan said. "You survived, and you're not paralyzed, and you don't have a head injury."

A miracle? I couldn't move, so I was relieved to know I wasn't paralyzed, but it bugged me that he hadn't answered my question. I just wanted to hear someone say yes. Just "yes," I was okay. A miracle is much more complicated.

This was on Friday, May 15, three days after the accident.

On the night of Tuesday, May 12, EMTs found me at the scene of the accident. Based on the initial hospital records for Jane Doe, I had probably been ejected from the train and was likely found amid the wreckage. I was covered in dirt and gravel. I suppose they cleaned off my face well enough because they could see that my skin was ashen, and I was turning blue. My breath was faint and barely perceptible. I was moving my legs and struggling to mouth words, but I couldn't make a sound. The EMTs placed an oxygen mask over my face and rushed me to the nearest local hospital, Frankford Aria.

The ER doctors at that small hospital worked to stabilize me, giving me multiple blood transfusions, putting me on a ventilator, and inserting chest tubes to draw out the blood accumulating there. They quickly realized that my pelvis was dangerously unstable and that I needed a higher level of care. Just before midnight, I was airlifted to Penn Presbyterian, site of the newest Level One Trauma Center in Philadelphia and coincidentally where the surgeon on duty at Aria had recently finished training. My trauma team at Penn would later credit the heroic work of the Aria team for keeping me alive during that initial hour after the accident.

The trauma team at Penn Presbyterian had been on alert since the accident hit the news, expecting an onslaught of patients. A poorly coordinated response effort, however, meant that some hospitals in Philadelphia were slammed with dozens of seriously injured patients, while the gleaming brand-new trauma unit at Penn sat empty. The helicopter that brought me in landed just before midnight.

The doctors unloaded me from the helicopter and wheeled me into the trauma bay. I was quickly given a series of X-rays and CT scans. One scan of my chest shows an image of my stomach resting up near my heart and a portion of my colon under my left armpit. I was prepped for emergency surgery.

The soft-tissue injuries were the first priority, and then the orthopedic surgeons would take over to address my fractured pelvis and ribs. The surgeons made a long incision to open up my entire abdomen. It was quickly apparent that, as suspected, the force of the accident had completely ruptured my diaphragm, the thick leathery muscle that separates the chest cavity from the abdominal one. My spleen was badly lacerated and bleeding uncontrollably. Both my colon and small intestine were perforated and torn in multiple places. Tests showed that my bladder was ruptured as well. Over the next several hours, the trauma surgeons eased my organs back into place, closed up my diaphragm, removed my spleen, resected sections of small intestine, repaired major tears in my large intestine, repaired my bladder, and then made way for the orthopedic team.

The medical literature describes a pelvic ring fracture in chilling terms. It is called "the killing fracture," and when the wound is open as mine was, there is an especially high risk of "early exsanguination" and infection.[14] Worse, studies show that when the injury is combined with other intra-abdominal trauma, it is "almost universally fatal."[15] For those who survive the immediate aftermath of the injury, it is "one of the most disabling injuries of the skeleton."[16]

The orthopedic surgeons stabilized the top of my pelvis by inserting two long screws through my broken sacrum and sacroiliac joint. That's the fixed joint just below the lower back that essentially connects the pelvis to the spine. More precisely, the joint connects the sacrum and the ilium bones, the two winglike bones at the top of the pelvis. Then they drilled holes into the bone just above my hip sockets and used two more screws to anchor a U-shaped bar that protruded outside my body, arching across my lap like a safety bar on a roller coaster, to hold the two broken halves together. They placed one leg in traction. They cleaned all the gravel, dirt, and bone fragments from the penetrating wound where my left hip had been crushed and ripped open. My broken rib cage would still make it impossible for me to breathe on my own without the ventilator, but fixing that would have to wait for another day.

They didn't close the huge abdominal incision. Stitching up my swollen abdomen was impossible and also inadvisable because the contents of my lacerated intestines had contaminated everything. Infection was a major threat. The doctors also knew more surgeries would soon follow, so there was really no point anyway. Instead, they packed my belly with gauze and bound it up with plastic wrap and some kind of girdle. My entire left side was a nest of tubes—multiple chest tubes, a feeding tube, and drainage for my wounds.

I had just come out of surgery when Jonathan found me, early Wednesday morning. The doctors spoke to him rapid-fire as they described my injuries, the surgery, and the danger I was still facing. Jonathan was too shocked to take it in. He was thinking of all the people who still didn't know what happened to me. He had calls to make. "Wait until her family arrives," he said. "They're all doctors. You can tell them."

I'm the oldest, but my career choices clearly had no impact on my three siblings. My brothers, Kent and Scott, both specialize in internal medicine. Scott's wife, Sheila, is a neurosurgeon, and Kent's wife, Hannah, is a pediatric emergency medicine physician. My little sister, Wendy, likes to remind me she is nearly ten years younger than me. She is a psychiatrist with the Veterans Administration, and I'm very proud of her work with traumatized women vets. Through my family, I had a personal shadow medical team—and over the next few years, I called on them all, day and night.

After the long search and the intense relief of finding me alive, Jonathan had shifted gears. He became all business as he focused on the task of informing and gathering my family. He tried to reach my parents first, but they weren't at home in Colorado. They were vacationing by the beach in Galveston, Texas, and their cell phones were turned off. They had actually seen the news coverage of the accident the night before. My mom, Geralyn, remarked to my father, Jim, "That's the train Sis often takes." She hadn't known I was traveling that day but nevertheless sent me a text message to check in. Uncharacteristically, she didn't worry when I didn't respond. She figured it was late and I was in bed.

Jonathan called Scott and his wife, Sheila, in Olympia, Washington, where it was about 4:30 a.m. Jonathan was distraught as he explained what had happened. He still didn't know much about my condition, but it clearly wasn't good. He wasn't sure what to do. Scott said he would call the rest of the family and fly out as soon as possible.

When Scott called Kent that morning, Kent immediately sensed something was wrong. No one calls that early just to chat. He answered by saying, "Hey, man, this isn't good, is it?" After Scott told him the news, Kent called Jonathan, who put him on the phone with the trauma surgeon, Dr. C. S. The doctor began her description simply, but tellingly: "Let's just start with her head and work our way down."

Kent grabbed an index card from his desk to take notes. As the doctor continued, he reached back for card after card, eventually just taking the stack. As Kent made his notes, he wondered, *How is she still alive?* Many of my wounds—the ruptured spleen, ruptured diaphragm, open pelvic ring fracture, and flail chest—were life-threatening even as stand-alone injuries. It seemed statistically impossible to survive all of them at the same time.

Kent had been on the academic faculty at the Baylor College of Medicine for more than a decade. He had seen terrible things, but nothing like this had ever happened to someone close to him. I was his big sister, just two years older. We were tight growing up, notwithstanding our differences. I was studious and careful, rarely in trouble but terribly self-conscious. Kent has oozed confidence since he was little. He's a Texan through and through—stubborn, blunt, and tough as nails. He is also hysterically funny and kind. His wife, Hannah, tells one of my favorite stories about my brother. To this day, he has been known to walk into his closet in the morning and boom out a question: "Who's the lucky shirt?!"

Still, Kent somehow looked up to me. To him, I seemed capable, strong, and invulnerable. Only now, I was fighting to stay alive.

Wendy got Scott's call in the parking lot of a Houston kolache shop, where she'd stopped on her way to work. Wendy was six months pregnant, and she'd been craving the Czech pastries. She also knew something must be wrong. When Scott told her the news, she forgot about the kolache and immediately drove home to figure out how she would get to Philadelphia. Wendy's young daughter was at preschool, and her husband was out of town. She'd have to wait for him to get a flight home before she could depart. Feeling isolated, lonely, and afraid, Wendy called her best friend, Alice, for moral support. They met up at a breakfast spot. For several hours, they read reports online about the accident and got updates from family. Wendy still didn't know how bad my injuries were, but she refused to even think that I might die.

After his conversation with Dr. C. S., Kent called Scott back and gave him the report on my injuries, doctor to doctor and brother to brother. Scott had been hurriedly tossing clothes into a suitcase. His plane was leaving from Seattle in two hours. Hearing Kent describe the seemingly endless list of injuries, Scott wondered aloud the question that was on both their minds: "What are her chances?" Scott reached into the back of his closet, where his dark suit hung. He ventured to ask Kent if he was bringing one, and Kent admitted he had been considering it. They left the question unanswered, but Scott decided the suit would be bad luck. Later, while waiting in the airport terminal, he sent a text to my phone. Scott knew the phone was lost and I was unconscious, but he felt like he had to reach out to me somehow. He wrote, "We love you and we're coming."

Back at the beach in Galveston, my mother woke up and rubbed her eyes as the sunlight streamed in the window of the rented condo. Hearing my father in the shower, and their friends in the kitchen, she smiled contentedly and reached for her phone. A voicemail from Jonathan. A text from Sheila. She clicked immediately.

"Call me. There's been an accident and Sis is hurt."

Mom gasped and ran to the bathroom, calling for my father. Neither of my parents remember who called Scott to find out where I was. They also spoke with Jonathan but don't remember that conversation, either. They knew little about my injuries—mainly that I was in critical condition and time mattered. They threw on clothes, grabbed their dog, and drove straight for the nearest airport. As Mom describes it, doors opened for them. They noticed a dog-boarding business near the airport and veered sharply off the highway. They walked in unannounced. The television in the waiting room was showing footage of the crash. Through tears, my mother tried to explain that they had been on vacation but had to fly to Philadelphia *now*. Without saying a word, the kind clerk took the puppy from her arms, handed her a business card, and gently turned my mom toward the door. "You go, ma'am. We've got him. Just call me later."

As they ran to the Southwest Airlines counter and took their place at the end of a long line, my mother remembers only the two of them standing quietly, holding on to each other and repeating, "She's going to be okay." The passenger in front of them turned around, stepped aside, and without a word waved my parents forward. Then the next person in line did the same, and the next.

When my stoic brother, Kent, called his office manager, he couldn't contain his fear. After explaining that I was in an accident, he spoke softly but firmly, asking her to reschedule all his patients for the next week at least. "I have to go now. I don't think there is any way my sister is going to make it. I don't know when I'll be back."

On the flight from Dallas/Fort Worth, he leaned over the tray table and put his head in his hands, visibly upset. A passenger across the aisle kept asking, "Is anything wrong? Can we do anything?" Kent's seatmate stepped in, waving her off. "Just give him space," he urged protectively.

Back in the hospital room, Jonathan's phone rang with an unfamiliar number. It was Ken Frazier, the CEO of Merck. Knowing my family was scattered across the country and that I might have little time left, Ken wanted to see if Jonathan needed help getting them to Philadelphia. Jonathan was touched but assured him that my family had found flights and were on their way. Ken sent his driver, Jim H, to the hospital to help in any way he could. Jim T, our FBI friend, also headed to the hospital to offer his support and took up a post in my room. He stood watch over me while Jim H steered an exhausted Jonathan out to get something to eat.

Jonathan felt better knowing an FBI agent was guarding my door. He was concerned about unwanted visitors. The accident was dominating the news, and just hours after finding me, a hospital staff person had handed him some papers and a business card. She said a representative from Amtrak had dropped them off. They were forms requesting the release of my medical information to Amtrak. The card was from one of Amtrak's lawyers.

"Are you kidding me?" Jonathan was outraged. He roared at the hospital staff, "I don't want any news reporters to come up here, and I don't want to talk to anyone from Amtrak. Keep them away from Geralyn."

That afternoon, another of our neighbors met my parents at the airport and drove them to the hospital. The doctors and nurses in my room made way for my parents as they entered. My mother introduced herself to Glenn before making her way over to my bedside. She knew my left side had been crushed and mistakenly had understood that I might have lost my left leg. For now, though, she focused on my face. Only my closed eyes and forehead were visible, but it was enough. They had made it. I was alive, and she was grateful.

Kent was the next to arrive, and then Scott. Kent almost felt relief when he saw me. It was not his sister. He looked closely and told Jonathan that there had been a mistake. Every part of my body was terribly swollen, bruised, cut, covered, stitched, or casted. "I really don't think that is her," he repeated, asking Jonathan several times if he was sure. Jonathan explained again that he hadn't recognized me at first, either, but he'd seen my jewelry and was now convinced.

Late that evening, Wendy was the last to arrive at the hospital. As she made her way through the maze of hallways, searching for my room, fear began to bear down on her. So far, she'd been able to convince herself that I was going to be okay, but as she reached the door of my room, she realized she was about to face reality, and she had no clue what that would look like.

As she walked inside and saw me—unconscious and intubated, my hair still covered in dirt—the magnitude of the accident finally hit her. My mom was gently wiping the track dust from my forehead. Wendy immediately grabbed a tissue and began to help her. There was gravel in my ears, under my nails, and embedded in my hair. They softly tried to swab it away, but my hair was full of grit, and I would feel dirty for weeks.

Another chaplain came by the room to offer counsel. My family is Christian, and both of my parents have a strong faith. The chaplain gave my mom a devotional with scriptural verses and quotations from various religions. She opened the book to a random page and read the first quote her eyes landed on, which was a Buddhist prayer: "Thy name, O God, art healing." In that moment, a feeling of serenity washed over her, and she sensed that, whatever happened, I would be all right.

To this day, I am grateful that in the midst of intense worry and uncertainty, my mother was able to experience a moment of peace. My brothers hadn't explained to her how severe my injuries were, and she didn't realize how slim my chance of survival was, which was probably for the best. In my mother's eyes, I was still her baby, born when she and my father were newlyweds in college in south Louisiana. The pain of seeing me injured devastated her, yet it brought forth the depth of her love for me. After so many years of cultivating positivity and faith, my mom was able to keep her focus on that love, determinedly holding her worst fears at bay. She kept the devotional with her for the next several months and whispered the Buddhist prayer to herself over and over: "Thy name, O God, art healing."

Earlier that afternoon, after my parents had joined Jonathan, Glenn finally left for home. When he pulled into the neighborhood, he saw Austin playing catch with a friend on the front lawn. Mercia was outside, too, waiting for Brad and Steven's school bus. Glenn walked over. He wanted to speak to Mercia about my condition, but he was afraid to tell Austin. *How do you break it to a fifteen-year-old that his mother is in critical condition?* My family had decided not to let the boys visit me yet. They worried it would be traumatic for them to see me in the intensive care unit, especially while I was unconscious and on the ventilator. Jonathan had explained to the boys that I couldn't talk to them right now and needed to focus all my energy on getting better. They seemed to understand.

Glenn tried to avoid Austin's eyes as he approached Mercia, but Austin walked right up to him.

"Mr. Prokopic," he said. "I want to know everything that happened."

Glenn realized that if Austin had the courage and the maturity to try to help find me by calling hospitals all night, he deserved to know the truth. He proceeded to tell Austin and Mercia about my injuries. Mercia began to cry, but Austin was stoic. It struck Glenn that Austin must have grown up a lot over the course of that night.

Other neighbors saw them talking and came over. Word of the accident had spread, and Glenn told them all the story of the search across Philadelphia the night before. It's a close-knit neighborhood, and now everyone wanted to know how they could help. Neighbors started to offer their support—volunteering to watch the kids and make dinner.

Soon the bus arrived, and Brad and Steven got off. Brad cast his eyes down and walked straight past, avoiding Glenn. He didn't want to talk and didn't want anyone to see him upset. I think he just wanted to focus on the simple fact that I was alive. Steven had the opposite impulse. He ran full speed at Glenn and threw his arms around his legs. "Thank you for finding my mom," he said, holding on tight. After keeping it together through the all-night search and then helping Jonathan manage the logistics of gathering my far-flung family, Glenn finally broke down. He reached down to hug Steven, and his eyes filled with tears.

That afternoon, Austin called Jonathan. Austin was scheduled to pitch a baseball game that evening. "Dad, do you think I should go?" he asked. Jonathan's first thought was no, but then he realized Austin absolutely should go. Like going to school, Austin found comfort in his usual routine. It would give him something else to focus on, instead of worrying. Jonathan asked a good friend to take Austin to the game and keep an eye on him. He could always leave if he changed his mind. As it turned out, Austin pitched five shutout innings—one of his best games ever.

The following day, I had another major surgery with multiple teams of doctors. It took six or seven hours. When I came out of it, I was submerged in a hazy cloud of anesthesia and painkillers. My whole family was eagerly looking for signs of responsiveness. My mother felt a wave of relief when she squeezed my hand and felt me squeeze back for the first time. I was still in there somewhere. As I drifted in and out of sleep and wakefulness, my family started talking to me. When they told me to blink in response to their questions, I blinked. This was a revelation for everyone. I was conscious; I was aware. Of course, from my perspective, it was all still one long, strange dream. The moment I fell asleep again, I would forget where I was and what they told me.

The doctors checked for reactions in my fingers and toes and assured my family that I was not paralyzed. I had fractured several vertebrae in my neck and lower back, but somehow my spinal cord was unaffected. What other way could my family describe this, except to call it a miracle? Not only had I survived the force of the crash, I would be mobile again.

There was, however, still considerable risk of a life-threatening complication. The doctors were concerned about infection, blood clots, internal bleeding, and whether my heart could stand the strain. It was more helpful than ever that all my siblings are MDs. They consulted with my doctors, kept close tabs on my condition, and translated the medical terms for the rest of my family.

There is a standard scoring system for rating the severity of traumatic injury. Known as the Injury Severity Score (ISS), the system is used primarily in research and by the National Transportation Safety Board (NTSB) in studying accidents. The ISS is considered the gold standard in grading trauma severity and is generally correlated with the likelihood of death, as well as length of hospital stay, need for major surgery, and the extent of permanent residual disability.[17] A score of fifteen or higher is considered "serious," and a score of twenty-five or higher is considered "severe trauma." I would later find out that my score was a fifty-seven. According to the NTSB's public report on all Amtrak 188 passenger injuries and their ISS scores, I was by far the most seriously injured passenger who did not die.[18]

The lengthy NTSB report is haunting. It's a sixty-two-page list, impersonal and clinical, of every injury suffered by every passenger (identified only by age, sex, and hospital location) including those who did not survive. Just to read the first several pages brings home the devastating power and scope of the crash.

As the seriousness of my injuries sank in, my family began debating how much to tell me. What should they say about the accident? Was I ready to hear that eight people had died? Was I ready to know that I might never walk? Would knowing these things make me more determined to live, or would it cause me to lose hope?

Kent was still wrestling with the experience of being on the patient's side of the equation. He noticed the little things that usually escaped his awareness at work—for example, when a group of doctors was chatting in the hallway. They were talking about their weekend plans and what club they were going to. Meanwhile, he was sitting on the other side of the door, worried that his sister's erratic heartbeat would stop any minute or that a deadly infection would take hold. He would return home from this ordeal with greater empathy for the disconnect or otherworldliness his patients and families must feel in the midst of a medical crisis.

Later, an older man in scrubs came by the room. He was a nurse. My mom was there alone, sitting by my bedside as I slept. He asked in a tentative voice, "Can she see?" Mom was confused by the question. I've worn glasses for most of my life, but it hadn't occurred to her to worry about my vision being affected by the accident.

"Yes, she can see," my mother replied.

"She was covered in dirt when they brought her in—you could hardly see her face— and I washed the grit out of her eyes while they operated," the man explained. "There were so many little pebbles in her eyes that it took over an hour to clean them out." Now his eyes were welling up with tears. "It seemed impossible to get it all out. I thought for sure her eyes would be damaged. I was so worried. I was thinking, *This young woman, she's not going to be able to see.*"

"She can see," my mother said again. She stood up and took his hand. "She can see just fine." She squeezed his hand and held his gaze, saying, "Thank you."

By Friday afternoon, my youngest son, Steven, wasn't doing well. He hadn't seen me since before the accident, and my absence worried him. He wanted his mom. Steven was very close to Mercia, who had been helping care for him since he was two years old. "Stevie, do you want to say something to your mom?" Mercia asked. "We can make her a video and send it to her."

Steven liked this idea. He got out a pencil and paper and sat down at the kitchen table to compose a song. When he was ready, Mercia held up her phone and started recording. Steven was solemn. His big blue eyes seemed impossibly sad and so unlike his confident and cheerful self. Steven read from his paper, beginning with a short introduction, "This is a song I made for you. It's called 'You are an angel.' Then it also says, 'Steven's song for Mommy.'" As he began to sing, his trembling voice was surprisingly soulful. "You are an angel, you make me happy, why did it have to be you? It should have been me." Then he seemed to express all the impossible questions that were playing in his mind as he sang off-key, "You are the best mom, but did it have to be at this time?" His childlike voice began to trail off as he sang, "You got what I need. You care so much for me," and then came in strong on the next verse: "I am so glad you are alive." He concluded in a whisper, "I love you so much."

Mercia sent the video to Jonathan. He watched it when he was alone. As he listened to our little Stevie singing, "It should have been me," tears poured down his cheeks. The video was almost unbearable to watch. He couldn't show it to me, not yet. He put the phone away and tried to gather himself. Jonathan was making a point of staying composed and cheerful in front of me. He cried often, but he never let me see. Sometimes he'd put on some music, lie down in the reclining chair next to me, hold my hand, and pray. I couldn't see his face, so he'd let the emotion wash over him, and the tears would flow.

Jonathan hadn't been home since the accident, but he knew the boys were being taken care of. In addition to Mercia, friends and neighbors had rallied around them. At one point, a friend sent a text: "There are eight women in your kitchen making dinner for your kids." Reading it, Jonathan felt a knot of tension in his shoulders release.

Mercia was less pleased. She was truly grateful that people wanted to help, but she wasn't so interested in sharing the kitchen with eight other women. She prided herself on knowing what the kids liked to eat. Now the entire neighborhood was clamoring to cook for the boys. The refrigerator overflowed with other people's Tupperware, but there was no stopping the avalanche of caring. Glenn volunteered to be the liaison with the neighbors so Jonathan wouldn't be inundated with text messages and phone calls. The neighbors created a schedule and assigned tasks, taking turns driving the boys to baseball and other activities.

By Saturday, I was more awake and eager to talk. It was hard enough being immobilized in the hospital bed, but to be completely unable to speak was agonizing. I had a million questions about the accident and my injuries, and I wanted updates about the kids. Most immediately, I had mundane little requests—I needed to tell someone when I was too hot or had an itch to scratch or when I needed the nurse. I would call my family over by banging my casted wrist against the bed rail. I probably did this fifty times a day. When someone came to my bedside, I'd try to mouth what I wanted and an exasperating game of twenty questions would ensue as they tried to figure out what I was asking for. "Are you in pain?"

Blink once for yes.

"Do you want more medicine?"

Blink twice for no.

"Hot?"

Blink twice.

"Itch?"

Blink twice.

"Pillow?"

Liz, one of my nurses, offered a solution. She brought by a board with the alphabet printed in giant, bright letters, like something stolen from a preschool classroom. To communicate, I was supposed to spell out each word by pointing at the letters one after another. We tried to use it, but it was completely maddening. It took forever to spell an entire sentence. I was still dazed from all the medications, so sometimes I'd be partway through spelling a word and lose the thread. I was beginning to think the letter board was a device invented to torture the infirm and anyone trying to communicate with them.

Finally, Dad went out and bought me a small whiteboard. My right wrist was in a huge cast, but my left wrist was free. What a relief to finally be able to communicate! If I was too hot, I could finally tell someone. I started writing "hot" fairly often, actually. In the state I was in, my body couldn't properly regulate its temperature. My family went out and bought a bunch of mini clip-on fans. They rigged them up around my bed, clipping them to the ceiling hoist, bed railings, and headboard. When I'd bang my cast and write on the whiteboard that I was too hot, my parents would turn on all the fans and carefully arrange them around me. After it was all set up, they would settle down into their chairs, only to hear me bang my cast again—now it was too windy, or I needed something else.

I had a call button to summon the nurse, too. When my family wasn't around and I needed something, I pressed the button. Then a nurse came on the intercom asking, "What can I do for you?" I'd stare at the intercom and try to make some kind of grunt through the ventilation mask. In other circumstances, it would have been comical. I couldn't say a word, and they couldn't hear my grunts. Eventually the nurse would hang up, and I would call again. And she would answer. And again—until at last a nurse would come to the room.

Now that I could write, I had a lot to say. I wanted to know about the boys and was eager to see them. *Boys?* I wrote. *Here?* My family explained that it was too soon. I didn't really understand. Too soon for me to see them or too soon for them to see me? But I didn't protest. I didn't want my boys to be frightened or upset. Maybe it was better to wait until I could talk, I thought. Jonathan and my siblings promised to leave the hospital for a bit and drive to our house to spend some time with them.

I also wanted to know about the accident. Jonathan had asked me what train car I was in. At the time, I didn't realize why he was asking because I hadn't seen the images of car one. Jonathan had watched the news footage and couldn't believe I had made it out of there. The car was completely decimated. In newspaper photos, it looked like a debris field between the other tumbled cars.

I asked Jonathan if anyone had died. He still felt it wasn't the right time to tell me, but how was he supposed to respond to such a direct question? "You're not going to die," he said. "You're going to be just fine." It was obvious he was dancing around the question.

I underlined the words on the whiteboard, "Did anyone die?"

He changed the subject again. "It's a miracle." Now I was exasperated.

Jonathan didn't want me to know about the deaths. In his mind, the topic of death was off-limits. He didn't want to be the least bit negative. I was going to get better, and that was it.

My whole family and all the hospital staff subscribed to the same belief. None of my family members cried by my bedside or talked about my chances of survival. Everyone seemed cheerful and full of purpose. They made jokes and laughed about the whiteboard and my dirty hair. They ate the cookies my friends sent that I couldn't have. Most of the time, I had no idea that I was walking the fine line between life and death. Instead, the focus seemed to be on fixing the long list of things that were broken and watching for any sign of infection. Everyone appeared confident that I would push through and get better.

When I asked about the accident, I didn't like the feeling that something was being hidden from me. With trembling, opposite-broken-handed scrawl on the little whiteboard, I kept asking direct questions until Jonathan told me at last. He said eight people had died. *Eight people.* Sorrow spread through me like burning leaves. I finally understood how serious the accident was. The fact that I was lying broken in the ICU might have been an indication, but I felt so detached from my body that it didn't register. With my neck secured in the cervical collar, I couldn't even lift my head to see myself. With my abdomen still wide open and my guts basically covered with Saran Wrap, I was immobilized, mostly numb, and mute. I only knew as much about my situation as others chose to tell me. Finding out that eight people had lost their lives changed my whole perspective on the crash; it was in a category that I hadn't considered. This wasn't a mishap—this was a tragedy.

At one point, I wrote a message to my mother asking, "Is my back broken?"

"Yes," she replied, "but it's going to be okay."

My injuries had been explained to me, but I complained to the hospital staff that they weren't telling me everything. My mother assumed it was because I was heavily sedated, and I was having trouble remembering. That was part of it, but it was also true that I wasn't being told all the details. For now, they were only giving me a high-level overview, and I couldn't get a sense of what it all meant. I got the feeling that it was hard for everyone to keep track of it all, including the many specialists and nurses. At one point, I was told my leg was broken, but it turned out that wasn't right. My pelvis was broken, but not my leg.

I wondered how serious my situation was. I hadn't even seen my own body—not that I really wanted to see it. I knew that whatever was going on from my neck down was probably pretty gory, and I was happy being protected from that. From Kent's and Scott's perspectives as doctors, I was extremely lucky. I'd had a slim chance of surviving, and I'd made it through the most perilous part of the journey. I wouldn't be bedridden for the rest of my life. I could move my arms and legs. Furthermore, if I could avoid major infection, my injuries would eventually heal. It seemed like I might have trouble with my left side, I might not be able to walk without a cane or walker, and I'd probably encounter issues with my digestion, but for the most part, I would lead a normal life.

Wendy didn't mention it at the time, but she had a serious concern. She was worried that I might have a cognitive dysfunction that hadn't been detected yet.

At one point, after she and my brothers returned from visiting the boys at our house, I wrote a note asking, "Did you see my farm?"

"Does that say farm?" Wendy said, thinking she must be confused by my handwriting.

"Yes," I wrote. Now Wendy was alarmed. Here was the sign she'd been on the lookout for. I was delusional. I didn't know anything about farming; I was a senior vice president at a Fortune 100 company. My grandmother had a peanut farm in West Texas, but that was as close as I'd ever come. I'd ended up in New Jersey by way of Duke University, Stanford Law School, and a decade as a Washington, DC, lawyer. But at that moment, I was insistent, looking at Wendy seriously and underlining my question, "Did you see my *farm?*"

"Sis," Wendy said softly, a bit hesitant to break the news. "You don't have a farm."

"Yes," I wrote with insistence. "I do!"

"No, no, you don't," Wendy said. She looked at Mom, wondering how she would deal with the realization that I was hallucinating. I underlined the word "farm" again with my red marker.

Finally, Jonathan noticed the confusion and laughed. "She planted a few things on the back porch—tomato plants and basil. She's very proud of it. They're actually growing, and she calls it her farm."

Wendy and Mom burst into laughter. "You had me worried," Wendy said. "I thought you were losing it!"

While there were funny moments, most of the time it was annoying to be misunderstood. Every time I'd start writing a long question, slowly and shakily drawing letter by letter with my left hand, people would try to save me the effort and finish the thought for me.

"Your leg—does it hurt? Is it hot? Does it itch? Do you need me to rub it? Fix the blankets?" Their guesses were never right. I kept thinking, *Shut up and let me finish!* The whiteboard was small, so I'd usually scribble a few words and then try to convey to the person holding the board that I needed them to erase it to make room for the rest of the sentence.

Eventually I wrote an announcement: "I have a lot to say." Pause. Erase. "Need bigger board." Everyone got a kick out of that. My usual bossiness was showing through. They went out and bought me a poster-sized whiteboard and propped it up beside the bed.

Getting a big whiteboard may seem trivial, but it meant a lot to me whenever someone acted on one of my requests. As the days wore on, the lack of control was getting to me, and I grasped at any chance to assert myself. Through these small offerings, my family gave me back some sense of control, of being in charge of my own body. They took me seriously, brought me multiple fans and whiteboards, and even duct-taped an iPad to the equipment on the ceiling over my bed so I could distract myself with Netflix. Having the power to *do* something is important for anyone dealing with trauma—patients and caretakers alike.

One day, as I was being wheeled out of the room for yet another surgery, I raised my arms for the nurses to stop. I motioned for the whiteboard insistently. I had been bouncing back and forth in my mind between the confusing present and what I thought of as my "real life." All of a sudden, it seemed terribly relevant that I hadn't looked at my email inbox for almost a week. I could picture the growing pile of unanswered emails. What would people think when I didn't write back for days on end? And now I would be going dark again for another major surgery. I felt compelled to scribble an urgent note to Jonathan as the nurses tried to convince me it was time to go. "Tell Lisa to answer only important emails," I wrote. "She should tell them I just don't have my devices."

Jonathan tried to suppress a laugh. I was fighting for my life, but to my mind, the only reason I wasn't responding to emails was because I didn't have access to my phone or computer. Still, he dutifully passed my message on to my administrative assistant, Lisa, who appropriately ignored it.

Lisa and my other colleagues were thrilled to hear I was well enough to worry about my unanswered email. The day after the accident, she says she stumbled around like a zombie. My boss, Bruce, was also visibly upset and had sent a mass email letting my colleagues know I was in intensive care. Bruce and I had worked together for ten years, and he had been a tremendous mentor to me. The announcement cast a solemn atmosphere over the entire office. My coworkers gave each other hugs and whispered words of comfort. As the days passed and I became more lucid and aware of my surroundings, I also became more aware of the pain. My family did everything possible to support me, but ultimately there was only so much they could do.

Nights were the most difficult. Around 7:00 p.m., my parents would leave for dinner, and the nurses turned the lights down low. The doctors weren't making rounds, and the hospital grew quieter (even if the beeping machines by my bedside did not). Jonathan sometimes stayed with me until bedtime. He'd move the reclining chair next to my bed, stretch back, and hold my hand. He played music or talked to me softly. For him, the evenings were a peaceful time as we sat in the quiet room, holding hands.

Jonathan's love and solace were a vital aspect of my recovery. I knew I would never make it through without my husband and the rest of my family to pray with me, clean the dirt out of my hair, and give me ridiculous things to laugh about. Yet despite their tenderness and care, deep in my bones I felt starkly alone. My family could stand by me, they could try to offer me all the empathy in the world, but I was the only one inside this body. Even if I had been able to speak, no words would fully express what I was going through. Jonathan was right by my side, holding my hand, but in my mind, there was a distance of a thousand miles between us.

My research since the accident has taught me that this experience of alienation from other people and from my own body is the state of dissociation, one of the defining impacts of trauma.[19] The experts say that in moments of agony, passing into a trance and forgetting where you are—forgetting that you even exist—is an act of self-preservation. When faced with danger, the body's instinctive response of "fight, flight, or freeze" and the accompanying rush of endorphins and stress hormones helps you cope. If the brain continues to sound the alarm for a long period of time, you get caught in a frightening, depressing fog of confusion that is only intensified if accompanied by a continuing bombardment of pain signals from the body.[20]

At one point, I was moved to a gurney and taken to another part of the hospital, where a specialist tested the repair of my bladder. Afterward, a technician strapped me back on the gurney and wheeled me into a quiet hallway. He assured me that someone from transport would be arriving soon to push me back to the ICU. Let's just say it didn't seem "soon" to me. As the minutes ticked by and I lay alone in the hallway with only a thin sheet covering my hospital gown, in pain, and unable to move, I began to cry. A few people walked by but avoided eye contact. I closed my eyes, trying to calm myself and consciously willing my mind to be anywhere else but there. My awareness of my surrounding blurred, and I welcomed the fog as I tried to leave that unbearable place. Weeks later, after I could move better and speak freely, I would still return to that same zoned-out place, sometimes involuntarily and sometimes by choice when I felt overwhelmed. I spent hours on end frozen in a distant, dreamy stupor, often staring at the same spot on the wall until it disappeared. This foggy disassociated state was a refuge, but over time, it became a bleak place to live. A poem by Emily Dickinson perfectly describes it:

Chapter Three

There Is a Pain So Utter

There is a pain—so utter—
It swallows substance up—
And covers the Abyss with Trance—
So Memory can step
Around—across—upon it—
As one within a Swoon—
Goes safely—where an open eye—
Would drop Him—Bone by Bone—[21]
—Emily Dickinson, originally published in 1929

In the evenings, as my feelings of isolation rose to the surface, the nurses came to clean my wounds and change the dressings. I never knew which two nurses would come. Sometimes they were both men, and usually people I'd never seen before. They took off the sheets and blankets, removed my hospital gown, and proceeded to wash the lacerations and surgical incisions from my neck to my knees, front and back.

"Okay, Geralyn," one nurse would say, "we have to roll you onto your side."

They asked me to grab the bed rail as one nurse rolled me on my right and then my left side while the other nurse cleaned the wounds and surgical incisions on my back. When I was rolled onto the left side, all my weight bore down on my crushed ribs and pelvis. I clung to the rail with one hand as pain crashed over me like a tsunami. Tears spilled down my cheeks. If I could have made noise, I would have howled. It didn't matter that I was on the strongest narcotics available; the agony tore right through them. The entire core of my body was broken. The slightest movement of my torso was excruciating, but to be rolled over onto my shattered ribs was unbearable. The forced movement and intensity of the pain also made it impossible for me to try to freeze and go blank.

Jonathan tried to distract me with talking and music, but I know this only from subsequent conversations with him. All I can remember is being alone, having no control whatsoever over my own body, and being undressed and touched by strangers in a way that felt like utter torture. I continually tried to force my thoughts to another place, focusing on a song we played on repeat. The words were "Lord, I need you, how I need you."

I'd heard people talk about turning to prayer in their darkest moments, but I hadn't fully understood what they meant until now. I couldn't speak and could barely move by myself—but I could pray. Prayer felt like the only act of volition I had left. I had my family around me, and I had excellent health care, but it wasn't enough. Every night for weeks, I felt that the only way I could endure the next thirty minutes was by reaching out to God. The song gave voice to my silent prayer: *Lord, I need you.* When I brought all my focus to those words, I was not alone.

As my existential struggle went on, it was, of course, just another weeknight for the nurses. Hearing them chat while they did their work felt like eavesdropping on a private conversation from another world. One of them talked about his cheap rent. He said the neighborhood was bad, so he got a giant dog for protection. I overheard another saying he switched to the night shift because the pay is better. Sometimes they'd mention "trauma drama"—I knew that meant it was busy in the ICU. We were in downtown Philadelphia, and gunshot victims were tragically commonplace. Other times they shared stories about disruptive people who had to be escorted out by security. It was hard to imagine. For my family and me, our entire world had been reduced to whatever happened within the walls of my room. We felt entirely disconnected from the world outside, which made it particularly jarring when that world entered our cocoon. My recovery was all-consuming, but on that same floor of the hospital, there were many other patients in their own parallel universe of agony.

Every evening, after the miserable cleaning ritual was over, I had trouble falling asleep. I'd begun to hallucinate that a stranger was in the room, and I was frightened. One such night, I pushed the call button for the nurse. Luckily, Liz was on duty. With her straightforward open manner and easy smile, I had come to trust her and welcomed the days she was on duty. I wrote her a note, "Could you make those people leave?" She and Jonathan looked around bewildered. The room was empty. Another time, I drifted off but awoke a short time later, terrified. My elevated heart rate must have set off the monitors, and alarms sounded. Nurse Liz appeared by my bedside and tried to comfort me. With a trembling hand, I wrote on the whiteboard, insisting she check the room for the person who was hiding there, trying to get me. She obliged, adjusted my medications, and sat by my bed holding my hand until I fell back to sleep.

Most nights, Jonathan went to the hotel to sleep. The lights were turned off, and I'd lie awake in the dark, watching the hours stretch on endlessly. Our bodies aren't meant to be immobilized, and it affected my psyche. Feeling powerless and overwhelmed, I continued to pray that I'd make it through the pain and fear of the nighttime hours. If I was hot or itchy, there was no one to tell. If the call button slipped out of my reach, I had to wait until someone came to check on me, whenever that might be. It was especially difficult to fall asleep knowing what it would be like when I woke in the morning.

I had a continuous drip of painkillers coming through the IV—a cocktail that the doctors told Jonathan was strong enough to knock out an elephant. In addition, I had a button I could push for a little extra to address "breakthrough pain," as they called it. During the day, I would push it whenever I needed to take the edge off. In the day, the pain felt less intense because I had my family there to distract me. At night, I didn't have the same relief. I was given medication to help me sleep, and eventually, I usually dozed off. When I woke up in the morning, after hours of lying still, not pushing the "breakthrough" button, the pain was monstrous. Each breath hurt, so I tried not to breathe until I absolutely had to, and then I would take a slow and shallow inhale, trying not to move my chest. My body was a prison. Tears streamed down my cheeks. It hurt too much to stretch my arm even an inch to find the pain button or call the nurse.

Eventually the nurse would come to my room, adjust my medication, and put the button in my hand. Even after I received a dose, it wasn't enough to assuage the crushing pain. I tried pushing the button every few seconds. If less than ten minutes had passed since the last dose, the heartless machine beeped its rejection, and the medication wouldn't release. Ten minutes seemed an eternity. I'd push the button over and over, thinking it must surely be time now. As the medication gradually built up in my system, the pain would fade, And I could begin to move a little bit. As the day wore on, I was able to write on the whiteboard with ease until the next evening, when the cycle repeated itself.

Four

By Sunday, my condition had been upgraded slightly, and my siblings flew back home to their jobs and families, promising to return soon. My parents planned to stay until I was well enough to return home, however long that would take. My parents and Jonathan have always gotten along well—fortunate because they all had to draw on that reservoir of goodwill during the tense weeks they spent together on the little couch in my hospital room. Everyone has their own way of dealing with stress, and this situation had pushed them to their limits. They still barely admit it, but I know they were driving each other crazy.

Jonathan hoped my parents would go stay in New Jersey to help look after the boys. One day when Glenn came to visit, my mother drew him to a corner of the room to speak privately. My mother is a cheery, petite woman, and when she smiles, her eyes turn into twinkling little half-moons. She can neutralize just about any disagreement, and never once in my entire life have I heard her swear. When something goes wrong, she might say, "Oh rats!" Usually followed by, "Well, this too shall pass." This time was different. Her daughter was hurt, and she was serious about staying with me. She held Glenn by the arm and looked him sternly in the eye. "If Jonathan thinks I'm leaving this hospital," she said, "he's got another fucking thing coming." Glenn laughed out loud and gave her a hug. Don't mess with a mama bear.

As the days in the ICU became weeks, my parents usually sat in relative silence in the tiny sitting area of the room, corresponding with friends and family on their phones and listening for any signal from me that I needed something. They found comfort in the stillness. Jonathan was far more prone to vent about his frustrations and fears.

Jonathan was angry with Amtrak. Representatives from the company had contacted my family. Kent and Scott found them to be sensitive and thoughtful, but Jonathan didn't trust their motives. Ever since the Amtrak workers in the ER refused to even speak to him the night he was searching for me, he had been pissed off at the whole company. The exact cause of the crash was still unknown, but it had been reported that the train was speeding, and it seemed clear that Amtrak was ultimately responsible.

He had become anxious that Amtrak was going to try to deny responsibility for the accident and that it might be financially ruinous for us. The company had offered to pay for our family's hotel bills, but what would happen if we accepted? Could they later build an argument that because we had taken this offer, they didn't owe us anything more? What would have happened if he had signed the forms releasing my medical information to Amtrak? Jonathan is a natural worrier, which is a good thing in a corporate transactions lawyer. He was always careful about what he signed and was trained to think about all the things that can go wrong or be misinterpreted.

Jonathan decided he'd feel more secure if he found a lawyer. Ordinarily, this was the kind of thing I would want to be consulted about, and I'd have an opinion on the arrangements. Jonathan tried to keep me in the loop, sitting by my hospital bed and outlining all the fees and agreements. In my dazed stupor, I couldn't follow a word he was saying. I didn't care and didn't have the headspace to think about anything besides getting through the next few hours. Eventually he asked, "Do you want me to just take care of this?" I blinked once—*Yes!*

Jonathan didn't want to bother me with his concerns about the future, but he talked to my parents about all his worries and suspicions. Talking about his feelings is one of the ways he manages stress. He spins out scenarios in his mind, coming up with various possible realities, and tries to deal with the contingencies of them all. Quiet contemplation isn't his style. My parents, on the other hand, process stress internally. The dynamic was draining for all three of them, and it would resurface in the coming months between Jonathan and me.

My parents have always had a subdued way of dealing with conflict.

They both grew up in Shreveport, Louisiana, and came from traditional Southern families that valued social graces and a calm exterior, even in the face of difficulty. Emotional outbursts didn't happen. I never have heard them yell or scream at each other or seen either of them sob uncontrollably. Even with four kids in the house, I don't recall anyone ever even slamming a door.

My parents married young, while they were still in college—not unusual for Baton Rouge, Louisiana, in 1967. Just twenty when she was pregnant with me, my mother often says she feels like we grew up together. I don't so much remember it that way. Mom had dedicated her life to motherhood, and she doted on all of us—but she was strict, and she was in charge. When grown-ups asked us questions, we were expected to address them as "ma'am" or "sir."

Shortly after I was born, my father got his first job as a geologist for a major oil company. We moved around Louisiana and Texas for the first ten years of my life. By the time I was in fourth grade, we settled in Houston permanently.

All of this is not to say that we were a particularly quiet or reserved family. Our house was rowdy and fun, and my parents were known for their offbeat, all-out costume and theme parties with dozens of their closest friends. My mother has always loved wearing loud colors, like lime green and flamingo pink. She says bright colors make her happy. A former elementary school teacher, she delighted her students with her extensive collection of kaleidoscopic patterned sneakers. We are both known for our riotous and easy laughter…but laughing out loud and thinking out loud are two different things.

Although I am outgoing, I don't generally think out loud the way Jonathan does. When I am going through something hard, I tend to retreat inside myself and push through. I speak when I've made a decision or reached a resolution. The disconnectedness I felt around my injuries only reinforced this tendency.

During the long days in the hospital, my mother found comfort in her church community and lifelong friends. One of her childhood friends was a nun named Meg Causey, who supervised a nursing home for retired nuns, as well as an elementary school for disadvantaged children in New Orleans. When my mother told Sister Causey about the accident, she soon sent back word that all 120 of her elderly nuns were praying for me. When my mom described the conversation to me later,

I was touched but also amused to imagine a nursing home full of nuns I'd never met, bent over their rosaries, saying prayers for the non-Catholic daughter of a friend of a friend two thousand miles away. Mom and I figured that if the ancient New Orleans nuns were with me, surely I was going to be okay.

In Sister Causey's school, the children came from different backgrounds and religions, but she had asked them to include me in their daily prayers. Two of the girls, one Muslim and one Jewish, even approached her in late May and asked that the last day of school be dedicated to me. One girl said that if she were in my situation, she would want them to dedicate the last day to her. The other said her family had been praying for me every night before dinner. These were the kinds of stories that sustained my mother and gave her hope. I am still touched by the kindness of these strangers who lifted my family and me up during that time.

Mom did her best to look at the bright side of things, but her grief showed on her body. The most difficult thing for her was seeing me in pain. Her hair began to turn white and fall out. She lost weight, and because she was only 110 pounds to start, she didn't have much to spare.

Dad, on the other hand, always enjoyed a good meal—he loved foods like Southern fried chicken with jalapeños and Tabasco sauce or a nice, sizzling plate of Tex-Mex fajitas. With all those hours hanging around the hospital, it was difficult not to indulge. At seventy years old and with a history of heart disease, he was supposed to be on a strict diet. My mom scrutinized everything he ate. She'd helped him lose weight, and his six-foot-one frame was now quite trim. Still, Mom was vigilant, and there was no "ICU-exception" to the rules. But Dad is resourceful, too, and just as stubborn.

One afternoon, my friend, Jen T, came to visit and offered to take my parents out to lunch. My mother declined, but my dad went. As they perused the menu, he knew he had to choose something healthy because my mom would ask. He chose soup and salad, but when the waitress took Jen's order, he interjected, "She wants onion rings." Jen shook her head. She told the waitress she didn't want any onion rings with the burger. "No, no," my dad insisted. "She *wants* the onion rings." Jen took the hint, and they didn't tell Mom.

Meanwhile, I was still on a ventilator and being fed through a tube in my side. I was desperate to get the ventilation tube removed so I could eat and drink, but most of all talk. Finally, a little more than a week after the accident, a doctor said it was time to take the tube out, right then and there. Just like that, I was going to get my voice back! Not only that, the head of my bed would be raised a little bit. I'd be able to see something other than the ceiling!

It turned out getting extubated was not as simple as I thought. The tube went all the way down my windpipe, so having it yanked out was more than a little messy and terribly unpleasant. After the nurses cleaned me up, my bed was inclined slightly, but I didn't have a chance to enjoy it. I immediately became dizzy and started vomiting all over again. The inside of my throat felt like it was being scraped with knives, so I couldn't actually talk like I had expected. When I did speak, my voice sounded like a two-pack-a-day smoker. Because the tube had affected my vocal cords, I'd speak with a raspy voice for months.

While intubated, I hadn't been fully expanding my lungs, which put me at a huge risk of pneumonia. Now, every time my white blood count ticked up, Mom worried. The doctors gave me devices to help me breathe deeply. They wanted me to try to inhale all the way down into the bottommost pockets of my lungs to open them up and reduce the risk of infection. I couldn't do it. With so many broken ribs, a deep breath brought a crushing wave of pain.

Most of the time, I continued to spend my days heavily sedated and drifting in and out of sleep. When I was awake, I could still only stare straight up. My view was of a large contraption on the ceiling that was used to lift and move patients. It looked to me like the giant hoists they use to pick up beached whales.

I needed something to focus on, other than the confusing present and the unknowable future. Jonathan and my dad took a roll of white medical tape and taped an iPad to the hoist on the ceiling so I could watch TV. My mom was a little nervous—what if they damaged the expensive hospital equipment? Who knows how much that giant hoist cost? Thankfully, the hospital staff didn't say anything. There was a chair that reclined all the way back, so Jonathan or my mom would pull the chair up beside my bed, and we'd watch the political drama *House of Cards* together. They each saw the same episode about three times because I kept falling asleep while we watched, finding it too mentally taxing to follow the plot.

A couple days after getting off the ventilator, I woke up in a cold sweat, engulfed in nausea. My abdomen was exploding with pain. When the doctors rushed in, they found my belly was so distended that the stitches were stretching and threatening to pop. Jonathan later said I looked like I was eight months pregnant. I was suffering from an ileus (a blockage in the gastrointestinal tract). My intestines were not moving—the muscles were simply not working—as a result of all the abdominal surgery. I'd begun drinking liquids and eating tiny bites of food, but my intestines hadn't woken up; now they were massively distended and blocked. A gigantic 13-centimeter bolus in my small intestine—larger than the average cantaloupe—had put me at high risk of an intestinal perforation that could be life-threatening. This was a new pain I hadn't experienced before. At one point, I reached out and took my mother's hand and whispered in my raspy, weak voice, "I can't do this anymore."

The doctors conferred with my family. My body couldn't handle more surgery at that point. Instead, they planned to insert a long tube through my nostrils, down into my stomach and another tube up the opposite end. The idea was to relieve some of the pressure on my intestines. They also decided to reduce the amount of pain medication I was receiving to try to "wake up" the digestive muscles. The doctors explained that this strategy of waiting for the problem to resolve somewhat naturally was probably the safest option, but it might take a while and would be quite painful.

"Then we *won't* do that," my mother said reflexively. She couldn't stand to see me in any more pain.

"Hold on," Jonathan said. "Nothing's off the table. If that's the best solution, I don't care if it's painful."

"How can you say that?" Mom cried. "You don't care if she's in pain?"

"It's not that," Jonathan said. "I'm just saying we can't change the course of action because it will cause pain."

"Jonathan's right," my dad cut in. "We have to let the doctors decide."

My mom had done a good job of maintaining her calm in the week and a half since the accident, but now she was ready to lose it. She couldn't stand the idea of sitting back and watching me cry out in pain, but Jonathan and my dad were firm.

Mom began to withdraw into herself—eyes closed, lips pursed, gently nodding as she prayed. Just then, a nurse with whom we had developed a genuine bond came in. She sat down beside my mom, put her hand on her arm, and leaned in gently. "Don't worry," she said, in a not-too-quiet whisper. "Geralyn is just full of shit." Mom's eyes flew open and she laughed in spite of herself as exactly enough tension left the room.

I have no memory of the next three days. Apparently, I alternated between moaning in pain and passing out, while everyone's attention was laser-focused on my bowels. My family and the medical staff were all waiting and hoping I'd pass gas, which would signal some intestinal stirring. Text messages were flying back and forth between my usually proper parents and siblings, saying things like, "Has Sis tooted yet?" and "Any fart news?" and "Still waiting for a BM." When things finally got moving, the whole room apparently stank terribly, and the news was shared far and wide, "Sis is pooping! Yay!" I was positively mortified when I learned about these conversations later, but I was glad they had amused themselves and found ways to smile.

The day after the ileus finally resolved itself, I woke up sad and frustrated. I thought I'd done a pretty good job of staying positive and keeping my emotions in check. I'd pushed through, but I couldn't stand another bleak day of the same routine. It had been weeks since I'd seen my boys. I needed them there. "Jonathan," I whispered in my new gravelly voice. "I want to see the kids."

"Okay, let's see when we can get them down here," he replied.

"Now," I said, both pleading and demanding.

"You want me to go get them?"

"*Now*," I repeated.

Jonathan got it. He left immediately, driving an hour and a half from the hospital to our home in New Jersey to pick up the kids and bring them back to me. I was grateful. My spirits were flagging, and I knew what I needed. It was another one of those moments in which a bit of my autonomy was restored.

During the car ride, Jonathan tried to prep the boys. "Don't hug her too hard. Don't make a big deal about how she looks or talk too much about pain," he advised.

"Dad, come on," Austin groaned. "We know. Just get us there."

The boys had become impatient, too. It seemed like they were the only ones who hadn't visited yet—their dad, grandparents, aunts and uncles, and even a couple of neighbors got to see me before they did.

In hindsight, I am not sure our decision to keep them away was the right one.

I prepared carefully for their visit. The physical therapist came to get me out of bed and into a reclining chair for the first time. I couldn't twist or lift my torso, so we'd have to use the ceiling hoist. I had been lying on a large mattress pad that was edged in a series of loops. They clipped the loops onto the ceiling hoist, and the physical therapist pushed a button. Soon I was dangling from the ceiling in my weird hammock. As I swung through the air above everyone's heads, it occurred to me that this was both insanely practical and hysterical. Once again, I just had to give in and laugh. Anyway, I was glad to get out of the bed.

I was lowered into the reclining chair, and blankets were draped over the hardware protruding from my hips. Mom put a bathrobe around my shoulders and rubbed some dry shampoo into my hair. I probably didn't smell that great, but I hoped I looked somewhat normal for the kids. I didn't want to upset them or scare them. I just knew that I had to see them.

The door of my room burst open, and the boys ran in. It was like someone had thrown open the window and finally let in the sun. We all started crying. I motioned for them to lean over the chair, and they gently hugged my shoulders and kissed my head. It felt like we'd been apart for months. After I wiped away my tears, I watched as Steven stepped back and examined the machines and monitors beeping and humming on all sides. Wanting to be encouraging, he turned to me and said in his most authoritative second-grade voice, "Mom, your numbers look good." We all cracked up.

I told the boys I wanted to talk to each of them one-on-one. Austin was first. Everyone else cleared out of the room.

"I brought you something," he said, settling his athletic teenage frame on the narrow couch and pulling a baseball out of his pocket. It was the ball he had pitched in the winning game the day after the accident.

I was so proud of him. I thanked him for helping to find me and for being so mature. I could see that even now, Austin was doing his best to be an adult for my sake. Highly intelligent and perceptive, he kept the conversation light and didn't ask me any details about the accident. He assured me everything was fine at home. My love for my sons had sustained me over the previous two weeks and given me strength to keep fighting. What an extraordinary gift to have a teenager who would do all the things Austin had done in the wake of the accident—staying up all night, calling hospitals looking for me, going to school the next day, pitching the baseball game, and now doing his best to reassure me. My oldest son was growing up, and he was turning out to be a really fine person.

Tall, lanky, and handsome, Brad came in to see me next. I held his hand and thanked him for helping find me, for thinking of me, and for being courageous. I knew Austin had gotten more attention for speaking with all the hospitals, but Brad had been there, too, just as concerned. I assured him I would be okay. He wanted to know exactly what each machine and monitor was used for. He also wanted to know which car of the train I'd been in. It seemed like he needed some concrete information he could hold onto so all of it would seem real. He asked me when I was coming home. That was the question I couldn't answer.

Steven was silly—smiling and deeply sincere at the same time. We laughed over a photo of him. He'd stayed over at a friend's house a few days after the accident, and in the morning, they'd found him in the garage. He was sitting on the roof of their minivan in a full lotus position with his fingers clasped in a yogic mudra, like a meditation master. The neighbors snapped the picture of him for me. I still don't know how he came up with it. No one in my family knew anything about yoga or meditation. I could always count on clever Steven to do the unexpected.

After the boys went home, I was drained. It was the first time I'd sat in a chair, and by the end of the visit, the pain was awful. It was completely worth it, though, and maybe the boost to my morale had a healing effect because in the days that followed, my recovery sped up. I could spend more time with the bed inclined—almost in a sitting position. Finally, I had a view of something other than the ceiling hoist. Sure, it was pretty much a sterile white box with fluorescent lighting, but it was a definite improvement. I joked with Nurse Liz about staring all day at the official hospital chart board that said the name of my nurse, my temperature, and what tests and procedures were scheduled for the day.

"You know," Liz said, "we could move the bed so it faces the window."

Mom and I looked at each other with wide eyes. "Really?"

It hadn't occurred to us that moving the bed was an option. Of course, with all the machines, tubes, and wires attached to me, a lot more than the bed had to be moved. The hospital staff was willing to do it anyway. From my new vantage point, not only was I able to get some sunshine, the window had a great view. I could see the whole city laid out before me, and my mood improved immediately. Nearby was the Philly Zoo, where they had a hot-air balloon. At first, there was something hopeful in the sight of that colorful balloon floating up into the sky, but after a day or so, I got a little tired of watching the thing go up and down and up and down, all the while tethered so it didn't rise too far. It was starting to seem like a metaphor.

I was getting frustrated that every time I made a little progress, a new complication seemed to arise. Unstable blood clots were found in both my legs. If a clot moves through your veins to your lungs, heart, or brain, it can be deadly. It's a complication that's rather common in cases of trauma. Surgery and prolonged bed rest also cause them. At this point, it felt like it was just one more thing that could go wrong, yet another reason for my family to be afraid.

During yet another surgical procedure, the doctors put a filtering device in my inferior vena cava, the major vein carrying blood back to my heart from my lower body. The filter was placed below my lungs to prevent the clots from going any higher. Now I had an additional specialist to see, the vascular surgeon, and I needed to start taking blood thinners on top of everything else.

Soon after the boys' visit, I got word that Bruce, my boss, wanted to come see me. As a longtime colleague and mentor, I had tremendous respect for Bruce, but I had mixed feelings about having him see me like that. I was anxious about being away from work and insecure about my position at the company.

"He really wants to come," my mom said.

Once again, I was raised up by the ceiling hoist and lowered into the faux-leather reclining chair. Once again, we did our best to make me presentable and hide the protruding tubes and hardware. As I sat there waiting for him to arrive, I realized that from this seating position, I could easily lift the drape and look down to see the external fixation bar holding my pelvis together. We joked that it was like I had my own personal towel rack attached to my lap at all times. I quickly discarded the idea of looking under the blanket. It seemed like a gross concept, and I knew deep in my bones that neither my body nor my brain could handle the visual image. I realize now that I was again trying to dissociate from my body, this time quite deliberately. Not once during my weeks in the ICU did I ever lift the blankets and look at my wounds or the many tubes and hardware protruding from me.

When Bruce arrived, he told me how worried everyone at work had been. As we talked, a nurse came by to put a soft cast on my left wrist—the one I'd been using to write. She informed me that a new review of the X-rays revealed it was broken, too. Bruce and I laughed at the casualness of the statement. Compared to the rest of my injuries, a broken wrist just didn't matter much. And the fact that I hadn't noticed said something about the rest of my body and the amount of medication I was taking. It was too early to talk about my going back to work, and I quickly realized my worries had been misplaced. Bruce had come to visit as a friend, and I was so glad he did. Connecting with someone besides my immediate family gave me a feeling of normalcy that I hadn't realized I was missing.

Several days and a couple more surgeries later, the doctors began to talk to me about leaving the ICU. They said I'd be transferred to a regular floor soon. After that, I'd have to spend time at an inpatient rehabilitation hospital before I would be ready to go home. "Can you believe we're talking about this?" one of the nurses gushed. "We never thought you would be out of the ICU in less than a month!" Everyone was complimenting me on my positive attitude and strength, which felt a little awkward. I wasn't doing anything especially heroic; I was only trying to get through each hour, each day, each night.

The day before my transfer to the regular floor, Jen T, my friend who is an orthopedic surgeon, came to visit again. We discussed some of the medical interventions my doctors were using. One of the surgeries I'd had about ten days after the accident was to secure metal plates to my ribs to hold them together while they healed. This amazed Jen. It was a new procedure in the United States, and the surgeons at Penn Presbyterian were some of the few performing it. The doctors had also replaced the external fixation device—my personal towel rack protruding from my hips—with an internal bar that went across my lap in a similar fashion, but underneath the skin. Jen taught me that this was another recent surgical innovation. At many hospitals, the external fixation bar stays in place for months until the bones are completely healed, and the patient has to stay in the hospital the entire time because of the risk of infection. I realized for the hundredth time how lucky I was.

About this time, I'd also started standing with the assistance of two aides and a sturdy walker. I couldn't put any weight on my left leg, and my broken wrist and fingers made it hard to bear weight on my hands. The walker had armrests, though, so I could lean on my forearms, stand on my right leg, and even inch the contraption forward. It wasn't graceful, but I was thrilled. Mom snapped a picture and cried.

Using the walker seemed like major progress, even if it was only to stand for a minute or two. I asked Jen when I would walk again. She frowned and warned me, "It's too soon to think about that. It'll be a few months at least."

I was stunned. None of my doctors had told me how long I would be in the hospital. Instead, they'd emphasized how quickly I was getting out of the ICU. I assumed that meant my whole recovery would be speedy.

"I don't understand," I said. "My legs aren't broken. Why would it take so long for me to walk?"

Jen explained that because my pelvis had been broken so badly in so many places, the pressure of my thighbones pushing into it to stand and walk would be too much. Not only that, the pelvis is the anchor point for all the connective tissues in the legs and abdomen. When my pelvis was broken, those connections were severed, and they couldn't be reattached until the bones had healed.

Talking with Jen, I was starting to realize that with so many separate injuries and specialists for each body part (trauma, neurology, orthopedics, vascular, pulmonary, urinary, gastroenterology, pain management, physical therapy, psychiatry...), it wasn't clear who I was supposed to talk to about my overall recovery. I couldn't figure out if there was a quarterback among my many doctors. I wasn't sure if anyone could provide guidance about my long-term trajectory. In the beginning, it had made sense to take it day by day, but at this point, I was ready to think further ahead. How long would this recovery take? When would I walk? When would I go home? Most of all, I wanted to know when I would get my old life back. When would things go back to normal?

Five

I n preparation for moving out of the ICU to the regular floor, I was
given the privilege of my first shower. It had been way too long, and
the sponge baths were not cutting it. My mom didn't want to insult me,
but later she admitted that I was quite pungent. I was most desperate
to wash my hair. We'd probably dumped half a pound of dry shampoo
on it, but I needed an industrial-strength washing.

Before I could get in the shower, Nurse Liz had to cover my wounds
and sutures with medical tape. It seemed to take her hours to wrap
me up. By the time she was done, I looked like a mummy. Nearly
every surface of my body from neck to thighs was zigzagged with plastic
medical tape. *How much of my actual skin is going to get wet?* I wondered.
Still, I was obsessed with washing my hair.

At last, I was in the shower chair, belted down, naked. Liz grabbed
the handheld shower nozzle and turned on the water. "Ooh!" she
exclaimed as ice-cold water sprayed out. She fiddled with the knobs
and waited a few minutes. Still cold. The hot water was broken. It was
too complicated to move me to another bathroom, so there I sat, shivering and covered in nothing but medical tape, as she hosed me down
with cold water and washed my hair. It was one of the worst showers
I'd ever had, but it was one of the best, too—it had been so long since I
felt ice-cold water running through my hair and down my face. Liz and
I laughed so hard and so loud; I think we disturbed the other patients
in the ICU.

My room on the regular floor was much smaller, but I didn't care. Moving out of the ICU meant progress. I think I was an unusual patient on the regular floor because I needed help with absolutely everything. In certain ways, I needed even more help than before. I no longer had a catheter, but I certainly couldn't get to the bathroom by myself. I required not one but two nurses to get me out of bed each time. Just a month earlier, I'd been giving a presentation to a group of some of the most accomplished CEOs and business leaders in the country. Just a few months before that, I'd been walking through the dusty streets of a peri-urban slum in Uganda by myself on a business trip. And now I couldn't use the bathroom without calling someone. I'll never forget the awful moment when I realized I wasn't able to twist or reach back far enough to wipe. Over the next several weeks, I'd swallow most of my dignity and surrender nearly all my privacy. And I'd try not to care.

Urinating took a ridiculous amount of mental focus. My bladder had been ruptured, damaging it and the surrounding nerves. While it healed, I was numb to the sensation of having to go. I had to rely on timing to figure out when I might to need to use the bathroom, and then I had to sit there for a long time, willing the necessary muscles to release. My technique was to breathe in gently and then exhale, telling myself, "Let go." I also had to guess when I'd completely emptied my bladder. Sometimes I was right.

After two days on the regular floor, I could recite the official list of my twenty-plus injuries from memory. Whenever a nurse was handing over the shift, he or she would come to my bedside, introduce the new nurse, and transition me by reading out the long list on the chart. For some reason, the very first thing at the top of my chart was my broken right ring finger. I thought that was hilarious—as if that was the most important thing for the next nurse to understand. I took to piping up from the bed, "Watch out for that finger!"

Pain continued to be my greatest struggle, especially during the nights and early mornings. Throughout the day, the nurses would ask, "How's your pain on a scale of one to ten?"

I'd say, "Fine, as long as I don't move or breathe." I wasn't being sarcastic. If I took shallow breaths and stayed as still as possible, the pain was bearable.

The nurse would usually cock her head and say, "So can you give me a number?"

Most hospitals use the same scale to rate the severity of a patient's pain. It has cartoons of a smiley face at zero, progressing to a deeply frowning, red, crying face at number ten. I would ask the nurse whether she wanted to know how the pain was when I was feeling the full effect of the medications, or when they'd started to wear off, or what my pain was like when I moved or took a deep breath. If I took a deep breath and reached to the side, the pain was ten. If I took shallow breaths and stayed perfectly still, the pain was a five, and the mouth of the smiley face might become a neutral straight line. Some days, the pain in my ribs was far worse than the pain in my back and hip; some days it was the reverse. The scale seemed useless to me, and I was almost offended that I was constantly asked to reduce the intense complexity of what I was feeling to a single number.

The reality, however, is that medical science has no objective barometer that can measure a person's experience of pain. Pain is meant to alert us we are in harm's way or that we need to protect a part of the body while it heals. Many elements contribute to this alarm system. Signals from the nerves, immune cells, and chemicals interact, causing us to take action, pay attention, or generate a memory or emotion. Everyone's experience of pain is different, and it cannot be gauged based on damage to the body because that's actually not what's causing the pain. It is the brain's *response* to these stimuli that determines what the patient feels. The only way to "measure" pain is by asking the patient.[22]

In her book *The Pain Chronicles*, Melanie Thernstrom quotes Virginia Woolf: "Let a sufferer try to describe a pain in his head to a doctor and language at once runs dry." Thernstrom goes on to say, "Part of the curse of pain is that it sounds untrue to people who don't have pain. Patients grope at metaphors that seem melodramatic, both far-fetched and clichéd."[23] My own pain was extremely varied, with so many sources, so many types of hurt, and so changeable depending on the time of day, my medication, my activities, my recent treatments. The only thing that didn't vary was my inability to describe it. This difficulty putting pain into words contributed to my sense of isolation and alienation. No one could really know what I felt like, and I couldn't even do a credible job of describing it. Pain is impossible to share, verbally or otherwise, even with those who want nothing more than to lighten the burden.

One thing that helped me push through the nights and the early mornings in the hospital was the thought of seeing my dad. He was the first to arrive each day. I was eating solid food now, so my dad started bringing me takeout to replace the hospital's bland offerings. Breakfast was one of those simple pleasures I had come to relish. I couldn't eat much. I had little appetite because of all the medications, and my digestive system couldn't handle more than a few bites. Still, my dad brought me a smorgasbord every single morning. I might ask him to bring me yogurt, and he'd show up with the yogurt as well as a bagel, a muffin, an egg sandwich, and a fruit salad. He'd stop off at three different places on his way over to the hospital—getting an item or two from the bakery, something from the deli, and another couple items from Starbucks. I had lost weight, and my dad wanted to help me get my strength back. He was also eager to *do* something for me.

Even though I could take only a few bites, I enjoyed tasting a little bit of everything. Breakfast became a sweet time for us—just Pop Pop and me. And, because Mom wasn't there, Dad made sure my daily leftovers didn't go to waste.

Dad also arrived early to eavesdrop on the doctors' discussion of my condition during their morning rounds. With so many specialists coming in and out all day, it was the only time he could hear the whole picture, a candid perspective on my status, the risks, and upcoming procedures and tests.

It was the same at lunch and dinner. Dad would ask what I wanted, and whatever kind of dish sounded remotely appetizing, he'd turn over every rock in downtown Philadelphia to find it. It didn't matter to him that I'd eat only one or two forkfuls. Before too long, though, he had to fess up to my mom; they had to venture out beyond the hospital to a local Target store to buy him pants with a wider waistband. I kept wishing he'd bring me a glass of wine, too, but no joy there.

I began to get a mysterious pain in my right leg—the supposed "good" leg—every time I tried to lift or move it from side to side. This pain was different from the other pain I was experiencing. My usual pain was like a constant, droning bass note. When I first woke up in the morning, the volume on that bass note was jacked up to ten, as though I were trapped inside a deafening wall of sound. As the day wore on, I was able to push the note into the background. By contrast, this new pain in my good leg struck intensely and randomly throughout the day. At first, it was an intense burning, but it rapidly evolved into a piercing, high-pitched siren that came and went without warning.

Several times a day, every day, the pain would suddenly shoot down my leg and set my outer thigh on fire. I'd scream as if a hot poker were being pushed into my leg. I felt like a crazy person: Why on Earth would my good leg have such strange pain? I was afraid to move it because the pain seemed more likely to strike if I engaged the muscle. When I was getting in and out of bed, someone would lift up my legs for me and try to gently set them down on the ground. Inevitably, I'd flinch, making the pain shoot through my leg. It made physical therapy nearly unbearable. I wasn't supposed to be putting any pressure on the left leg, so I had no choice but to use my right leg and pray that the electric shock of pain that struck at random intervals would be quiet that day. Sometimes when it hit, I'd uncharacteristically shout curse words as I froze or doubled over. It somehow made me feel a little better, though it was embarrassing when everyone turned to stare. The therapist gave me a long stick with a loop on the end so I could use my arm muscles to move my leg when I needed to readjust my position in the bed. But using it still required me to lift my head and shoulders, and I barely had the abdominal strength to do it.

I kept thinking that if I had just one of my injuries, I could deal with it, but with all of them put together, I was overwhelmed. We'd been so excited to move out of the ICU, but that enthusiasm clashed with the reality that I still couldn't do a single thing for myself. Medically, I was out of the woods, but my body still didn't work right.

Three weeks after the accident, I was discharged from Penn to a rehabilitation hospital. I was transferred sooner than anyone expected, and we cheered the progress. My condition was stable, but delicate. I was wheeled out on a gurney and loaded into an ambulance for the ride to the new site. It seemed a bit incongruous to be *leaving* the hospital in an ambulance, but I was happy to be moving forward. We even snapped a picture of me waving and smiling on the gurney.

It turns out riding in the back of an ambulance is like riding in the cargo hold of a truck. Now I knew what boxes of tomatoes felt like as they barreled down the highway, battered by every little bump and dip in the road. Jonathan rode in the back with me and tried to help me relax. By the time we arrived, I was exhausted.

I was wheeled through the lobby, where visitors were waiting. The EMTs had to check in with the nurses and get paperwork approved before I could be admitted. It felt odd to be stretched out on a rolling bed in a public space, wearing nothing but a hospital gown. It seemed like everyone in the lobby was staring. We waited for what seemed like an hour. I wished I could disappear into the wallpaper. As the pain built, I retreated into my zoned-out place and let the noise around me fade and my vision blur.

At last, the nurses let me through. As I was wheeled down the halls, I looked around curiously. A bad feeling crept over me. I'm not exactly sure what I had imagined this next hospital would be like. Maybe I was picturing one of those sneaker commercials where they show a high-tech gym and a top athlete recovering from injury. This was not the scene as we made our way to my room. I saw old people. Very, very old people. Several were slumped over in wheelchairs with dazed expressions. It didn't look like these people were being rehabilitated. I was forty-six years old. I wasn't ready to move into a nursing home.

After they moved me into my new room and I took a nap, my mom offered to take me on a tour of the new place. I agreed. Maybe there was a better part. I was sure that shiny high-tech workout gym was around there somewhere. It wasn't. As Mom wheeled me around the halls in my wheelchair, past the drab institutional cafeteria and so many of my fellow inmates, I began to sob. It wasn't that it was so terrible. Objectively, it wasn't. I just couldn't stand that I belonged there.

"Just take me back to my room," I whispered to Mom, who obliged and knew better than to say anything to try to make me feel better.

Like the patients, most of the nurses seemed to be in their golden years, too, but a few were very young. All were kind enough, but right off the bat, I could tell I wasn't a typical patient for them. My first night there, a young nurse came to the room in the evening and said hesitantly, "I'm supposed to clean your incisions." I could tell the prospect scared her. I showed her my stomach and did my best to walk her through the process, as I understood it. I'd grown accustomed to retreating into a passive state when my wounds and incisions were cleaned. I didn't want to have to pay attention.

She gently informed me that a new, painful element had been added to the wound-cleaning ritual. At the hospital, my abdomen had been terribly swollen. Now, as the swelling went down, the stitches around my long incisions had to be hand-tightened. Each night, the nurse would need to drag a thick strand of gauze beneath the stitches, all along the incision, and then tug each stitch tighter, as if tightening the laces of a loose shoe. I liked it best when she didn't try to talk to me or comment on the procedure, and I could squeeze my eyes shut and try to find the fog until it was over.

The first day waking up in the new place, I was frozen in pain, locked inside my morning prison, but more tightly than usual. My chest was exploding, and I had to convince myself that I could breathe. Eventually, I opened my eyes enough to look at the clock. It was nearly 6:00 a.m.; the nurse would come soon. I willed myself to hold on just a little longer. My move to the rehab hospital had meant a transition away from continuous IV pain medication, and I hadn't adjusted. Tears streamed down my face; sweat beaded on my forehead. I couldn't move a muscle, even to find the call button that was hidden somewhere in the covers. Every few seconds, I opened my eyes and looked at the big clock on the wall. The hands finally reached six, and I listened intently for the sound of footsteps in the hallway, the creak of the door—some signal that the nurse was coming. The clock ticked on. I shut my eyes and tried to disappear. The pain was so all-consuming that it wasn't centered in any particular part of my body. Everything throbbed. I tried to breathe as shallowly as possible. Had I been forgotten? How long would it take? I repeated my prayer: *Lord, I need you.*

At 7:00 a.m., a nurse swept into the room. She looked at my pale, tear-stained face and said, "What's wrong?"

"I need my meds," I gasped with effort. "I needed them an hour ago."

She recoiled and took a lecturing stance. "I have a one-hour window to deliver meds," she said. "And I have a floor full of patients."

My heart dropped. This nurse didn't seem to have a clue about the level of pain I was dealing with. I couldn't move and was in too much pain to even press the call button. As she raised the head of my bed and handed me the little plastic cup of pills with disinterested briskness, I closed my eyes, took the cup, and swallowed them without another word. It occurred to me that although I had thought that leaving the ICU meant freedom, progress, and a step toward normalcy, it was perhaps a terrible demotion. I was still in the hospital, only far less comfortable. This was not going to work.

Soon after, my dad arrived with breakfast, but I wasn't in the mood to eat. The pain was still blaring, and my body needed more time to tamp it back down to a manageable level. He dropped the food on a table across the room, sat by my bed, and stroked my hand as I slowly regained my composure over the next hour.

All of a sudden, it was 9:00 a.m., time to begin physical therapy and time to get out of the hospital gown I'd worn for weeks. Just as I started to realize that I had no clothes, Mom burst into the room all smiles and laden with shopping bags. I tried to refocus and shake off the memory of the morning.

As Mom pulled camisoles, T-shirts, and shorts out of the bags, I smiled but rolled my eyes. Everything was neon orange, turquoise, and every other loud color imaginable. Even the underwear looked like bits from a clown costume. "Mom, didn't they have any beige?" I groaned.

"No, sweetheart, they didn't have *any* beige." She smiled mischievously. "Doesn't it just tickle you to look at all these fun colors?" she asked. I thanked her in what I hoped was a convincing tone.

Not only was my mom picking out my clothes, she had to put them on me because I wasn't able to move freely enough to dress myself. Never did I expect to be in a position as an adult where my mother would have to put on my underwear for me. I let myself zone out again. My mind drifted away, as if my body were an empty shell—something I almost didn't recognize as my own.

The morning session of physical therapy was what I'd expected and feared. A group of about twenty people in wheelchairs were gathered in a circle, and we did mundane little exercises to build strength, like squeezing a ball between our knees. It was the same crowd I had seen when I arrived. The woman seated next to me asked what happened to me, and I told her I was in a train derailment. "Oh my God!" she exclaimed. She'd seen the accident on the news and wanted to know details. I decided from then on, I was just going to tell people I was in a car accident. It was simpler and far less interesting.

When I'd been admitted to the facility, I'd been informed that meals were served only in the cafeteria and that a nurse would transport me at mealtimes to eat with the other residents. I get that this encourages self-sufficiency, but, umm…no. I wasn't going to the cafeteria for lunch that day, or any day, for any meal, ever. I know it was snobbish, but I could not bear to sit around a table eating Jell-O with old ladies dealing with dementia, strokes, or a fall in the shower. Their issues seemed so different from mine, and I couldn't imagine any of them returning to robust activity in this lifetime. I was far too busy feeling sorry for myself to have much time for empathy. Luckily, my parents were happy to continue bringing me takeout for all my meals. They had decided to stay at a hotel nearby, so we basically kept the same routine. Mom and Dad spoiled me rotten, indulging my desire to separate myself from the rest of the patients, as if I alone had ended up in this place by terrible mistake. I'm not proud of it, but I needed that space.

In the afternoon, I had occupational therapy to learn how to do everyday tasks to prepare for life at home. In the first session, they had me practice getting an empty carton of milk from a refrigerator. Using a walker, it was impossible to carry the carton and walk at the same time, so I was taught to put the carton on the counter and then slide it as far as I could reach, inch the walker forward a step, and then slide the carton a little farther. There were endless tedious tasks like this. In a later class, they showed me step-by-step how to get onto a special bench in the bathtub. After that, we used a life-sized model of a car as they taught me how to get in and out of the seat. Getting in the car was one of those things I always did automatically. Now, I had to think through every little move, and the whole painful procedure took ages.

With all the focus on my survival and "miraculous" recovery, I had continued to believe I'd bounce back pretty quickly. Now, it was becoming obvious that I wasn't bouncing anywhere. I wouldn't be able to get in or out of bed by myself, use the bathroom by myself, dress myself, drive myself, or cook for myself. Maybe the doctors at the hospital didn't want to tell me all this because if I'd known what was coming, I would have been too upset and discouraged to focus on my immediate recovery. I probably wouldn't have believed them anyway. Then again, if I'd been better prepared, maybe I would have been less crushed when reality hit. Maybe the rehabilitation hospital wouldn't have been such a cruel wake-up call.

I started asking for more information about what to expect. How long would I be in this hospital? What targets would I need to reach before I got to go home? I wanted some general sense of the timeline. If I knew where I was heading, at least I'd have a goal to focus on. No one was willing to give me a real answer. I asked doctors, nurses, physical therapists; they all had vague responses like, "We have to see when you're ready."

As the week wore on, every day followed the same dull routine. I'd wake up and pray the nurse would come soon with my morning pain meds. Later, Dad would bring me breakfast, and Mom would get me dressed. I'd go to physical therapy in the morning, go back to my room for a nap, eat lunch, get rolled out into the garden for fresh air, go to physical therapy again in the afternoon, have another nap, eat dinner with my parents, and then wait for the nurses to make their evening rounds.

Some evenings, I asked for a shower. I usually had to beg. It was such a time-consuming process, the nurses had multiple explanations for why it wasn't possible that evening—I hadn't scheduled it far enough in advance, or two nurses were required, and only one was available... It was one thing when Nurse Liz and I had laughed through the process in the ICU, but now the indignity of begging a different person every time to strip me, tape me up, strap me into a chair, and spray me down was wearing on my pride. Afterward, I always needed an extra dose of pain meds and a sleeping pill. But I had clean hair.

Of course, the facility wouldn't allow me to have a razor for shaving. My mother bought me an electric razor like the one she had given me when I first started shaving as a teenager. I couldn't maneuver enough to shave my own armpits, so my mom did it for me. She also shaved my legs and brushed my hair. Once again, my dependence stirred up intense feelings. I was so grateful that she did all those things without fuss and with good cheer—but I still hated it and am quite sure my gratitude went unexpressed.

My dad was also eager to help in any way he could. Sometimes, I'd mention a tool we'd used in physical therapy that was helpful, like a stick with a claw on the end to grab things that were out of reach. The next day I had one by my bedside—Dad had been to the oh-so-strange rehab gift shop.

Jonathan was my lifeline to my "real" life, and I looked forward to his visits when he brought news of the boys, messages from friends, and plans for my eventual homecoming. He visited much less often during my time in rehab, however, and I chalked it up to his needing to spend time with the boys. I later learned, however, that he was struggling mightily as well. He was spending hours on end at home, alone in our master bedroom with the door closed, worrying, sleeping, stress-eating, and putting on weight. His dreams of starting up his own business were on hold, and he was frustrated, angry, sad, and exhausted.

During that time, I finally got my cell phone replaced. I began reading headlines about the accident and for the first time saw photographs of the crash scene. I also found photographs and short profiles of the eight passengers who died. I wanted to know more about who they were, but there was only a short paragraph about each person. I gazed at the image of a young mother. Was she the dark-haired woman who had been standing behind me as we boarded the train? She'd sat just a few rows away from me. My mind couldn't make sense of the fact that I was here, lying in bed in a hospital, and she was gone. I felt intensely guilty that I had been complaining about trivial things. Soon, I would go home to my sons, but her little boy would grow up without his mother. I continued to think about that woman and the others who did not survive the accident. I revisited that article again and again to look at the photographs and reread the brief descriptions of who they were and why they were on the train that day. I prayed for them and prayed that God would help me remember how lucky I was.

For weeks, Glenn had been sending mass emails and regular texts to all our friends with updates he got from Jonathan. Now that I had my own phone, it seemed unnecessary. I told Jonathan that Glenn could conclude the phone/email tree. If friends and neighbors wanted to ask how I was doing, they could contact me directly. I wanted to speak for myself.

When the text messages began to pour in, however, I realized I wasn't ready to do that. I was still having terrible difficulty concentrating and couldn't focus on anything written for more than a few sentences. But there was so much I wanted to say. When people asked how I was doing, it wasn't like I could just reply, "Fine." I was soon overwhelmed and found I often couldn't respond at all. I would lie in bed staring at my phone, stymied and exhausted by the effort of writing a simple text to a friend.

On Friday, at the end of my first week at the rehab hospital, I had visits scheduled with my many specialists at Penn. I was taken there in a van that could hold a wheelchair strapped down in the back. It was my first time riding in a seated position, and it was torture, and the ride took more than two hours because the van driver got lost. Once again, I could sympathize with a box of tomatoes in the cargo hold of a truck, only this time the ride felt a lot longer and a lot bumpier.

By the time I arrived at Penn, I was already miserable, ready to lie down for a long nap. Of course, now I had to go see the doctors. I had to see at least three specialists—one to remove a surgical drain, another to check my neck to see if I was ready to have the cervical collar removed (I was not), and another to run some neurological tests.

At the end of the day, after another two-hour drive in the back of the van, I was done—done for the day and also done with the rehab hospital. The relatively cheery and upbeat patient from the ICU was long gone. I wanted out. No one would give me a clear answer on how long I was expected to be there or what milestones I'd have to reach to be released, so I decided to set my own goal. I was going home in one week, on June 12, Steven's birthday.

I asked my parents to bring me a large piece of poster board and a fat red marker. I wrote June 12 on the board in giant letters and had it hung on the wall beside my bed. From that point on, whenever the doctor, nurses, and physical therapists came to my room, I pointed to the date and said, "That's the date I'm leaving." They smiled, and no one challenged me directly.

There was something else I was determined to do. Sunday was Austin's confirmation at church. His confirmation-class peers had chosen him to deliver the sermon at the Sunday service, and I couldn't stand the thought of missing it. We talked about other options—I could see the video later or watch on my phone through FaceTime, but the idea of seeing Austin give his speech from my hospital bed seemed awful.

It's not so easy to get a day off from the hospital. Jonathan had to request a special dispensation from our insurance company. We also needed our own transportation. Thankfully, our neighbors across the street kindly offered their wheelchair-accessible van. It was another rough ride getting there, but as we entered the church and they rolled me down the center aisle over the plush red carpet and parked me beside my family in the pew, I felt an enormous sense of gratitude and pride. I'd made it. I was there for my son. Not only had I made it to his confirmation, I was alive and surrounded by my family, praying with gratitude for God's grace.

I watched Austin walk up to the high pulpit in his dark suit with a red confirmation shawl draped over his shoulders, his blond hair gelled back. I was so proud of him. His speech was about the accident and how the experience changed him and strengthened his faith. His voice was steady as he described the moment when Jonathan told him about the accident, making frantic calls to hospitals, and praying with Mercia. "The only comfort I had in this whole situation was God," Austin said.

It seemed like all two hundred people in the congregation were crying as he spoke. He went on to tell about receiving the text message that I was alive. He said he realized in that moment, "Not only was my mom alive, but God, too, is alive. My faith is alive." Austin said he'd come to recognize God's grace in the world—through others' kind gestures and love, supporting us in times of need. I was amazed and honored to see my fifteen-year-old son stand up and speak in front of so many people with such openness, bravery, and wisdom.

Brad, too, had given a recent speech about the accident. As the school year drew to a close, his teacher asked each student to speak to the class about how they had grown and changed since September. Brad began his speech by saying, "How have I grown in the past year? A better question would be, 'How have I grown in the past month?'" He went on to describe the moment Austin told him about the train crash and said, "That night when Austin came into my room, it changed me forever." He spoke about praying for me all night. When he heard I was alive, he said he felt that their prayers had worked. He explained that he was changed by the accident because he had become a more spiritual person. He believed that the prayers of the family and our neighbors were the reason I was still alive and concluded, "God was listening to me, and I had never felt that way before."

He also spoke about feeling more responsible for his performance in school. He knew I would want him to do well, and he felt it was his duty to keep up good grades for me. When I read Brad's speech, I was filled with love and pride. He's more reserved than Austin, and writing doesn't come easily to him, so I knew that sharing something so personal with his seventh-grade classmates must have been challenging. He did it beautifully.

Two days after Austin's confirmation, on June 9, it was Brad's thirteenth birthday. If there had been any chance of making it, I would have set my homecoming for that day, but I knew they weren't letting me go yet. Jonathan took a picture of the three boys standing in the kitchen at breakfast. Brad was in the middle with a hopeful expression, his braces showing through his grin. He was holding up a plate of pancakes formed into a slightly lopsided number 13. Austin was wearing his backpack, like he was about to head for the bus. Steven was looking up from his plate of chocolate-chip pancakes. He had probably just rolled out of bed because he hadn't put his shirt on yet. There were glasses of orange juice, a few sliced strawberries, and an open bottle of syrup. Seeing them among all the familiar trappings of home filled me with longing. I ached to be there, sitting around the kitchen island, feeding them breakfast, laughing together, and showering Brad with birthday hugs and kisses.

Preparations for my homecoming began to intensify. One requirement for my release was for the house to have an accessible living space. We were getting a bed that could be raised and lowered, installing a ramp over the side steps leading into the house, and refurbishing the first-floor guest bedroom and bath to accommodate me and my wheelchair. Neighbors had offered to take care of our dogs so their exuberance wouldn't jostle me.

My friends, Jody and Tracy, volunteered to organize all our friends in the neighborhood to help renovate and decorate our "new" bedroom. Jonathan asked if I wanted to give any input, but I told him to leave it to them. They had way better taste than me anyway.

Another friend, Jen A, coordinated contributions to a giant gift basket. This was no random collection of trinkets. There was a fluffy robe, pajamas, and other gift-store items from the Hershey Spa in Pennsylvania, where our group of friends had taken midwinter trips together for the previous few years. Another friend gave me a Kindle because she figured I had a lot of time for reading. A friend who sells upscale beauty products included all the best body lotions, moisturizers, and lip balms. There were soft blankets for my bed. The greatest of all was the joke gift—a hideous housedress made of paper-like material in a garish print with a zipper up the front and a condom slipped inside the pocket. We howled with laughter as it fell out on the floor beside my bed. It was difficult to imagine a less-relevant gift than that tragically lonely condom.

I started to have a few more visitors. The kids and Mercia came one afternoon, and Scott flew in from Seattle for another visit. I still wasn't ready for many friends to drop by, partly because I didn't have much energy, but also because I was embarrassed to be seen in the rehab hospital. I did see Tracy one day when she was in the area. Lisa also visited, bringing a huge shopping bag stuffed with get-well cards and letters that had been sent to the office.

Seeing all the cards astounded me; there had to be at least 150 in every color and size. We had to set up an assembly line to open and read them all, with my dad opening envelopes and my mom writing the sender's name before I read the card. I wanted to keep track of each one so I could send thank-you notes. I soon realized that was impossible.

Some cards came from close friends and colleagues, others from company executives and people in the industry I deeply respected. There was a hand-drawn card with notes from families and staff at The Children's Inn at the National Institutes of Health. The Merck Foundation makes grants to that residence for families with children receiving treatment for rare and life-threatening diseases. I had always been touched by the bravery of these children and now, here they were, sending *me* a get-well card.

There were cards from people I'd never met. One was from a Duke alumna named Ginny who had seen me speak the night of the accident. Her granddaughter, Charlotte, had asked if her grandmother knew anyone on the train after the priest at church said a special prayer for the people involved in the derailment. Ginny told her about me. Charlotte went into the other room for a while and then came back to ask how to spell my name. A little while later, she brought out her hand-drawn card and asked her grandmother to give it to me. Ginny only knew that I worked for Merck and mailed it to the company headquarters, assuming it would find its way to me.

So many people—some total strangers—were praying for me and offering to help in ways seen and unseen. It was a humbling experience, and there were moments when I was overcome with gratitude. The support of all these people was truly palpable to me. I felt it in my heart and in my bones.

But there were still other moments when I felt utterly isolated. Some part of my mind was stuck on the horror of what had happened and couldn't move past it. I felt disconnected from everyone I loved, because they hadn't been in the accident. It was a strange dichotomy—to have moments of intense loving connection with family and strangers alike and other moments of complete alienation. The ups and downs were exhausting.

The pain and fear of pain were also exhausting. The dosage of some of my medications kept going up and up as the doctors tried to provide relief. I was also facing the physical reality that there are some levels and kinds of pain that they simply cannot relieve.

I started to feel that my progress had plateaued. The days blended together, and any advances weren't terribly obvious. One good session of physical therapy might be followed by a particularly painful one the very same day. I pestered my doctors nonstop to let me go home.

Finally, I got the news I wanted. My doctors had agreed I could move home and continue my recovery there, with support from a visiting nurse. My excitement was tinged with annoyance, though; my release date was set as June 13. I felt like I'd been pretty clear, with my giant poster board sign, that June 12 was an important date to me. Apparently, however, there were too many other discharges scheduled for that date, and I would have to wait a little longer. I was disappointed to miss Steven's ninth birthday. That morning, Jonathan sent me another breakfast-time photo. This one was only Stevie, his little fingers wrapped around the edge of a plate, holding up a chocolate-chip pancake in the shape of the number 9. The corners of his mouth were turned up, but his eyes weren't smiling. His hair was poking up in the back, and maybe he was just tired, but it looked like reaching this milestone of nine years had left him a little world-weary. I wished I were there to gather him up in my arms and give him a hug.

My many new accessories had been delivered to the house—the wheelchair, walker, shower chair, and special toilet seat (one of those raised seats with handles that fits over the bowl). On the one hand, it felt like progress; on the other hand, it stunk to know that all that stuff was for me. Jonathan sent me a picture of everything set out in our driveway. "We're ready!" he texted. I thought, *Okay, that's great. Can we get the granny toilet out of the driveway now?*

Then there were the prescriptions. From now on, it would be up to Jonathan to keep them filled. This turned out to be a way bigger deal than we expected. I was taking sixteen different medications, three or four times a day. When we were sure the doctors had given us all the scripts, Jonathan drove to the pharmacy in our neighborhood. It turned out they didn't have all sixteen drugs in the necessary dosages in stock. Jonathan filled what he could and drove to another pharmacy. The next pharmacy didn't have everything I needed, either. Filling my medications was like a scavenger hunt: Jonathan had to continue driving from pharmacy to pharmacy until he found each one. We didn't yet know how much of his time this hunt would take over the next two years.

But I was going home! At last I could say good-bye to the hospital. This was momentous. No one (except blissfully ignorant me) had expected me to leave so quickly, and it renewed my optimism. I couldn't wait to see my boys every single day. I could sit on the porch with friends. No one would wake me up in the night to check my vital signs. I could have a glass of wine! It seemed like I could ride this momentum all the way to a complete recovery. I estimated it would take another six weeks. I might still be on crutches at that point, but I began telling everyone I'd be well enough to jump back into normal life by the end of the summer. Getting back to home and work, resuming my usual routines would mean I'd moved on and put this awful episode behind me.

Six

As Jonathan drove up our street, brilliant sunlight spilled through the windows. The sky was pure Titian blue, and the neighborhood lawns glowed a vibrant green. A crowd was gathered in the driveway and, as we pulled up, my friends and neighbors erupted into cheers and clapping. At their feet were colorful chalk drawings by the kids and enormous chalk letters spelling out the words, "Welcome Home!" Only one element ruined the postcard-perfect picture. A long, black metal ramp slashed across the front yard, covering the steps to the house and extending to the sidewalk. The harsh ramp felt like a giant billboard, announcing to the world that the two small steps up to my front door were too much for me now and that this house was not the same.

Jonathan opened my car door and placed the walker next to me so I could show off by standing up and taking a few steps for everyone. As he eased my legs out of the car, I felt the sun kissing my face and warming my back. I'd been indoors for so long; the touch of the sun and the fresh air was blissful. Gentle one-arm shoulder hugs wrapped around me, as the parents cautioned the kids to be careful. While my wheelchair was vacant, Brad took the opportunity to test it out on our long, sloping driveway. In what would be the first time of many, I called after him to bring it back to me. Later, my crutches would often mysteriously find themselves on the other side of the house, too.

Well-medicated, I made my way with the walker to the foot of the ramp and then took a seat in the wheelchair. I think I mostly looked normal, except that I was still wearing a cervical collar that cupped my chin and extended all the way down to my collarbone. Everyone was eager to show me the inside of the house. Brad wanted to be the one to push my chair, so he wheeled me up the steep ramp. Hanging over the doorway was a colorful banner saying, "Welcome Home, Geralyn." As Brad attempted to push the wheelchair through the entrance, it got stuck on the threshold. He backed up and pushed again. It still wouldn't go. He turned me around backward and tried lifting and pulling. Jonathan came to help. He gave one big push, and I rolled inside. For as long as I needed the wheelchair, I wouldn't be able to make it up the ramp or through that doorway by myself.

As we entered the kitchen, it was like wandering into a wonderfully familiar florist's shop. Every surface was covered in beautiful, fragrant flowers. It looked like there were dozens of bouquets in all varieties. Friends had strung up balloons and streamers, and there were stuffed animals, fruit baskets, too many cards to count, and gifts—many from people I'd never met.

The far reach of people's kindness amazed me: flowers and cards from the local dry cleaner, hair salon, and taxi service; a gorgeous handmade quilt with a butterfly motif from Linda W, a longtime family friend; and a hand-knitted prayer shawl from a local Catholic church I'd never attended. Members of a church in Minnesota sewed a third quilt. A couple I didn't know had heard my story when visiting my parents' church in Colorado. When they went back home, they had organized a quilting project at their own church. The parishioners tied knots of prayer into the vibrantly colored fabric. Then they sent the quilt to my parents' church in Breckenridge, Colorado, where more prayer knots were tied before the quilt made its way to me in New Jersey. The knots were more than symbolic. More than one hundred people, most of them strangers, had prayed for me, each of them calling on God in their own way. Those rows of knots held God's love.

Finally, it was time to see our new temporary bedroom, which was just off the kitchen. The room had been a guest room of sorts but was mostly a junk room full of mismatched furniture, a few dim lamps, and carpeting stained with urine from our poorly trained puppies. I knew Jonathan and my friends had been making some changes to accommodate my first-floor existence, but I hadn't imagined the extent. As we entered the room with a dozen people watching my reaction, I gasped.

It was like one of those home remodeling TV shows when they do the big reveal. The room was completely repainted, with new hardwood floors; bright overhead lights; new curtains, furniture, and bedding; and even a flat-screen television. All my friends from the neighborhood had pitched in to help. What touched me most of all was a wall of framed family photos, including many from years ago. Jonathan had helped my friends find pictures of the boys and us, as well as photos of my parents and siblings. I loved seeing our happy family memories filling the wall.

It was when I caught sight of the bathroom that the made-for-TV moment ended. Jonathan explained that the renovation hadn't gone quite as quickly as planned. The bathroom was still a construction zone. I didn't want to fixate on what was wrong because I was so grateful for all the effort my family and friends had made, but this was going to be a problem.

The trip home had exhausted me. Happy but tired, I thanked our neighbors and friends once more, and after exchanging hugs, they cleared out.

After a much-needed nap, I tackled the chore of getting my pills organized. I rolled my wheelchair up to the kitchen table, where my sixteen different prescription bottles and boxes were spread out. Jonathan had bought every kind of pill sorter he could find, but it appeared there wasn't one on the market with enough slots for all the pills I had to take throughout the week. Some I took every three days, and I took others two, three, or four times per day. There were some pills I took before lunch because I was supposed to have them on an empty stomach; others I took after lunch because I was supposed to have them on a full stomach. (The fact that I had absolutely no appetite for lunch or any other meal complicated things further.)

Because I worked for a pharmaceutical company, I understood the importance of strictly following prescribed medication schedules. I had assumed that remembering which pills to take when was a problem only for elderly patients or those who were simply irresponsible. Again, the arrogance of good health. I finally made a giant calendar chart listing my medications and their schedules, and then I dumped all the pill bottles into a giant salad bowl. It was the best solution I could come up with.

That first night, Jonathan and I settled into our new adjustable bed with its new down comforter and about a dozen fluffy pillows in all shapes and sizes. He elevated my head and legs and collapsed beside me on a flat mattress. On my bedside table, he'd organized the necessary nighttime pill bottles in a neat line, with a glass of water and my phone. I wish I could say that we savored and celebrated the moment, finally at home in bed together. In reality, I took my sleeping pill and lay in bed, staring at the ceiling in a daze. The feeling was familiar and incredible, yet foreign and weird. The feeling of differentness clashed so loudly with feelings of homecoming, love, and gratitude. I wondered if he heard the noise as well.

"What are you thinking?" Jonathan asked softly as we lay in bed taking it all in.

I shook my head. I couldn't put it into words.

He started snoring; my sleeping pill took effect, and the moment passed.

Sometime around 2:00 a.m., I woke up. My whole body hurt. I nudged Jonathan. I had to use the bathroom, and I needed a pain pill, but as usual, I couldn't move enough to reach it. He got up, raised my headrest, lowered the footrest, handed me the water and pill, and waited for me to take it. Then he took the cup, put it down beside the bed, and carefully uncovered my legs. He lifted them gently as I braced for the pain, slowly turning my torso 90 degrees so he could set my feet down on the floor. He then positioned the wheelchair beside me and helped me rise and turn just enough to sit down in the chair. He then pushed my wheelchair across the house to the small powder room that had the only working toilet on the first floor. Next, he had to run back to the bedroom to get my walker and set it up in front of me so I could navigate the last few steps to the toilet in blessed privacy. Ungrateful and self-absorbed, I grumbled repeatedly about the construction.

When morning came, I once again felt immobilized from pain. Just as I would bang my casts on the rails of the bed in the hospital, I tried to move as little as possible while jostling Jonathan next to me with my right forearm to wake up and help me reach my pain pills on the bedside table. Jonathan got up again, helped me adjust the bed, and handed me the pills. Then he readjusted the bed and turned the light off again as he went to wake the boys and get them ready for the day. We'd repeat this process every four hours every night for weeks to come.

As I lay in bed in the mornings, actively trying to separate my mind from my body, I couldn't completely shut out the everyday sounds of the busy household I had rejoined. I would hear Jonathan calling the boys to breakfast, readying their backpacks, and hustling them out the door to catch the bus. It was the last week before the start of summer vacation—a time filled with end-of-school concerts, parties, and tests—but those were a distant concern. An hour after the boys left, Jonathan often brought me a cup of coffee in hopes of getting me up. It was 8:00 a.m. I had to get out of bed because the crew was coming to work on the bathroom. This frustrated me—I had this special adjustable bed and a new room, but I couldn't stay in there. My mom would come in to help me get dressed, and then they would wheel me out to the living room and settle me onto the couch.

Often, I didn't feel comfortable enough to fall back to sleep. I had some breakfast, but I couldn't eat much. I couldn't climb stairs, so showering was not an option. If I didn't have physical therapy or a doctor's appointment that morning, what was there to do? My parents, Jonathan, and I sat around making small talk and trying to be positive, but the day seemed to stretch out before us. My mind was too foggy to read a book. Sometimes, we sat on the back porch until it got too hot. Maybe I'd write a few thank-you notes that all sounded pretty similar.

My mom was wonderful and would take me for short "walks" down the street to get me out of the house. Pushing my wheelchair with the leg supports extended out straight in front of me, she navigated the bumps and dips in the street carefully to try to avoid setting off the right-leg shocks. Going to the end of the street and back was a major outing, and we both love the sunshine.

My friends stopped by often with food and to check in; their visits were a highlight that often pulled me out of my funk. At the same time, while I appreciated all the cooking my friends were doing, I wanted things to go back to normal as much as possible. I think we all did. I finally asked everyone to stop bringing us food. Mercia and my mom are great cooks, and I needed my normal. I tried to explain and hoped they weren't offended. No more labeled dishes piled up on the counter waiting to be returned; no more overflowing fridge.

My friends sought other ways to reach out to me. Soon after I arrived home, a group of women from the neighborhood told me they wanted to organize a girls' night, a house party at my place. They said I didn't need to do anything; they would bring all the supplies. My mom bought me a casual dress that was loose enough to wear easily over my bandages.

When the evening came, the doorbell rang and a crowd of women streamed into the house, carrying bottles of wine, wheels of cheese, and bowls of dip. Everyone congregated in the kitchen, spreading the food and drinks out on the island. The room was filled with laughter and excited chatter. More guests trickled in—there had to be about thirty women. It was wonderful...for about half an hour. Then my stomach started to bind up in knots. It was the revenge of the opioids. To combat the problem, I was taking all kinds of prescription laxatives, but nothing really worked. Whoever came up with the phrase "shitting bricks" was definitely on fentanyl and OxyContin. Bent over the handles of my walker, I excused myself and retreated to my bedroom, embarrassed. My friends, Jody and Joanne, helped me get into bed. As much as I wanted to be up for a party, my body wouldn't cooperate.

Jen A popped her head in the door and told me not to worry; they were moving the party to someone else's house. I was disappointed, but there was nothing I could do. Jody and Joanne said they would stay, and Jen said she was staying, too. Tracy, Vicki, Liz, Kim, Lynette, and a few others joined us. They gathered in my bedroom, and a few of the girls crawled into bed with me. The chatter from the kitchen died down as the crowd dissipated. Then it was just ten of us sitting and talking in my room.

Now that I was lying down, my stomach felt better. I pointed out all the things I loved most about my new room. Jody showed us a "before and after" video she'd made of the renovations. I recounted some of the funny stories from the hospital, and we laughed about the lonely condom in my gift basket. I talked about my worries, too, and about my plans to get back to work later in the summer.

Our after-party went on for an hour or so, until Lynette said, "We should go and let you rest." The ladies began to get up and gather their things.

"No! Don't leave," I pleaded. I wasn't ready for the night to end.

Nighttime was so difficult. I would have preferred to stay up talking with my friends rather than face the darkness and the quiet.

I had expected to settle back into my old life, albeit with some restrictions, but to be with my family in the same way we always had been. Instead, my days mostly revolved around my body's constraints and needs. I had enough energy for only one main activity per day. It might be a physical therapy session or a friend coming over for lunch. Sometimes, I'd be lying in bed, half-awake, staring at the walls, and I'd realize friends would be arriving in ten minutes. It took all my willpower to perk up, get out of bed, and run a brush through my dirty hair.

I was referred to a nearby physical therapist who was affiliated with the rehab hospital. On my first visit, Jonathan pushed me up to the entrance in my wheelchair. Two sets of imposing glass doors confronted us. Jonathan opened the first door while I wheeled myself inside the vestibule. He then struggled to position my wheelchair so he could open the second door with enough room for me to wheel through. *What kind of physical therapy office doesn't have a wheelchair-accessible doorway?* I wondered.

When my name was called, I rolled myself into the treatment space. A nervous young therapist sat at the computer. "So, what happened?" he asked. I stared at him blankly. "What are your injuries?" he repeated.

"You don't know?" I sputtered in disbelief. "You don't have my records?" I assumed this would be a seamless transition. Why else would I have been referred here?

Still staring at his computer screen, he explained that the office didn't work that way. I was starting from scratch. It didn't seem right that they were relying on *my* recollection of a complex constellation of injuries to determine my treatment. I got through the first appointment and never went back.

Jen T helped me find another office with excellent physical therapists, and she lent her expertise in explaining my injuries. My new therapist's name was Brian. He was hugely supportive, but going to physical therapy was difficult because I was in much worse shape than all the other patients. I felt out of place among the high-school athlete getting rehab after knee surgery, the obese woman dealing with lower back pain, and the elderly man working on building strength. Only once did I see another patient in a wheelchair. I had to get over myself and accept that the world wasn't built around people who had been crushed by trains.

In addition to physical therapy three times a week, I was going to occupational therapy for my hand twice a week. Those hour-long sessions were utterly mind-numbing. I had much more serious medical issues to deal with than trying to straighten all the fingers on my right hand, but I wasn't willing to compromise on getting back full functionality. As a lawyer, I had always spent my days at a computer, typing... so there I was, gripping a pencil with my fist and stabbing holes in a piece of clay, over and over. Ball up the clay and press it flat. Stab, stab, stab. Meanwhile, the occupational therapist would tell me all about the latest comic-book convention he had attended. Roll out the clay. And the superhero costume he chose for the occasion. Stab, stab, stab. I felt like I had been dropped on another planet.

A visiting nurse came to check on me twice a week, and I started seeing a primary care physician whose office was close to my home. Like many women, I visited the ob-gyn once a year, but it had been ages since I'd seen a primary care doctor. Now all my medical forms asked for the name of this nonexistent doctor, so I had to find one. A friend recommended Dr. P.

Jonathan came to my first appointment. He knew things about my time in the hospital that I had either forgotten or been unconscious for. My independent feminist streak rebelled at the idea of bringing my husband to my doctor appointments, but for the time being, it was necessary.

In the waiting room, I chose to stand, leaning over my walker, because getting in and out of a chair was too painful. A heavyset woman with dark curls coated in gel was seated in the corner of the room. She stood and approached me, carrying a tote bag full of files, notepads, and papers. She asked, "Excuse me, are you Geralyn Ritter?" I nodded. "I'm Leslie, your nurse case manager. I was sent by your insurance company, and I'm here to help you." That last line sounded like a joke. The canned sentiment certainly didn't win my trust. I was fortunate that my medical expenses were covered by worker's compensation insurance. The meeting, however, was my first introduction to the byzantine bureaucracy of health and disability insurance. Insurance companies are legendary for creating hoops to jump through and obstacles to surmount when someone tries to claim their benefits. Navigating the myriad forms, documentation requirements, phone calls, emails, and delays would become my new job and a near-daily chore.

A rep from my insurance company had told me they were assigning a nurse case manager due to the complexity of my injuries and the number of doctors I was seeing. I wasn't very clear on her role or why

she'd been sent to meet me at Dr. P's office. Leslie said she'd be tracking my case and began asking me questions about my medical care. Jonathan eyed her suspiciously. Still bent over my walker, I felt unsteady and too distracted by pain to pay attention to what Leslie was saying. Thankfully, the nurse called my name, and I had an excuse to walk away. I began to inch forward with Jonathan by my side. I'd made it a few feet when I realized Leslie was following us. I looked at her, my brow furrowed in confusion.

"I'll be accompanying you to all your appointments," Leslie explained. She must have seen the look of shock on my face because she quickly added, "Of course, I'll step out if you need to disrobe." It never would have occurred to me that the insurance case manager would actually come to the exam room and sit in on my visit with the doctor.

"Is this really necessary?" Jonathan asked gruffly.

"Yes, it is a stipulation of your insurance," Leslie replied.

I didn't have the energy for an argument (with either of them). "It's fine," I said.

When Dr. P opened the door, her eyebrows shot up. "Well, hello!" she said to our uneasy little group crammed into the tiny exam room. I was seated on a chair with Jonathan by my side and my walker folded up next to him. Leslie was in the doctor's swivel chair, and she jumped up when the doctor entered and squeezed herself into the corner behind the exam table to make space. Leslie introduced herself. Dr. P turned to me and asked, "Are you okay with this?"

Jonathan muttered under his breath, and I shot him a warning look that meant *not now*.

"It's fine," I said, shrugging. If I were being truthful, I would have agreed with Jonathan. Aside from the fact that the exam room was the size of a closet, it felt like a tremendous invasion of my privacy. A total stranger was going to be listening in as I described my pain, ailments, and fears. She'd hear everything, including all the details about my difficulties using the bathroom. For what reason? All I could think was that she was there to judge me—looking for reasons to refuse my benefits. The old me would have been furious.

I did my best to put it out of my mind and focused my attention on the doctor. She was a trim and stylish young woman with shoulder-length, wavy strawberry blonde hair. I liked the flashy red heels she wore with the requisite white coat. Trauma wasn't her specialty, but she didn't seem intimidated by my condition. Dr. P took her time with me, and our conversation went on for well over an hour. The hospital wouldn't send over my medical records for another six months, so she had to rely on what Jonathan and I told her, along with the laundry list of injuries on my discharge form. She asked about my pain, how I was eating and sleeping, issues with digestion, and so on. I liked that I could tell her everything because she wasn't focused on one narrow area of expertise. As she made notes on the computer, she remarked that she'd never used the insurance code for a train accident before. Dr. P recommended that I find a pain specialist nearby, given the assortment and high dosages of pain medications I was taking.

After the appointment, Leslie gave me a pile of forms from the insurance company to sign. One was the agreement for my nurse case manager to accompany me to my doctors' visits, have access to my full medical files, and be allowed to speak with my doctors without me present. "This is insane," Jonathan said, seething. I, too, wanted to refuse, but in bold text, surrounded by asterisks, the document said something like, "Failure to agree may affect your benefits." We couldn't afford any risk to my benefits, and I didn't have energy to spare. Giving Jonathan a severe look that he knew meant I alone was going to make this decision, I signed the form. As it turned out, I was given not one, but two insurance caseworkers—one for appointments in New Jersey and one for appointments back at the hospital in Pennsylvania.

The visiting nurse the insurance company sent to our house twice a week annoyed the hell out of me, too. Nurse Susan had to drive two hours to get to my house, so she liked to settle in and stay a while after she arrived. I wanted nothing more than for her to draw my blood, check how my various surgical incisions were healing, and leave, but a quickie conversation was never what she had in mind. She would make small talk, sit down and get comfortable, and then pull out a mess of folders stuffed with forms that she was required to fill out for every visit.

She'd ask my least-favorite question: "How's your pain?" I never had any idea how to answer. How's my pain in this very moment? When I first wake up? Before I take my meds or after? When I'm moving or trying not to move? When I'm breathing or trying not to breathe? When lightning bolts unexpectedly shoot down my right leg? In those random moments, my pain was eleven out of ten, but when the moment passed, that part of my body was back to near-zero pain. The pain varied from hour to hour, from day to day, and from body part to body part, jumping around the scale between unbearable to background noise. As always, Susan just wanted me to give her one single number. I'd arbitrarily pick one: "It's a five" or "It's a nine." It didn't really matter. She marked it down on her form, making sure that the number showed through on all three copies.

"Are you constipated?" Susan asked.

"Yes," I said, "I haven't gone for a week, and I'm not eating."

"Okay," she replied, dutifully marking it down on the form.

She checked my pulse and blood pressure and then asked where her box of supplies had gone. Because she was coming so often, she kept the supplies at my house. Someone often seemed to have moved the box, and we spent the next twenty minutes hunting for it, with me rolling around in my wheelchair, pointing to closets or cabinets where her all-important Band-Aids might have migrated. Then Susan took my blood, had me sign a few forms, and blessedly left. A day or so later, I would get a call that my blood was too thick or too thin, and I needed to pick up a new prescription to adjust the dosage of blood thinners.

The constantly fluctuating dose of blood thinners was one reason keeping track of my meds was nearly impossible. Dr. P didn't know why the vascular surgeon at Penn had prescribed this particular medication, and I certainly couldn't enlighten her on his reasoning. She tried calling him to find out, but he wasn't returning her calls. I knew from my health-care policy work that coordination of care is not the US healthcare system's strong suit. I had just never experienced those disconnects in such a personal way.

As the weeks passed, tension began to mount between Jonathan and me. From midnight to 8:00 a.m., I needed Jonathan, and he helped me cope with the basics of life. During the day, however, I kept feeling that his initiative was exactly zero. Something needed fixing? Pop Pop was on it. Meals? Mom and Mercia had those covered. Ask Jonathan to take out the trash, and he'd grumble and complain about this being his own house and promise to do it later. During our worst arguments, I told him he was wallowing.

A few days after I arrived home, I was sitting on the toilet when I doubled over in pain. My abdomen felt like it was going to explode. I lost my balance and tumbled over to the floor. Now I was curled up and whimpering on the floor of our tiny powder room with my pants around my ankles. I was in so much pain I couldn't get up. I couldn't get enough air, and I started to panic. I realized I had no choice but to call out to Jonathan for help. He came running. We didn't know what was causing the pain, so he made a desperate call to Jody, hoping that as a doctor, she might know what was wrong. Between breathy gasps, I argued with him not to call her. It was too embarrassing. "Just hang up!" Wisely, he ignored me. Jody suggested it was probably severe constipation. My bowels were so impacted that it was causing intense belly pain. Jonathan would need to address the situation himself or get me to a hospital where they could. My last shreds of dignity were swept away.

After we resolved the issue and the initial panic was over, I felt disgusted with my whole situation. This was not how I wanted to rely on my husband. We'd been married for eighteen years, but since the night of the accident, our relationship had been pushed into new territory. I didn't want him (or anyone) to see me like that or have to care for me that way. Jonathan stood by me faithfully, but that didn't make me feel any better about being so dependent on him. My frustration over the whole situation started to bubble up as little resentments, snappish comments, and impatient criticism.

After much discussion, Jonathan had quit his job as a lawyer a few years earlier to start his own tech business. He was interested in 3D printing and other new technologies—he had a ton of ideas. I had recently received a promotion, and there were advantages to him having more flexibility to help around the house, so we agreed we would try it out for a year and see how it went. Then one year became two, and two years became three. None of Jonathan's ideas had come to fruition. We'd been arguing about the fairness of the arrangement since well before the accident, and now I was out of work, too, making me even more anxious about our finances and the future. It seemed to me that Jonathan should start looking for a "real" job at a real company or perhaps go back to a law firm.

I still needed him to take care of me, but I couldn't face the reality that this was a 24/7 undertaking. I started to fixate on all the little things he wasn't doing. Why didn't he notice that we'd run out of milk? Why did it seem like dirty dishes were always piled in the sink over the weekend? One day, he took a nap on the porch in the middle of the afternoon. "Why are *you* so tired?" I snapped. Jonathan was flabbergasted. To him, it seemed obvious and my question the height of ingratitude and thoughtlessness.

And I suppose it was. But no worse than his remark to me, asking what I was doing to help the family: "Just sitting around and waiting to get better?" he asked sarcastically.

Umm. "Yes," I said, seething.

Ever since that night spent searching for me, Jonathan had been grappling with a mix of emotions. At the forefront, understandably, was his anger with Amtrak. Years before, Congress had ordered all passenger railroads in the United States to install the safety measure of positive train control (PTC), which automatically slows a speeding train, but time and again, the railroads had lobbied Congress to extend the deadline. If PTC had been in place, Amtrak 188 never would have derailed.[24] On top of this, federal law also severely limits damages for passengers injured or killed in railroad accidents. So the railroads got to skimp on safety and avoid full accountability for the broken lives that inevitably resulted. It's an unfair rule that still exists. Jonathan had reason to be upset, and I understood that. I was just tired of hearing him rage on about it.

What I didn't know at the time was that decades of research have shown dramatically high rates of PTSD among the families of ICU patients,[25] along with very high rates of depression.[26] The long-term psychological effects in family members appear similar to those experienced by ICU patients.[27] Family caregivers are also substantially more likely than non-caregivers to suffer physical health consequences, including higher rates of obesity, high blood pressure, and heart disease, among other ailments.[28] My petite mother lost far too much weight, and most of her hair fell out over that summer and fall. Jonathan, by contrast, gained thirty pounds in short order, and I now recognize that his constant fatigue was undoubtedly a sign of depression.

Jonathan's openness, spontaneity, sensitivity, and enthusiasm were all qualities that initially attracted me to him. The flip side of those wonderful traits was volatility and quickness to anger that had long been a point of tension. When Jonathan is worried, he tends to talk, and venting his anger seems to relieve a certain amount of stress. But during those difficult months, it was sometimes less of a conversation than a furious monologue. Talking through his frustrations made him feel better. Hearing the same frustrations over and over again made me feel worse. We are a matched set in many ways, but not this one. His expletive-filled tirades would go on for ages about the unfairness of everything, and he wanted me to be angry, too. If I started to respond with a neutral comment like the fact that caps on damage awards are commonplace in the law, he'd get even madder and start directing his anger toward me. I didn't feel angry, though. I just felt sad. I was compartmentalizing my hurt, trying to be positive and to focus on things I could control. To me, Jonathan was obsessing about things we couldn't control. Our resentments grew, and being stuck in the house together 24/7 wasn't helping.

All too often during those early months at home, we simply couldn't give each other what we both needed—and didn't even know how to ask. Jonathan was looking for a sympathetic ear with no judgment or opinions that challenged him; he wanted encouragement and recognition of his efforts. I needed positivity and encouragement in the peace I was trying to make with my situation. For the next two years, we would struggle. Major blowups happened infrequently; however, the constant tension, unspoken resentments, and passive-aggressive comments were just as poisonous. Despite our best intentions, empathy and emotional security were in short supply, and we both worried that our marriage would break under the pressure.

Lack of sleep certainly didn't help. After dinner, in addition to the continuous dose of 100 micrograms of fentanyl supplied by the large patch on my left upper arm, I took melatonin, Ambien, my nighttime dose of OxyContin, Lyrica, and blood thinner. When the house grew quiet and dark, a veil of sadness and isolation settled over me. I stayed up after Jonathan had fallen asleep, binge-watching shows on my phone, trying to distract my restless mind and hurting body. By 3:00 a.m., I would get desperate and add an oxycodone plus some Benadryl or Tylenol PM to the mix, washed down with another glass of wine. I still shudder at my recklessness.

During the day, I was in a daze. Everyone offered me useless, unrealistic advice to beat the insomnia, like *get up early in the morning* or *don't nap during the day*. It was impossible not to doze off in the morning and daytime, and sometimes those naps felt like my only relief from stress, worry, and pain.

I've read memoirs of other survivors of serious illness or trauma, and insomnia seems to be extraordinarily common. It seemed like my body had forgotten how to sleep normally. I felt constantly jet-lagged. My psychiatrist later suggested that my body simply didn't feel safe "going dark" at night.

Scientific studies affirm that sleeplessness is intertwined with trauma. One researcher writes, "Trauma-induced insomnia is a highly prevalent, disabling, and under-recognized phenomenon."[29] Although disturbed sleep is a core feature of PTSD, there is also evidence that "trauma-associated sleep disorder" can be a completely separate phenomenon, experienced by trauma survivors who do not develop PTSD.[30] Worse, there is also substantial evidence that serious insomnia following trauma puts a patient at *higher risk* for developing PTSD. The evidence suggests that addressing insomnia early on can actually prevent full-blown PTSD in trauma survivors.

Insomnia in the weeks following a trauma is essentially a marker and a risk factor for susceptibility to future disability, including PTSD, depression, substance abuse, and other anxiety disorders. Despite this evidence, the optimal management of insomnia following trauma is still poorly understood, and little authoritative guidance is available.

What we do know is that the reason for this close connection between trauma and insomnia traces back to the part of the brain that regulates our fight-or-flight stress responses. The nervous system is essentially stuck on high alert, long after the danger has passed. Trauma may generate an intense, sustained hyperarousal state by activating the amygdala, a key structure in the brain that is critical to the stress and fear responses. Amygdala activation, in turn, kindles heightened arousal in the brain stem, promoting alertness. Studies of patients' heart rates, blood pressure, respiratory rate, EEGs, stress hormones, and whole-body metabolic rates have demonstrated this state of hyperarousal, as have neuroimaging studies.[31]

Insomnia is also a frequent partner of chronic pain. It may seem obvious that pain makes it harder to get a good night's rest. What is less obvious, but has been proven, is that poor sleep actually makes the feeling of pain worse. "Pain worsens sleep patterns, and sleep disturbances worsen pain—it's a vicious cycle," says Robert Bolash, MD, from the Department of Pain Management at Cleveland Clinic.[32] In fact, sleep impairments are actually a stronger, more reliable predictor of pain than pain is of sleep impairments.[33] Studies have shown that even modest changes in a night's sleep can affect a patient's sensations of pain the next day.[34]

The exact mechanisms in the brain that cause this response are poorly understood, but recent studies using sophisticated brain-imaging equipment suggest that sleep deprivation enhances pain responsivity within the primary sensing regions of the brain's cortex, yet blunts activity in other regions that modulate pain processing. In other words, a lack of sleep interferes with the brain's natural ability to moderate pain.[35]

All I knew at the time was that my body had changed. I would get into bed around 11:00 p.m., but I wouldn't fall asleep until around three or four o'clock in the morning. A few hours later, I'd wake up in damp sheets, my skin clammy from sweating through my nightgown, sticky hair matted against my face. My legs would be tensed in a rigid position that I could unlock only with deliberate concentration. My arms would float mysteriously above my head. Intellectually I knew I was safe, but my body had a mind of its own.

My friends talked among themselves about how I wasn't the same person they knew. Their previous Geralyn had a loud, wild laugh and a vibrant, energetic personality. She worked at a high-level job, went on business trips to far-flung places, spent time with her three kids and husband, and could still throw a late-night neighborhood party on the weekend. Now I was rarely out of bed before noon. I tired easily and couldn't handle the simplest things. They hoped that once I was healed and off the medications, the old Geralyn would come back. No one knew for sure.

I didn't realize how strongly the pain medications were affecting me or how long it would take to wean myself off them when the time came. When my doctor friend, Jody, heard about the large quantities of fentanyl, OxyContin, and oxycodone I was taking, she was shocked. She told her husband, "The amount of medicine Geralyn is on would kill a horse." My own surgeon once told Jonathan the exact same thing. Apparently, I am a sturdy horse. My friends later told me that they wondered to each other how Jonathan and I would manage all these drugs. Seeing how groggy I was, some feared I would forget how many pills of Oxy I'd taken. They were probably right to worry, especially during the long nights when sleep wouldn't come, and I'd search the medicine cabinet for anything I hadn't taken yet.

Although I was clearly moving at a different pace than before, my mind still hadn't synced up with my new reality. I constantly talked about going back to work. Some of my friends wondered why I was so eager to jump back into my former life. After enduring such a harrowing experience, why didn't I want to take a breather, slow down, and spend time with my family? I have wondered about this as well. I care a great deal about my job and career, but I have always prided myself on keeping some kind of balance and taking every single day of my vacation time. I think I was fixated on work because I was desperate to return to normal. My mind was stuck somewhere between denial and deliberate optimism, and I continued to believe I would return to the office in a matter of weeks. Whether this was healthy or not, I still do not know.

Now that I was out of the hospital, my parents decided it was time to head home. They'd flown across the country on no notice, and they'd devoted themselves to me completely for months. On the one hand, I was grateful for the way my dad heard the tiniest suggestion of a request from me and responded immediately. I might mention the only thing I felt like eating was ice cream, and the next thing I knew, our freezer was stocked full. My mom had been a godsend. I absolutely could not have managed without her praying with me, dressing me, brushing my hair, and shaving my legs every day without a single complaint. Of course, with all the doting came concerned remarks about whether I'd eaten enough and the perennial question, "Did you remember to take your pill?" which I resented. I was forty-six years old. I wanted privacy, independence, and the right to make my own decisions.

Mom and Dad were exhausted, too. My progress was heartening, but the emotional and physical demands on my caretakers were nonstop, and my marriage tensions were adding to everyone's stress. We all needed a break.

They knew I was on the mend, but they were still worried. A week or two after they left, my dad sent me a pleading text suggesting I wasn't calling or texting my mom often enough. They needed to hear from me. I understood this, but it felt like a burden. I was deeply grateful to my parents, but I didn't want to be checked on every day. It was easy to text them when I felt fine, but when I didn't feel fine, I didn't want to talk about it or fake it.

Since I'd returned home, my emotions were all over the place. One moment, I was looking out the kitchen windows at the grassy expanse of the backyard, the swimming pool, and the hillside beyond. Gratitude welled up inside me. This was a beautiful place to spend my days recuperating, and I was so incredibly fortunate. I'd get teary-eyed and write gushy thank-you letters. The weather was warm, and often, I would sit on the back porch in my wheelchair. I planted myself out there with my water bottle and my phone. My friends were very kind about coming to visit or planning things around what I could do. They brought their kids and wheeled me down to the pool so we could sit and talk while the little ones swam. I'd usually take off my neck brace because it was so hot. Inevitably, someone would scold me, saying I needed to keep it on, and I'd playfully show them my middle finger.

Then my mood would unexpectedly shift in the other direction. There were flashes of red-hot anger when the pain shot down my leg, and I'd scream and yell. There were moments when I was pushed to tears because it seemed like I couldn't do even the smallest thing without help. Often, it was a crushing sadness. The pain was relentless—almost like I was wearing a heavy coat all the time, its weight dragging me down.

One day, I was writing a thank-you note, and I dropped the pen. There it was, on the floor three feet away. I stared at the thing for a while and felt my irritation grow. It was so close, but I would have to call someone to come to the kitchen to pick it up and hand it to me. I decided to try getting it myself. I pushed the walker away, slowly bent over, bearing most of the weight on my good leg, hoping the shock didn't flare. I reached for the ground and made it down on my hands and knees. I immediately regretted it. My chest, back, and pelvis seized up in pain as I froze on all fours. I cried out. Now I was stuck.

Jonathan heard me and came running into the kitchen in a panic.

"What happened?" he yelled. It looked like I had fallen.

I angrily snapped, "I was just trying to get my pen," as if it were obvious.

"Next time, ask for help," he chided. I glared at him. "You have to ask for help," he repeated. Everyone was offering to help me all the time, but I was tired of calling people two floors away to come pick up my stupid pen.

Feeling confined made me snappish, too. The smallest thing would set me off—Jonathan hadn't done the laundry, or the kids had left a mess in the kitchen. Maybe I was looking for a way to assert some bit of control over my life. I'd been in the hospital for so long, I felt like I'd lost my role as a parent in some ways. When I tried to take charge with the kids, they would retreat upstairs where I couldn't follow them.

I was getting on the boys' nerves, too. They were used to my busy work and travel schedule, and now I was always home, always camped out on the first floor near the kitchen. If I noticed they were eating too much junk food or weren't going to bed on time, I'd be on their case. Then there were the mood swings: they never knew which version of me they would get—teary-eyed and emotional, or pissed off, sleep-deprived and zombie-like, or bubbly and talkative, making plans to return to work soon. I know it was a relief to have me home from the hospital, but I didn't make it easy.

The kids wanted normal, too. Sometimes, Steven would ask, "Mom, can you go swimming yet?" and I'd have to say no. He also missed jumping together on the trampoline. One day he suggested, "What if you just *sit* on the trampoline?" I felt so guilty. Another day, he asked to play Monopoly. This was something I could do…but I just didn't feel like it. I couldn't go to their sports games like I used to, either. I made it to one baseball game when Austin was pitching. Rolling up in my wheelchair and neck brace, I was glad for the change of scenery and to see the other fierce baseball moms. They wished me well and said kind words that I appreciated. I cheered for Austin as he pitched a few innings, and then the exhaustion and the bittersweet sensation hit. I was nodding off in my chair, even as the pain was building. I had made it to the game (so grateful!), but I couldn't stay (so pissed!). I didn't go to another game until I was out of the wheelchair and could pretend that it was all behind me.

I looked for new ways to spend time with the boys. The accident had brought up such intense emotions for all of us; I thought eventually we would have deep, heart-to-heart conversations. Whenever the boys came home from school or camp, I called out to them from the bedroom, hoping they would hear and come talk with me for a while. When they came in, I would ask, "How was your day?"

In the tradition of teenagers everywhere, they gave me the usual one-word answer: "Fine."

"What did you do at school?" I asked.

"I don't know. Regular day."

Most moms try to get their kids to watch less TV or spend less time in front of screens. I became the opposite.

"Don't you want to watch a show?" I pleaded. "Anything you want. You could get a snack…this bed is cozy…"

Sometimes, the boys indulged me. Some of my most peaceful memories of those difficult months were the long, lazy afternoons with one or more of my boys keeping me company as we binge-watched one sitcom after another.

In the evening, if I was awake, I joined Jon and the boys at the dinner table. Most of the time, I wasn't eating, or I might just have a bowl of ice cream, but I sat at the table anyway because that is what people do. Afterward, we might hang out together in the bedroom, where they curled up on Jonathan's side of the bed to watch TV or play cards with me.

One day when I was in the kitchen with thirteen-year-old Brad, he asked about the accident. It had been almost two months since that night, and until then, he hadn't wanted to talk much about what happened. He'd asked Jody some medical questions about what the spleen does. The day he visited me in the ICU, he asked about the various machines and monitors.

But that day, he had a different kind of question: "Mom, are you *sure* you were in the first car?"

"Yes," I said, puzzled at the question.

"Are you sure?" he asked again. It was clear he'd been thinking a lot about this.

"Yes," I said again. "I'm sure because I was in business class, and that was the only business car."

"Have you seen the pictures?" he asked.

The pictures?

"No," I said, reminding him that I was unconscious in the ICU when most of the news stories were first published. Since then, I hadn't been able to focus sufficiently to read very much about the accident. I also hadn't really let my mind go there.

Brad was insistent.

"But have you seen the pictures?" he asked again. He had to know whether I was really in the first car. He brought the iPad over and pulled up photos taken the day after the accident. He found the one he was looking for and zoomed in all the way, so every detail was enlarged. He held the screen about two inches from my nose, asking again whether I was sure.

It was the first time I'd seen that image from the crash. There was car one, twisted and bent like a coil of wires. The front half was turned upward so you could see the driving wheels. The other half was ripped open, its insides spewed out onto the tracks—scraps of metal and broken glass strewn alongside blue upholstered seats and shredded carpeting.

"Mom, how did you survive *that?*" he asked.

"I don't know," I said at first, taken aback by the sight of it. I looked at him and touched his shoulder. I repeated, "I just don't know, sweetheart." We sat in bewildered silence as I pulled him close. "I guess... that's how great God is." I hesitated to use the word "miracle." It sounds so self-congratulatory. I told Brad, "We can't always understand, but we can be grateful. God can do things, baby, that we don't understand."

To this day, I don't know a better answer.

Seven

"What do you think would look better?" I asked Bruce. "If I show up with a walker or in a wheelchair? I'm thinking the walker," I said, pleased with my progress.

I was going to the office. It was early July, and Bruce had been encouraging me to visit. He said everyone had been so worried about me; it would be reassuring if I stopped by. I figured it made sense to visit because I was planning to get back to work at the end of the summer.

"Definitely the wheelchair," Bruce advised. "The wheelchair looks temporary."

"Got it," I agreed, somewhat relieved as I thought of the long hallways in the office.

Luckily, all my scars were hidden under my clothes, so aside from the wheelchair and the cervical collar, it would probably look like nothing was wrong. Jonathan helped me dress in one of my favorite summer suits. I wanted to appear professional.

My admin, Lisa, and I planned a schedule of people to see during my visit. We kept it light, taking my lack of stamina into account. Bruce sent a car to pick me up. The drive was only about forty minutes, but by the time we arrived, I was overcome by nausea.

"I'm not feeling so well," I told Lisa as she met me by the elevator.

"Do you want to head back home?" she asked. My face had drained of color, and I was beginning to slump in my wheelchair. "We can reschedule."

I considered the offer. If I could have been back in bed right that instant, I would have done it, but the thought of riding back home when I already felt nauseous was daunting.

"I don't know," I said.

"Let's go inside," she suggested. "Maybe if you have a few minutes to rest, you'll start to feel better." She wheeled me into a conference room. "You can take some time alone in here," Lisa said. She brought me a bottle of water and turned out the lights, saying, "I'll be back in a little bit."

I took a sip of water and put my head down on the conference table. The nausea would not subside. The time for my first meeting came and went. I tried, but I couldn't muster enough energy to get my head off the table. Minutes ticked by.

The conference room door opened suddenly, and I picked up my head. I was astonished to see Ken Frazier, the CEO of the company, standing in the doorway. "Geralyn, how are you doing?" he asked.

"I'm so sorry," I said. "I just got a little carsick. I'm fine. I just needed a minute," I babbled, no doubt unconvincingly.

"Please, don't apologize," he replied.

"I'm getting stronger," I said. "I'm just using the wheelchair for convenience today," I explained, "but I can stand on my walker now. I just have some pain and stamina issues to work through."

"Do you mind if I have a seat?" Ken asked. He sat beside me in the darkened room and took my hand in his. "I'm sorry you're not feeling well," he said.

Ken and I had worked together for a few years, but I never would have expected the CEO of the company to take a personal interest in my recovery and to be so kind. Ken is one of the most remarkable people I've ever met. Under his leadership, Merck evolved from a company whose very existence was in question as a result of an avalanche of lawsuits to the top-performing stock in the Dow Jones Industrial Average in 2018. When he was serving as Merck's CEO, he was among the small handful of Black CEOs heading Fortune 500 companies. (In 2021, Ken retired from Merck as CEO and now serves as Chairman of the Board.) A deeply principled man with a strong moral compass and abiding faith, Ken has spoken of the values instilled in him by his parents. Growing up in a rough neighborhood in Philadelphia, he lost his mother when he was twelve, and his no-nonsense father raised him and his sister on a school janitor's salary. Ken graduated from high school at sixteen and went to Penn State University as an undergrad and then to Harvard Law School. In 2018, *TIME* magazine named him one of the Top 100 Most Influential People of the Year.

As we sat in that windowless conference room, I started again to broach the subject of work. I was insecure regarding my position in the company and wanted to assure him that he could count on me. Ken cut me off before I'd finished my sentence. He is known for being direct—when a subject is off-limits, it is off-limits. "Geralyn, I know that you believe. Would it be okay with you if we prayed?" he asked. I was too surprised to respond with words and simply nodded, trying not to tear up again as the tension and anxiety left my body and was replaced by deep gratitude.

As we bowed our heads, Ken held my hand and prayed aloud. I listened to his soothing words, my heart deeply touched. Ever since the accident, I'd seen that, when something really serious happens, people reveal their true colors. People from all aspects of my life were doing extraordinary things to take care of me and my family. I felt almost overwhelmed at being the object of so much kindness. Ken asked me to keep in touch and visit again. I tried once more to reassure him that I would be back at work soon, but he waved me away. Every month after that, Ken sent me a note checking in and asking how I was doing. He continued to be influential in my recovery.

My first series of follow-up appointments at Penn came after I had been home about a month. Despite my resentment, I appreciated that my insurance-company nurse case manager was able to use her clout to schedule all the visits with my specialists on the same day. I was going to see the neurologist, orthopedic surgeon, vascular surgeon, urologist, trauma specialist, and a hand specialist. Each doctor was in a different section of the hospital, with another waiting room, a separate set of medical-history questionnaires, and different screening processes.

Each visit began the same way. While staring into a computer screen, the nurse or physician assistant would ask routine questions. In every office, I tried to assure the nurse that my file was up-to-date, but each one insisted on asking me the same string of questions, including my all-time favorite: "What's your pain level on a scale of one to ten?" The computer program seemed ill-equipped to document polytrauma. It required that you give one number, but the pain in my leg, back, pelvis, and ribs were all at different levels. "Just pick one," I was told. The nurse only wanted to enter a number so she could click through to the next screen. I guess we both knew it didn't actually matter what number I chose.

After going over my medical history, we'd review the list of medications I'd brought. It was up to me to tell each doctor what I was taking so they could check for interactions between the drugs and understand the universe of the chemicals running through my body. Electronic medical records are supposed to facilitate this process. In theory, at least within the same hospital system, every specialist can see a common record and have an up-to-date understanding of the patient's history. In reality, every specialist still wants to verify the accuracy of the record at every appointment. So a patient with six appointments in a day will fill out the same questionnaire, tell the same story, and go through the same interview six separate times, as each doctor has his or her nurse confirm all the same information in the record.

I had only a few precious minutes with each doctor, and I wanted to be sure all my questions were answered, but Jonathan kept chiming in with his own questions—some helpful, others not. His tendency to interrupt and to deal with his anxiety by talking constantly and making lame jokes grated on my nerves. Even worse, sometimes he indulged his intellectual curiosity and tried to explore his own business ideas about medical imaging with the doctor. I was appalled at what seemed the height of self-centeredness. I clenched my teeth each time he spoke, screaming inside my head for him to just shut up.

When I had been in the hospital, unable to make my own decisions about my care, thankfully Jonathan was in charge of making them for me. Now I needed to take back control. I used every diplomatic skill I could muster to ask him to hold any questions until after I'd gotten all of mine answered. Intellectually, I knew he was entitled to have questions about my health; I knew that my health affected him, too. Emotionally, however, I just couldn't get there. I couldn't get past the feeling of resentment at the intrusion on my time with the doctor. I couldn't suppress my annoyance if he dared to correct me, add his own interpretation of my recent pain levels, or ask about a subject I had deliberately decided to avoid. It wasn't fair, but I've spoken to enough survivors and caregivers to understand that this difficult dynamic is a common one.

Dr. M, my kind and straightforward orthopedic surgeon, sent me for a series of X-rays on my chest, neck, back, and pelvis. When we met to go over them, he told me the news I was most eager to hear: I could start bearing weight on my left side. My pelvis was healing, and I would be able to walk again! I could begin using a pair of crutches. He said putting weight on my left side would hurt, but it wouldn't do any damage to my body. He looked me straight in the eyes with a serious expression and pointed his finger. "Come back in six weeks," he instructed, "and I want to see you walk through that door when you do." An almost-mischievous grin spread across his face, and I felt tears well up in my eyes.

When I'd gathered my emotions, I asked about the jolts of sudden pain I had been feeling in my right leg. Dr. M explained that the pain was caused by the internal fixation hardware in my pelvis. The metal bar screwed into each side of my pelvis, holding the right and left sides together, and it was lying directly on a major nerve on the right side. He explained matter-of-factly that it was unavoidable, given where they had to place the bar and screw it into my hip bone. I felt better knowing what was causing the strange, debilitating pains down my "good" side. I had wondered if it was all in my head. "We'll remove the bar in September," he said. "That may solve the issue, but there are no guarantees."

Once again, I felt like a yo-yo. The benefit of the leading-edge orthopedic surgery I had received allowed the hardware to be placed inside my body and allowed me to recover at home instead of spending many more months in the hospital with giant metal bars protruding from my hips. But the searing, burning nerve pain down my right leg was the price I would pay, with only an assurance that it "should" go away.

"What about my ribs?" I asked. "Do you know how long they will hurt?"

Dr. M again looked at me intently but kindly, his dark eyes serious. He sighed. "Geralyn, people complain that the pain from one or two broken ribs can last for months. Your rib cage—he paused, searching for the right word—"was annihilated." Dr. M never sugarcoated anything.

As that statement sunk in, he explained that the problem with broken ribs is that they are constantly moving—they expand with each inhale and contract with each exhale. So healing is slow and painful.

We weren't dealing with a few clean breaks either. My ribs had been crushed into maybe twenty pieces. When Dr. M was putting them back together it was like gluing together a broken vase. That's why he decided to put metal plates on my ribs, although not all the breaks could be healed that way. Some of the ribs were left to heal in a disconnected, zigzag manner. "You might have pain for six to eight months, or a year, or the pain might never go away."

"Never" is a big word. I chose to focus on the low end of his estimate—pain for six to eight months. This was depressing enough. So far, with the help of massive doses of fentanyl, OxyContin, and other pain medications, I had made it to month three.

"I wake up in the night from the pain," I explained, "and sometimes I feel like I can't breathe because they hurt so much."

"You need to practice deep breathing," Dr. M said. He told me I needed to get the air down to the bottom of my lungs to stave off the threat of a lung infection. He'd given me an incentive spirometer, a plastic device that measures the depth of your breath. "Remember to use it a dozen times a day to fully inflate your lungs." I couldn't imagine ever getting used to the heavy painful sensation of taking a deep breath.

As I made my way to my next visit, the good news Dr. M had given me was still ringing in my ears. I would walk again! And soon I would be free of the wheelchair and the walker! That same day, my neurologist also gave me permission to throw away the cervical collar, declaring that the broken vertebrae in my neck had sufficiently healed, and the danger of damage to my spinal cord had passed. And the vascular surgeon told me the large blood clots in my legs had resolved, so the filter implanted in my vena cava could soon be removed as well, with another surgery later in the fall. This was progress.

The last appointment of the day was with Dr. C.S., my original trauma surgeon. She had been the first doctor to work on me when I was taken off the helicopter.

"How are you?" she asked. All my appointments had begun with this question—the doctors wanted to know about my bones, my bladder, the blood clots, and so on. I began to tell her how each injured part of my body felt. She interrupted me. "But how are *you* doing?"

I opened my mouth to answer, but the tears began before I could find the words. Somehow, I hadn't thought about this. How *was* I doing? It was easy to describe my digestion issues or the nerve pain in my right leg—these things were concrete and hopefully transitory. It was more difficult to know how I was doing. My mood was constantly ping-ponging between awe and gratitude that I was alive and feeling dazed, depressed, and deeply uncertain about my future. I was thankful that the doctor cared and had asked, but her simple question brought me up short. I had become so detached from myself that I felt like a collection of broken body parts. I didn't know how to answer it. The silence grew as I wrestled with how to describe how I was doing and tried to brush off the tears that kept flowing.

"I recommend all my trauma patients see a specialist for PTSD," she said gently, tucking a wayward strand of strawberry blonde hair behind her ears.

Her words were jarring. I had my own biases about post-traumatic stress. I began to sputter lame arguments: "But I don't have PTSD. How could I? It's not like I was in combat. No one *tried* to hurt me. I can't even remember the crash."

Dr. C.S. nodded and said simply, "Well, keep it in mind."

I nodded and looked away. "You think it's necessary?" I whispered.

"I advise all my patients who have been through severe trauma to see a psychiatrist," she repeated. The word *all* struck me. *All* patients—even the strong ones, even the ones hurt in a freak accident, even the ones who never set foot on a battlefield or stared down the barrel of a gun. The doctor went on: "When your body is seriously injured, the brain releases stress hormones. The change in brain chemistry can affect your mood and emotions."

This was the first time anyone had explained to me about the brain's reaction to trauma. The revelation dawned slowly. Later, I would take comfort in the fact that there was an actual physical reason, backed up by science, that might explain the lousy way I'd been feeling. I wondered if she was right. "I'll think about it," I said.

Dr. C.S. took her time with me, and I was able to ask her all the questions that didn't fit into any other specialist's line of work. We talked about how I was eating and the importance of good nutrition. I told her that my hair was falling out and my nails were weak and shredding.

"That's trauma," she said definitively.

I later learned that hair follicles truly are sensitive to trauma and major surgery. The condition is called *telogen effluvium*. The body focuses attention on more urgent matters, and the hair follicles transition early to their resting or death phase.[36] I needed to start asking someone to clean out the shower drain on a regular basis because hair clogged the drain every time I washed it.

My fingernails and toenails had given up, too. I'll never forget the poor manicurist assigned to give me a pedicure. She looked up with an entire toenail in her hand as if to say, *"What am I supposed to do with this?"* I grimaced and shrugged. I didn't care too much about my hair or my toenails, but it seemed an overly apt metaphor. My body—head to toe—was not right.

Toward the end of the visit, Dr. C.S. asked, "Do you think you will ride on a train again?"

I felt the tears coming back. This was the first time I considered the question, and I resented my own uncertainty. "I have to, for work," I said quickly. "I don't know if I'll be afraid or not." I wiped my eyes and began formulating a plan that I would take a train trip as soon as I could, to prove that I could do it.

By the end of the day at Penn, I was worn and wary, but also triumphant. I'd received confirmation that I was getting better. I could throw away the huge cervical collar and make plans for two more surgeries in the fall to remove some of the hardware in my body. On the way home, we stopped at the first pharmacy we saw to buy a beautiful set of crutches.

But I'd also been told to expect at least six more months of serious pain. It was depressing just thinking about it, and I chose not to believe it would last that long. Surely I'd be on the "strong" side of the recovery range the doctors had given me. There was also Dr. M's vague warning about ultimately needing to go through withdrawal from the pain medications. I naively chose to believe this would be no big deal and decided not to think about it, either. *It's not like I'm addicted or anything*, I thought.

Later that week, Jonathan and I took the kids out to Chili's for dinner. I used the crutches instead of the walker. I wasn't too steady on them because I could barely put any weight on my left foot. I crept along bit by bit, taking a careful step with my right foot and then inching my left foot forward. Jonathan walked beside me and held me up as I maneuvered to our table. I almost tripped a few times, and it seemed to take forever to move a few feet, but I didn't care—I much preferred the crutches. When I was out in public on the walker, a forty-something woman with three kids, strangers stared and gave me pitying looks. Crutches didn't look like such a big deal. One step closer to normal.

The following Friday, I got a call from Lynette. She said a bunch of our girlfriends were going out to a new movie that weekend that looked hilarious. She wanted me to go but was a little concerned if I would be okay. I assured her that I was fine, but maybe we could just make sure I had an aisle seat.

"It's not that," she said, hesitating. "It's the new Amy Schumer movie...have you heard of it?" I laughed and told her that at this point, it would take a lot more to upset me than a silly movie title mocking the main character's disastrous love life. So it ended up that my first big outing with friends would be to a movie called *Trainwreck*.

My friends organized everything. They bought tickets at a theater where we could reserve seats in advance. They had a backup plan, too, which they didn't mention to me. They brought two cars, knowing I might get tired and need to leave early. One of them volunteered to take me home if I couldn't make it through the movie. It was a realistic plan because when it was time to get ready that evening, I had to drag myself out of bed and force myself to get dressed. I was able to move past my fatigue: when we were in the car, my friends' energy was infectious.

As we sat down at the dine-in theater, the usher approached me to take our order. I wasn't hungry but ordered a glass of wine.

"ID please," he asked.

I laughed. It hadn't occurred to me. I'd been hospital- and home-bound for months, and my purse was lost in the accident. I had no ID, but I really wanted a glass of wine. No one thinks I look under twenty-one, by the way, but I understood policy. I decided to resort to sympathy. I started to explain to the poor usher who had twenty other rows of patrons waiting to order. "I was crushed in a train crash and lost my wallet. This is my walker. I haven't needed ID in a really long time..." His arched eyebrows conveyed his disbelief as my friends giggled in the background. Yes, he remembered reading something about that accident, and yes, it was quite a coincidence with the title of the movie, but...he'd still need to get his manager. Two levels of management later, I emerged victorious and happily spent the movie sipping my Chardonnay, ordering a refill for good measure.

In the last week of July, I asked Jonathan if we could plan a party for my birthday at the end of August. I don't usually care much about celebrating my birthday, but this year, just thinking about it stirred my emotions. Gratitude and sadness churned inside me as my mind circled around "What if?" scenarios. I wanted to mark this birthday and give thanks. After all, if ever there were a time to celebrate another year of life, this was it. Jonathan was excited about the idea, which made me feel lucky. With everything else he was dealing with, he was still happy to throw a party for me. Even more than celebrating my birthday, this party would be an opportunity to thank all our close friends who had helped us through the accident and my recovery. I was envisioning it as a bookend. It would mark the end of my recovery and this scary chapter in my life. Sort of like: "Thank you for coming; thank you for being here; the show is over, and we're all good now." Just thinking about it made me smile.

Jonathan and I planned to make the celebration easy and manageable so we wouldn't end up overwhelmed. We'd invite our closest friends, and our boys would be the only kids. We'd have it catered and keep it simple. I started to write up a guest list and think about the menu.

Now that I had permission to bear weight on my left side, physical therapy became much more exciting. Up until now, my exercises seemed to be focused on the parts of my body that were not injured, to avoid losing strength in those areas. I would do simple, dull movements like lie on an exam table holding a light bar above my hips, raising it over my head while inhaling, and then lowering it back down while exhaling. With Dr. M's mandate that I walk through his office door in six weeks, the focus immediately shifted to relearning to walk. The PT center had an antigravity treadmill. It looked like a regular treadmill equipped with a harness and a big, plastic, air-filled bubble that covered the whole platform from my waist down. The controls could be adjusted to set the level of gravity. So at the highest setting, the patient could literally float through the motion of walking. I held onto the handrails and, as Brian turned on the machine, I lightly touched down my toe, the ball of my foot, and then my heel—one foot in front of the other, in a slow, steady stride. I was walking! This simple act felt like a revelation. I asked him to take a short video and send it to my family. The accident had a way of reminding me that even the most mundane aspects of life were a blessing.

Of course, getting back to walking came with its struggles. Over the next few weeks, the white-hot pain in my right leg flared up again and again. It had seemed like it was lessening, but now it came back even worse than before—striking multiple times a day. Every time those electric jolts ran through my leg, I'd scream, curse, and collapse. Brian said it was because I was more active now, using the crutches most of the time. All the movement was irritating the nerve, still crushed by the hardware implanted across my lap. One step forward, one step back.

I'd been trying to stay positive, but most of the time, I was still caught in that distant, foggy, depressed feeling, and it wasn't getting better. I cried easily, which was unusual for me, and angered easily, which was even more unusual. I could be quite a bitch. I ignored my mother's daily texts asking how I was doing, snapped at the boys, and resorted to yelling up the stairs when they retreated to their rooms. Most of my venom, however, I saved for Jonathan. Why was he so tired and eating all the time? What was he really doing all day other than running a few errands? We have a nanny, for goodness' sake! And why wouldn't he shut up about Amtrak and the cap on damages? *Deal with it*, I thought. *You are* not *the one who is actually hurt.* I cringe as I think about my preoccupation with my own needs and my inability to connect with my husband emotionally. But my guilt is tempered by the reality that I felt like Jonathan didn't understand—because he didn't. He couldn't. We were on parallel, but utterly separate, paths through the darkness, and I felt alone.

For his part, Jonathan marveled at my ingratitude. Our entire world had been reordered to revolve around me. The calls, the gifts, and support network were all focused on me. What about him? The normal give-and-take of a marriage seemed to be, for him, mainly about giving during those days.

For me, the nights were the loneliest times. I'd stare at my phone for hours, clicking on the same news sites over and over. I'd haunt the kitchen, fixing a bowl of cereal or eating Ben & Jerry's out of the carton at 3:00 a.m. I'd pour a glass of wine and take another pain pill and then flip on the gas fireplace and sit staring at the flame, sometimes till dawn. Sleep would come with the morning, and as everyone else started the day, I found it almost impossible to get out of bed.

Often, when I woke up, I'd find my arms stretched straight up in the air, palms slightly open and fingers curled, as if holding a bar above my head. I had done this in the hospital as well and ignored the strangeness of the position, figuring that my body was stretching the only part that could move at that point—my arms. As I continued to wake up regularly with my arms stretched toward the ceiling, I became increasingly aware of the oddness of it. I knew intellectually that I could put them down by my side, but it felt as if it would be deeply uncomfortable to move them. Sometimes, I lay there, fully awake, in almost a trance state, staring at the ceiling with my arms stretched up toward the ceiling, for what felt like hours. I fought the fatigue in my arms. Only when the discomfort of holding them in that position became too great, or someone entered the room and shook me from my trance, was I able to allow them to fall to the bed. I puzzled over this—my arms seemed to have a life of their own. It freaked Jonathan out. He would wake up in the night to find me moaning, arms outstretched to the ceiling, like a zombie toy someone had tipped over on its back.

One day, as I described my last memory before the crash—people were constantly asking whether I remembered the accident—I explained that I was standing in the aisle of the train with my arms outstretched, holding on to the luggage rack above my head. It clicked. I realized the position I was waking up in day after day—my arms reaching out, my fingers curled around an invisible bar—was my position when the train derailed. All I can figure is that this position was imprinted in some deep part of my brain and that my mind found odd relief in reenacting my last moment of safety. I discovered later that many trauma survivors find comfort in reenacting the event. They may not remember or want to retell the story of what happened, but they will repeat certain actions, emotions, and sensations related to the trauma.[37] It was like my body took a picture of the moment of impact and was having trouble filing it away.

On the last day of July, I visited a psychiatrist for the first time. I'd been hesitant about going. I'd long had biases against mental health counseling, and it didn't fit with my self-reliant self-image. I could deal with accepting help to straighten out my broken finger. When it came to my thoughts, mood, and emotions, however, I preferred to work through issues alone. But even I had to admit I hadn't been so successful lately. The other issue was that it was difficult to get worker's compensation insurance to cover psychiatric care. If they did, I would have to go to the doctor they assigned, and it seemed likely the insurance company would require access to records of my sessions. That's where I drew the line. It was hard enough for me to accept that I needed to see a psychiatrist, let alone do it with an insurance company's rep looking over my shoulder. I decided to try it and pay out of pocket. I swallowed my pride and called a doctor who had been recommended to me.

In our first session, I told the doctor I'd been trying to focus on the good things, telling myself how lucky I was to have survived, but as the pain wore on week after week, it was getting harder. As I spoke, the well of grief opened up, and tears flowed once again. I wanted to know why I wasn't strong enough to deal with this. I'd always prided myself on my self-reliance and self-control. Why was I so crushingly tired during the day and wide awake at night? I knew my body needed time to heal, but I didn't see why a bunch of broken bones and busted-up organs would have such a dramatic effect on my emotional state. As I'd said to Dr. K, I didn't even remember the accident. How could I be mentally traumatized by it?

Dr. K reinforced what Dr. C.S. had told me, explaining that there is interplay between the physical body and the mind. When the body is severely injured, or one's life is in danger, the most primitive part of the brain, the so-called "lizard brain," automatically reacts. In an attempt at self-preservation, it floods the body with stress hormones like cortisol and adrenaline to support in fighting back or escaping. Sometimes, the nervous system stays on high alert long after the initial threat is gone, and the body continues to be inundated with stress hormones.

Dr. K acknowledged that he couldn't precisely pin down the reason I was always exhausted—sleeping mainly during the day and not at night—but it could be my brain's reaction to trauma. Or it might be depression, side effects from my medications, or simply that my body was still healing. The easiest answer was to say that it was all the above. He advised me to go easy on myself and not to beat myself up. "It's okay to stay in bed," he said. "Give yourself a break."

After talking with Dr. K, I was willing to accept that I might be experiencing post-traumatic stress, but I wanted to know how much of my dazed stupor was due to the painkillers. What would it feel like to be me, without the medications? Shortly thereafter, I had a day when the pain was minor, almost just soreness. I had stopped taking the breakthrough doses of oxycodone over a week before, and my digestion had been somewhat better. That afternoon, I tried skipping one dose of OxyContin to see what would happen. I took the next dose that afternoon on schedule and didn't notice much difference, so the next day, when it was time to change my fentanyl patch, I decided to delay putting on the new one. I knew I would feel it, but I just wanted to experience the "real me" at that stage. I figured my hips and ribs would hurt, but I could stand it for a little while, and then I'd simply put on the new patch. Any transitory increase in pain would be worth it to know what state my body was really in.

It happened all at once, as if the ceiling had crashed down on me. The main sensation was that I was suffocating. Before I realized what was happening, I was curled up in a ball on the bed, crying. I couldn't move. My ribs felt like they were closing up around my lungs. I was trying to breathe and simultaneously trying not to breathe so I would not move my throbbing chest. On top of the pain from my injuries, I'd thrown myself into withdrawal, and it was horrible. No one was home; I'd left my medicine in the kitchen. I felt like I was right back in the hospital, trapped in my bed, struggling for breath, unable to move or call for help. I finally steeled myself and got up the will to reach over to the bedside table and pick up my phone. I called Jonathan and whispered, "Come home."

Jonathan rushed home and applied a new fentanyl patch, and he gave me my regular dose of OxyContin, a breakthrough oxycodone dose, and the Lyrica. Two hours passed, and I was still curled up on my bed, breathing easier, but still unable to move. I gave in and threw another oxycodone into the chemical cocktail swirling in my body. By the evening, the wave of drugs finally kicked in, and I felt enough relief to raise the headboard of my bed. I lay there, playing a simple card game with Steven, trying to assure him that Mom was okay, just having a bad day.

I would discover in the coming days that my effort to discover the "true" state of my body had thrown off my equilibrium and sent my nervous system back into high alert. It took more than a week to get regulated to the medications again. There is a reason doctors always advise patients to "keep ahead of the pain." There are complex biological and chemical reasons why a hyper-aroused nervous system can't immediately calm down after the pain has passed (or the pain drugs have restarted). This came as a shock. I had no idea how dependent I was on the painkillers. People had been remarking on how quickly I was healing and how well I was moving around, but apparently, it was all an illusion. I couldn't even function for a few hours without the medications. Until now, I'd been feeling impatient—when was I going to start feeling like myself again? It turned out the real me was in much worse shape than I'd suspected. Dr. M had warned me that I would have to wean off the drugs, but I hadn't appreciated what that meant, nor had I realized that I was far from healed enough to handle it.

Throughout August, I spent half the day in bed and much of the rest of the time at health appointments. We'd managed to get rid of the visiting nurse, but now I had to go to a lab twice a week to have my blood checked, on top of the daily physical therapy and occupational therapy sessions and multiple doctor appointments. On the days that she took me to my physical therapy sessions, Jen texted an hour before it was time to leave. Jonathan would raise the head of my bed, open the curtains, and bring me coffee to help me wake up, but I often dozed off after he stepped away, several times spilling hot coffee all over the blankets. When Jen pulled into our driveway, Jonathan would gently pull me up and help me put on a pair of sweatpants. I usually went straight from bed to car, tying my messy short hair into a ridiculous stubby ponytail.

One day at physical therapy, I was feeling particularly low. As I lay on the exam table, doing my exercises, my mind was mired in dark thoughts. My idea of a six-week recovery had obviously been wildly unrealistic. What if my idea of a full recovery was also unrealistic? The future felt like it was shrouded in bleak uncertainty. Brian came over to stretch my legs. He piped up, cheerfully, "Things getting back to normal these days?" Lying on the exam table, I shook my head, my eyelashes suddenly wet with tears. I couldn't give any other response. Jonathan and I had had a tense morning, my whole body hurt, and the doctor's caution about significant pain for an entire year loomed over me. *How can he even ask me that?* I wondered. Things were nowhere near "normal," and it wasn't clear if they ever would be.

Everyone else was enjoying the end of the summer, going on vacation, and getting ready for the start of the school year. I was going nowhere, but at least my birthday party was something to look forward to. We set the date for August 21. Our closest friends turned out to be a group of fifty people, so it was going to be a pretty sizable crowd.

Jonathan and I got more ambitious and decided to make it an elegant sit-down dinner. We wanted this to be a special and memorable thank-you to everyone who had helped us through the previous few months. There would be fresh flowers, cloth napkins, and tablecloths. We'd start with appetizers and cocktails before dinner. For dessert, we splurged and ordered 150 mini-cupcakes in special flavors, like cookies and cream topped with fresh strawberries, red velvet, and carrot cake.

As the plan got bigger and bigger, I wished my parents could come. They did so much for me; I wanted them to be part of this grand thank-you celebration. When I invited them, they said they couldn't make it. The more I thought about it, the more disappointed I was. I really wanted them here. I started calling my mom nearly every day to tell her how the plan for the party was progressing. Every time I called, I asked her if there was any way she and Dad could come. I was whining about it so much, she finally had to admit the truth. "Sis," my mom said, "we wanted to surprise you. We booked our flight weeks ago."

The week of the party, I tried a new medication. I'd been resistant to taking any mood drugs, but Dr. P had prescribed Cymbalta, in addition to the Lyrica I was already taking, to try to dull the nerve pain in my right leg. "It's also an antidepressant," she said as an aside, "which might not be a bad thing." There was no trace of sarcasm in her voice. I accepted the new prescription, telling myself I was doing it only because it was primarily for the pain, and I was desperate for some relief from the electric shocks still plaguing me on a daily basis. If I were being honest, however, I was glad for this "cover" to try out a new drug that might make me feel even a little happier.

In hindsight, the fact that I needed an excuse for taking medication to treat my depression seems ludicrous. I now know that, like the connection between pain and insomnia, chronic pain and depression are profoundly linked.[38] Chronic-pain patients have far higher rates of major depression, and depressed patients report far higher rates of pain than nondepressed patients.[39] This makes sense intuitively, but the relationship is complex and important to understand. As Judy Foreman explains, "At its most basic level of brain anatomy, an emotional response is intrinsic to pain. It's part of the deal. It's how we are hardwired. It's neurobiological. The parts of the brain that process emotions (the limbic system) are literally connected to the parts (the somatosensory cortex) that detect bodily sensations."[40]

In fact, brain-imaging scans reveal similar disturbances in brain chemistry and changes in brain structure in both chronic-pain patients and patients suffering from depression.[41] Both conditions involve the neurotransmitters serotonin and norepinephrine, which play a role not only in mood disorders, but also in controlling pain.[42] Properly understood, anxiety and depression are not merely psychological responses to pain; they are physiologic, biologic consequences of it.[43] Somehow, understanding that there was a biochemical reason why I felt depressed—that it wasn't simply because I couldn't handle the pain, stress, and disruption to my life—made me feel less like I was failing at my "job" of getting better. Learning about these underlying mechanisms helped restore a bit of my confidence that I was still a strong person, just maybe not one who could fight basic neurobiology.

Unfortunately, just as chronic pain can lead to serious depression, the effect also runs the other way. Pain and depression can reinforce each other in a vicious cycle. Serious depression can actually intensify the way that the brain perceives pain and interfere with its natural ability to try to lessen it. Our natural pain relievers, endorphins, become less effective. The best prescription for this "double hurt" is just what Dr. P did: treat both. As I ultimately figured out (much later), there is an important role for both pharmaceutical and nonpharmaceutical interventions aimed at both issues.

I woke up with a bittersweet feeling on August 21, the day of the party and my first day on the new antidepressant. I wasn't anywhere close to where I'd expected to be in my recovery. Jonathan and I planned to give speeches to thank our guests that night. I sat up in bed to work on mine. When I had had the idea for this party a month earlier, I had thought I'd be healed. The party was supposed to be the finish line, a triumphant and clean ending to an unpleasant interlude. All month, I'd been seesawing back and forth between feeling okay and feeling exhausted, or moody, or woozy, or dealing with the unpredictable pain shooting down my right leg. As the chairs and tables were delivered and the caterers began setting up, Jonathan had to take the lead in directing things. My parents arrived, and I showed off our fancy preparations, only to then apologize for going back to bed. I was feeling dizzy and exhausted and wondered if this party had been a big mistake.

As the evening neared, I gathered my willpower and resolved to try as hard as I could to have fun. When Mom came in to wake me, she found I was already up, dressed, and putting on lipstick. I had forced myself out of bed and put on the new dress Mom bought me for the occasion. I'd remarked several times that the one good thing to come out of the accident was that I'd lost twenty pounds, and I was ridiculously pleased that the slim cut of the dress fit well. She gave me a big hug, cried a little, and then helped me cut off the tags and decide which flat sandals to wear.

By evening, when our guests began to arrive, the backyard was cast in golden light and the air held the sweet smell of summer. We gathered on the patio by the pool for drinks and appetizers. We'd had parties out on the patio many times before, but this one was special. We'd gone all out. Tracy said it felt like we'd been transported to a resort. The bartenders were working at full speed, servers came around with shrimp cocktail and a variety of sushi appetizers, and there was a spread with caprese salad and crudités. As friends and family hugged and snapped pictures, my mood continued to brighten, and my energy returned. Laughter could be heard across the yard, and God treated us all to a magnificent orange and pink sunset that spread across the sky. It was almost like old times.

We stayed outside talking and enjoying cocktails until the sun slipped away behind the hillside. It was time to gather inside for dinner. We'd turned the open foyer, dining room, and living-room space into a banquet hall, with round tables covered in cheery lime-green textured tablecloths and decorated with bouquets of blue hydrangeas and fragrant white lilies flanked by tall taper candles. Crystal glasses glimmered beneath the chandelier. We'd pulled out my grandmother's china that she'd given us for our wedding present. Gold-rimmed plates were already heaped with green salad, and teacups were brimming with my favorite, spicy gazpacho.

Jonathan and I gathered our guests around the foot of the staircase to offer our thanks. He walked up a few steps so everyone could see him. He began by saying, "This year is a very special year for us to celebrate Geralyn's birthday. I have long known how very precious she is to me, and these past few months, I've really come to know what she means to her friends." Jonathan went on to thank our friends for their acts of kindness since the accident.

There were a few specific people he wanted to thank individually. He thanked Glenn for helping search for me and for his support and friendship since. As Jonathan spoke, tears came into his eyes. It was never really possible for him to talk about that night without getting tearful. Listening to him recall the terror and uncertainty of the search, everyone became a bit emotional. Mom's shoulders tensed, and she looked at me protectively. It was difficult for her to hear details about the night of the accident. Jonathan thanked my parents, our sons, and Mercia. Mercia had helped keep our lives as normal as possible during a tumultuous time, and he thanked her for praying with our boys the night of the accident and staying with them whenever they needed her.

Then Jonathan presented me with a small box wrapped in gold paper—my birthday gift. I smiled as I pulled the paper away. Inside was a little velvet jewelry box. I immediately knew what was inside. The night of the accident, when Jonathan was brought to the ICU to iden- tify me, he was handed a plastic bag with the jewelry I'd been wearing. The moment he saw the cut-off twisted wedding rings and bracelet was the moment he realized he had found me. Now, I snapped the lid of the box open and saw a sparkling re-set engagement ring and wedding band nestled there. They were perfect. I hugged him and tried to gather myself to say my piece.

With the help of one crutch and the banister, I got myself up a few steps. My friends all gave me a round of applause. I struck a silly pose, wiggled my hips, and laughed. Looking out at their faces, I felt their kindness and love raising me up once again. We were all so lucky to have such a close, caring community. Before the accident, I'd been so busy with work and my family that I hadn't been truly aware of the significance of this bond with my neighbors. I thanked them for their support. "I'm happy for my kids to see this," I said, referring to the ways they'd helped us, "for my kids to see that this is what it means to be a friend."

I also had to be honest about how I was doing. "One of the hardest things about this experience is—not being in the hospital and going through all the surgeries, or being the youngest person in the rehab hospital by thirty years. The hardest thing is that it isn't over." That was the other reason I wanted to thank everyone. Not only did they have my back in a moment of crisis; they were still there for me now, months later, and I knew I still needed them.

It was like the Academy Awards. I had to thank everyone, and happily for me, they couldn't cut my mic. I thanked my siblings, even though they couldn't be there that night, and I thanked my parents for sitting by my side in the hospital, scratching every itch; responding to every request scribbled on the whiteboard; and bringing me breakfast, lunch, and dinner many tines. I thanked Jonathan for his love, care, and constant support.

It was important to me to acknowledge the boys in front of all our friends and say how proud I was of them. "I'm proud of you for staying strong, for doing what you needed to do in school, in church, or with your teams, and for understanding that I couldn't be the mom I want to be for a while." I recalled the day they first visited me in the hospital. To this day, I am completely convinced that I would not have made it through this experience without them. Needing to be their Mom was what got me out of bed most mornings (or afternoons).

Finally, I thanked God for His mercy and blessings. Most of my friends practice their faith quietly, and it isn't a frequent topic of discussion, but that night, I felt it was important to me to thank God out loud and without fuzzy euphemisms, in front of everyone. Before now, I thought I could work my way through anything. This was one of the few situations in my adult life that I couldn't solve by hard work. Everything was out of my control, and that was impossibly hard for me to accept. Even with fantastic medical care, a supportive family, and an incredible community of friends, it still wasn't enough. Only God was enough.

That night, everyone stayed late, eating, drinking, and celebrating—perhaps not in that order. My hip was killing me, and I resorted to my crutches by midevening, but it was by far the best birthday I have ever had. I needed a reason to celebrate, to say thank you, to see my friends, and to hear them tell me I looked good. While we were planning the party, there were difficult moments—times when I was zoning out and staring at the wall when I was supposed to be calling the caterer. And I'd had to rely on friends for some things, like giving me a ride to the florist to pick out the flowers. But I'd found that making myself take on a project like this felt good. It pushed me out of my funk and made me look forward to the future.

Looking back on that evening, I realize how therapeutic it was to throw that party. The experts say it's a basic lesson of survival: *Do something*. Even something as trivial as throwing a thank-you/birthday party for my fifty closest friends. Take control. Find the good. Do something.

Family photo taken about 5 months before the accident. Austin is 14, Bradley is 10 and Steven is 8.

"My guys" preparing for a charity run, just weeks before the accident.

My pre-accident career involved lots of travel, national conventions and public speaking.

The suit I was wearing the day of the accident.

Car #1 is barely recognizable in the middle of the crash site.

When Jonathan couldn't reach me by phone, he used the Find my iPhone feature. The results confirmed his fears; my phone was at the reported scene of the accident and off the tracks.

The bag of jewelry Jonathan used to identify me at the hospital after he couldn't recognize my face or body.

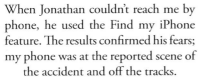

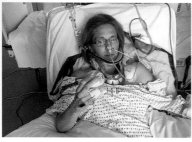

I have few pictures from my first stay in the hospital. Jonathan did not take photos because he said he didn't want to think of me that way. This one was taken a couple weeks after the accident. My kids had finally been allowed to visit, and Austin presented me with the Game Ball he had won after pitching his team to victory on the day I was found.

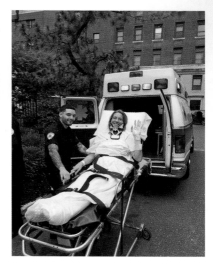

The irony of being *discharged* from the hospital strapped to a gurney and in an ambulance struck me, but it represented progess as I headed to the rehabilitation hospital.

Missing Brad and Steven's Birthdays while in the rehab hospital.

Coming home!

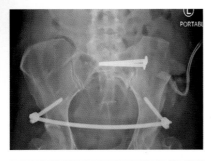

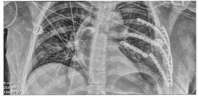

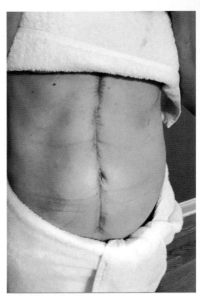

Some of the hardware required to put
me back together.

And the scars.

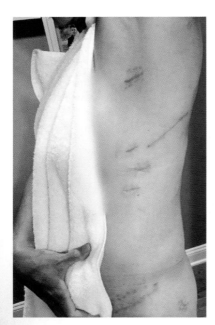

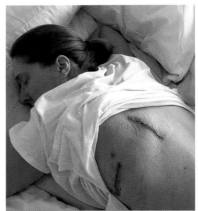

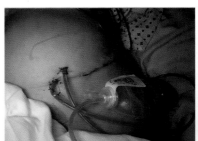

Pills and pain – and the unconscious reach for safety.

Physical therapy 5 days/week

My parents flew out to be with us for every single surgery.

I found sharing my story difficult, but healing as it strengthened my faith.

Bermuda, Spring of 2016 with Jonathan

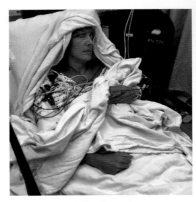

Fall of 2015

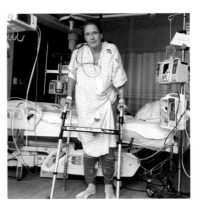

Back in the ICU in summer 2016

In the years following the accident, I was able to travel, albeit with accommodations and plans for only short outings. These glimpses of normality, spontaneity, and pure fun were incredibly healing. Even though interspersed with more surgeries, we made progress in overlaying the hurt with beautiful memories and building the confidence of my sons that Mom would be OK.

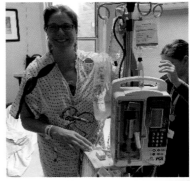

Unexpected emergency surgery in 2019

Japan 2017 with Steven

Hawaii 2017 with Bradley

Portugal 2018 with Austin

We were all honored to cheer on
Mercia as she received her Masters
of Theology in 2018.

I proudly went back to work part-time in 2017 as a Senior VP at my company. I worked to rebuild my professional credibility, my professional network, and generally convince others that I was up to the job–while still dealing with chronic pain, intermittent disability leaves for more surgeries, and the never-ending complications of a compromised body.

In 2021, Merck spun-off its women's health products into a new and fully independent major company. I was chosen as a senior executive of the new company and was thrilled to help ring the opening bell of the New York Stock Exchange.

The Ritter Family, 2021. Our card games are legendary and fierce!

Jonathan and me, 2021

My pride and joy–Austin, Steven and Bradley, 2021

Eight

Before the end of August, I called my pain-management specialist, Dr. S, to make an appointment. I was put through to the nurse, who asked what my issue was. "I have pain from injuries caused by an accident." At that point, I was still a relatively new patient, having seen Dr. S only twice.

"What body part was injured?" the nurse asked.

I began to go through the laundry list, almost by rote. "Crushed ribs, open pelvic ring fracture, massive abdominal trauma, fractured vertebrae, pain from the implanted hardware crushing a nerve..."

The nurse thought I was joking. I assured her I was very serious. "Dr. S is out on medical leave," she said.

"What?" I asked, panicked. "Who will do my prescriptions?"

"I'll check on that and get back to you," the nurse replied. After my experience of going off my pain meds for just a few hours, I knew I couldn't make it long without them. I tried to stay calm as I waited for the nurse to call back. They couldn't actually leave me stranded without my medications, could they?

Dr. S's nurse called back and informed me that I wouldn't be able to make an appointment with the doctor while she was on medical leave, but the doctor would continue to refill and update my prescriptions. Because of scrutiny around the prescription of pain medicine, other doctors in the practice would not cover for my pain specialist in this capacity while she was out of the office. It seemed a bit strange, but I was just pleased to have a continuing source of the prescriptions without the need for another office visit that month.

Because of the opioid crisis, there are strict rules around prescriptions for pain medications. While well intended, these rules can be a nightmare for pain patients trying to adhere to the regimen their doctor has prescribed. Filling a legitimate prescription for fentanyl or OxyContin is a multistep process. During my recovery, the rules provided that a script couldn't be written for more than a thirty-day supply. The prescribing doctor was not allowed to refill the script until the twenty-ninth or thirtieth day, just before the medication ran out, so that the patient was never left with any excess patches or pills that could be sold or shared. Today, many states have limited that time frame to a seven-day supply, forcing pain patients to refill their prescriptions every single week.[44]

For me, paying strict attention to exactly how many pills were left of each prescription and exactly when the refill would be required became of paramount importance. I would show up at my pain appointments with a purse full of bottles to count out every pill and plan for when refills would be required. In addition, pharmacies required a hard copy of the prescription form—no e-prescribing or doctor call-in allowed—necessitating a trip to the doctor's office for every refill, for every single medication, every time.

After the supply of one of my medicines dwindled sufficiently for me to successfully get the refill order from the doctor, the clock started ticking—we usually had, at most, forty-eight hours to get the prescription filled before the meds ran out. Jonathan drove me to the doctor's office to present my driver's license so I could pick up the hard-copy prescription. He then took me home and drove immediately to a pharmacy to drop off the prescription.

At that point, it was time to deal with the obstacles the insurance company had created. Initially, my insurance company told us they required forty-eight hours to approve any narcotic pain relievers. They eventually relented a bit, but I can't even count how many times Jonathan would drive to the doctor to get my new prescription form, rush it to the pharmacy, and wait for the refill, only to be told that it required (yet another) prior approval and I would have to call my insurance company. My call was always to Leslie, my nurse case manager, who could often help me work the system and navigate the bureaucracy to ensure eventual approval.

After insurance approval, the next hurdle was the pharmacy itself. By now, I was incredibly anxious. There were only a few hours left before the meds ran out and my body crashed. Many pharmacy chains have been accused of lax oversight of opioid dispensing in the past and have tightened up their systems considerably. I never experienced such laxity. They kept limited stocks of drugs such as OxyContin, oxycodone, and fentanyl. So, after running the gauntlet to get a new prescription slip, get the prescription to the pharmacy, and get insurance approval before I ran out of the medicine and went into withdrawal, Jonathan frequently was told the pharmacy was out of stock, and they had to put in a special order for the dosage I needed.

Sometimes, the pharmacist suggested we blame "those" people from closer to New York City for coming out to our part of New Jersey and filling what he implied were bogus prescriptions that depleted the pharmacy's stocks. Other times, the pharmacist looked at Jonathan skeptically, shrugged his shoulders, and suggested he try the pharmacy across the street to see if they had any. Still other times, the pharmacist explained that they almost always ran low during the last week of the month and were not allowed to order more until the beginning of the next month. Jonathan tried to explain calmly that next Monday, or the first of the month, simply wasn't good enough. Sometimes the pharmacist called around town for him and saved him time by directing him to a pharmacy that had the drug in stock. We became experts on the locations, hours, and dispensing practices of every pharmacy within a thirty-mile radius of our town.

My father once drove me to pick up the prescription myself. I was told the familiar story that it was the end of the month and no supplies were available. I tried to explain my predicament to the pharmacist, but my protests were met with a suspicious sideways glance.

"I was crushed by a train," I implored. "What am I supposed to do?"

The pharmacist's eyes opened wide. He paused, and then he shrugged and suggested maybe I should try the pharmacy across the street or in the next town. Bottom line: not his problem. Rules are rules.

An undercurrent of suspicion (if not overt hostility) ran through every interaction, as if I were intentionally causing all these complex issues. If pharmacists weren't pointing fingers at me, they were blaming some other actor in the system.

My pain doctor explained apologetically that the drug test was required by the insurance company. The insurance company blamed the legal system or the "abusers."

When most people hear the phrase "drug test," they think of peeing in a cup to prove you don't take drugs. In my case, I had to submit urine every month to prove that I *did* take them. The problem was that my bladder had ruptured during the accident, damaging the surrounding nerves, and it was quite difficult for me to urinate at all, much less on demand. I would chug an entire bottle of water before and during every pain appointment, dreading the inevitable request. Once asked to go to the one-person bathroom, I often tried the old trick of turning on the sink and letting the sound of flowing water motivate my bladder. Unfortunately, the bathrooms at my pain doctor's office were equipped with the latest water-saving faucets. I would sit on the toilet and try to make it happen, shuffle over to the sink with my pants around my ankles, and wave my hands in front of the sensor to make the water run. When it did, I'd hobble as quickly as I could back over to the toilet. I'd grab the rail, sit down gingerly, close my eyes, exhale, and try to get my numb and injured bladder to relax, all while holding the specimen cup awkwardly. Just then, invariably, the sink would automatically turn off, and I would end up repeating the back-and-forth routine over and over. A few times, I tried to use a scarf or my purse to trick the sensor. I waved it beside me as vigorously as I could while leaning sideways on the toilet. I once threw a roll of toilet paper at it. More than once, it occurred to me that this would be a great stand-up routine for a desperate comedian. After half an hour or more, I emerged both victorious and humiliated, carrying a little plastic cup with a couple of drops of yellow gold, proving to all that I indeed was taking high-dose narcotics daily as promised.

Leslie tried to assure me she had told the insurance company that I was a legitimate pain patient who didn't require extra monitoring for abuse. It didn't matter that there was no freaking way that I was going to *sell* my prescriptions. I had to resign myself to a system that didn't trust me and seemed designed to be uniquely challenging to a pain patient who couldn't drive, who couldn't use the bathroom normally, and for whom organizing basic tasks was overwhelming. I wouldn't have survived without Jonathan's dedicated support and patience in spending many hours every single week to keep my medications filled and available to me in the correct dosages.

I understand the rationale for each of the rules. At every step along the way, conscientious professionals are concerned about supplying addicts and feeding the epidemic of tragic overdose deaths that have consumed so many communities. Hundreds of thousands have died of overdose, and millions have had lives disrupted or destroyed by unscrupulous doctors, negligent pharmacists, and misleading marketing by a few pharmaceutical companies. But somehow, some way, there needs to be an avenue for those truly suffering from cancer, severe postsurgical pain, and polytrauma to have access to medication that allows them to breathe through the day, to get out of bed, to be a mother or father, and to claim some shred of normalcy and independence.

I feel certain that there must be a better way to distinguish legitimate patients and prescribers from those who have abused the system and the drugs. Every dental procedure surely doesn't require a thirty-day supply of oxycodone, but by the same token, a complex polytrauma or cancer patient might indeed need weeks or months of fentanyl or OxyContin without excessive regulations adding daily hurdles to the difficulty of recovery. Just being a few hours late with a dose left me breathless and paralyzed and set me back in my efforts to move beyond the post-traumatic symptoms of a nervous system stuck on high alert.

One expert, a bioethicist at Johns Hopkins University and a former pain patient himself, writes that the challenge physicians face is the need for nuance. "The benefit of opioids doesn't mean that we should take them like candy, and the risk of opioids doesn't mean that we should lock them away and forget about them," he writes.[45] But nuance and good judgment are far harder to teach and enforce than simple rules and one-size-fits-all guidelines. Knowing when opioids will help more than hurt requires a lot of data that have been hard to collect, analyze, and make available to practitioners.

The current system is incoherent.[46] There is still far too much abuse, and at the same time, efforts to curb the abuse of prescription pills have fed the underground market for more dangerous drugs like heroin and made good doctors throw well-managed pain patients off their medications and into withdrawal and depression for fear of lawsuits.[47] Doctors need more training and guidance in distinguishing pain patients, legacy patients, and patients at risk of developing an addiction. These are all vulnerable and sometimes overlapping populations that have suffered from bad medical practice and bad policy.[48] In fact, in 2019, the CDC and FDA warned physicians against forcing well-controlled patients to abruptly taper off opioids. They noted multiple reports of patients taken off their pain medicines who were suffering "serious withdrawal symptoms, uncontrolled pain, psychological distress, and suicide."[49]

Coincidentally, while Dr. S was away on leave, there was a change to my fentanyl patches. I noticed they looked different. The shape was more rectangular, and the material was transparent rather than Band-Aid beige. I put the patch on and didn't think too much about it, pleased that it would be less obvious on my arm.

I was well acquainted with the seventy-two-hour fentanyl cycle. The first day I put on the patch, I felt like a zombie; I would zone out and stare at the walls or my phone for hours. I sleepwalked through physical therapy but marveled at how easy it was to do the exercises. By the second day, my mind was sharper, but the pain was still held at bay, and I moved around the first floor of the house and the porch with ease, reading or doing minor chores like watering the flowers on the back porch. The second day was usually when I'd be motivated to call a friend to come over and share a glass of wine and chat on the back porch, or I'd email my work colleagues, write thank-you notes, and make journal entries. Second days were the good days. Second days were when I'd call my boss to "check in" and assure him I was doing great and would be ready for action in another few weeks.

On the third day, the medication would begin to wear off. The patches were supposed to last seventy-two hours, but they never did. Those last eight hours were difficult, and I usually retreated to my bed, took the oxycodone I was supposed to use for "breakthrough" pain, and binge-watched old TV shows to distract myself from counting the hours till I could replace the patch with a new one. I was careful never to put it on too soon, knowing that the ten-patch prescription had to last me all month and "early" refills were not allowed. So I waited and checked my watch.

That September day after I received the new patches, I knew something was wrong. Only halfway through the second day, I already ached all over. I was short of breath. *Maybe that patch was a dud*, I thought. I put on a fresh one, knowing I was going to have to explain to my doctor, the insurance company, and the pharmacist why this month's prescription ran out a day early.

After thirty-six hours, the medicine began to wear off again, and I started to panic. It was Sunday; the doctor was unavailable, and I could feel thunderous pain approaching as I struggled to expand my chest and take a real breath.

I called the pharmacy in tears. After listening to what seemed like an eternity of keyboard clicking, I tried to explain and impress on the pharmacist the seriousness of my problem. He listened patiently before explaining that they had recently switched suppliers of the medication. The pharmacist tried to tell me that "many" other customers preferred these new patches because they were clear and less obtrusive (as if other customer's preferences should matter to me). I knew enough to suspect that the pharmacy had gotten a better financial deal from this new manufacturer or distributor. I'd already been taking a generic version, but a different company made this one. I had never heard of anyone having a preference between two generic manufacturers of the same drug, but I couldn't deny my own experience of the dramatic difference between the two manufacturers' products.

I have since learned that patches, in particular, are difficult to replicate. Even if the medicine is exactly the same, the material of the patch can affect how it is absorbed through the skin. I didn't care what the patch looked like; it could be neon green and the size of a pancake. I just needed my old version back.

I argued with the pharmacist that the patch wasn't working for me in the same way. He said I'd have to try another pharmacy that sourced their fentanyl from the particular company I was accustomed to. *Really? I* thought. *How does one go about that?* It would be nearly impossible to get another pharmacy to fill the prescription since it had already been filled once. Not to mention, I'd now need to find another pharmacy that sourced its generic fentanyl patches from the company that made the ones I had used for the first four months of my recovery. I marveled at the absurdity of my situation. I was a fentanyl connoisseur. I pleaded with my pharmacist and every supervisor I could reach, begging them to return to their previous supplier.

I called the pain doctor's office and explained the situation to the nurse, hoping someone could call the pharmacy and help me get this straightened out. Meanwhile, I was starting to go into withdrawal. I was getting that claustrophobic feeling of my ribs crushing up against my lungs, making it impossible to breathe.

Several hours later, I got word back from my doctor's office that the doctor was still out on leave, but she had prescribed a 50 percent increase in the medication to address my out-of-control pain. Given the complications around reaching the doctor during her medical leave and getting the prescription filled, I was grateful. I took the new super-dose of fentanyl for the rest of the month.

The Centers for Disease Control published guidelines for prescribers of opioids in 2016 that suggest avoidance of—or extreme caution in—prescribing more than 90 MMEs per day of opioids.[50] MMEs stands for morphine milligram equivalents. It is how the strength of different opioids are compared. Before the 50 percent increase in my fentanyl dose, my fentanyl/OxyContin/oxycodone combo was approximately 450 MMEs daily, or 500 percent of the recommended daily maximum. After the increase, it was about 570 MMEs.[51] Let's just say that I didn't have an issue with the medicine wearing off anymore. The rest of September passed in a blur.

At the end of the month, I had surgery to remove the metal bar from my pelvis. For so long, I'd felt that hard piece of metal across my lap just beneath my skin. The lightning strikes of pain from the compressed nerve continued to torture me at random, frequent intervals. Dr. M cautioned me that removing the hardware might not address the nerve pain. Some of the nerve damage might be permanent or at least take some time to heal. I tried to lower my expectations but still counted the days to the surgery.

The surgery was a fairly simple one. The surgeon made two incisions on either side of my pelvis, removed two large screws from each hip bone, and pulled out the long metal "lap bar." I was later assured that the surgeons had tested my bones by pressing, twisting, and stressing my pelvis on the operating table. After more than four months of fixation, together with the two 9-centimeter screws that would remain in my lower back permanently, it was "rock solid."

When I woke up from the surgery, I was immediately nervous about whether it had worked—was the pain in my right leg gone? Still groggy, I placed my hands on my hips and tentatively tried to wiggle my right foot. Soreness…but nothing else. I bent my left knee and moved it side to side. Same thing. I took a deep breath and closed my eyes, saying a silent prayer. Then I raised my right knee. Cautiously, protectively, I let it drop to the side. Nothing. I squeezed the tears out of my eyes and dared to hope that the lack of pain was a result of removal of the surgical hardware, not the lingering effects of the anesthesia.

I was up and walking the next day. I took tentative steps, ready for the familiar zap, but it never came. As it turned out, the nerve pain really was permanently gone. Never again was I doubled over by a shock in my right leg. Finally, I could stop feeling like a lab rat in some cruel experiment. Within a week, physical therapy and walking became much easier. Jen and I began taking strolls together up our street. I couldn't go very far or walk very fast, but I was getting out of the house. Dr. M had advised me that the numbness in my outer thigh from the nerve damage would almost certainly be permanent. He called it "his gift to me." I still smile when I think of those words. The fact that my right thigh is curiously numb, yet sensitive to pain, is a small price to pay. His real gift to me is that I lived and that today I walk with no assistance or visible limp. Dr. M deals in miracles.

As Halloween decorations were going up around the neighborhood and everyone was ready to set a bowl of candy by the door, my giant mixing bowl full of pill bottles became a running joke among our friends. "Woo! It's Halloween at the Ritters'!" I was pretty sick of my bowl of pills—sick of being dependent on them, sick of the way they made me dependent on Jonathan, and sick of the way they gave everyone else the right to ask about my pharmaceutical status. At that point, I was juggling blood thinners, prescription meds to unfreeze my bowels, five different pain medicines, Ambien for sleep, an antidepressant, iron, and a host of vitamins, as well as every over-the-counter laxative and sleep aid on the pharmacy shelves. I'd lost thirty pounds, and far too many of my days still revolved around lying in bed, trying to use the bathroom, and going to physical therapy or doctor appointments. Even though I was walking well, and my ability to concentrate and read was returning, I'd missed my goal of returning to work in the fall.

On weekday afternoons, when Stevie bounded in the door, finished with school, and bubbling with news of the day, only to find that I was still lying in bed, wearing pajamas, and staring at the walls or my phone, I felt a sense of failure unlike any other I could remember. Later during my recovery, I read a book that my sister-in-law, Hannah, recommended called *Surviving Survival* by Laurence Gonzales. The book follows survivors of extraordinary life-threatening incidents, examining how they handled the year after their survival, the real recovery process, and the unexpected challenges along that path. Many spoke of incidents in which they struggled during their recovery with what the author called their "personal scum line,"[52] the level below which they must not sink or else lose all respect for themselves.

I was embarrassed I didn't have the willpower to get out of bed. I was embarrassed I hadn't showered. This was my own personal scum line. My three boys would raise their eyebrows and tease me, saying, "Mom, you really should put on a bra." I laughed with them, explaining that crushed ribs and bras are not natural partners, and they would just have to deal with the fact that God gave me the biggest nipples in the house. But under the laughter, I felt terrible. What kind of Mom is still in bed, half-dressed at 3:00 in the afternoon?

Once again, I suspected it was the pain drugs, but I had learned my lesson about suddenly stopping the opioids. Given that my nerve pain had resolved, I figured I would experiment with cutting the Lyrica to try to address my fatigue. I had been on twice the maximum recommended dose—600 mg daily—for months.[53] I figured, since the nerve pain from the bar was gone, I wouldn't need to take it anymore. It surely wouldn't matter if I took less, so I cut my daily dose in half.

The morning I changed my dose, I began to feel sick to my stomach, lethargic, dizzy, and particularly zoned out. I stared at the walls for hours on end. Somehow it didn't occur to me that it had anything to do with cutting my medication. This was the non-narcotic drug, the less controlled one. One day in physical therapy, as I was overcome by dizziness, I finally called Dr. S in tears and told her that something was wrong with me and I couldn't figure out what. She asked a few questions, and then I mentioned that I was halving my Lyrica dose. "That's the problem," she replied immediately.

"But it's not a narcotic," I protested. Dr. S explained that I was on such a high dose that I absolutely couldn't cut it in half without having a major reaction.[54] I needed to taper down more gradually.

I made a similar mistake with the antidepressant Cymbalta. My supply ran low, and I didn't feel like asking Jonathan to go to the pharmacy again. We'd been arguing, and I hated asking him for help when we were fighting. I skipped my dose for three days, but I didn't notice an adverse reaction. On the third day, I texted Jen A to see if she wanted to take a walk. She said she would come by my house in an hour. When it was time to get ready, I found I was gasping for air. My heart was pounding in my chest, and I began to sob. That's when Jen came knocking at the door. I thought about not answering. If I waited a few minutes, she'd probably give up and go away. No, I couldn't do that. I was the one who had asked her to come over. I brushed away my tears, forced myself to open the door, and stepped outside. I made it twenty steps, and then I froze. I could hear myself gulping for air. My mind was spinning in circles. I burst into tears again. "Jen," I gasped. "I can't. I can't. Everything hurts."

Jen held on to me and walked me back to the house, where she sat me down. She and Mercia gathered around me. Jen looked me in the eyes and said, "Geralyn, I think you're having a panic attack." She coached me to take a deep breath. Mercia brought a glass of water.

Jen was one of the few people who knew I was taking an antidepressant. It was something I found embarrassing and didn't want to share. Jen asked if I'd missed a dose. I told her I hadn't taken it for three days but was too proud and mad to ask Jonathan to make another trip to the pharmacy to refill it. "Geralyn," she scolded. "You have to be more careful. You can't play around with that stuff."

As someone who worked in the pharmaceutical industry, I knew about the importance of sticking to a prescribed dose and following doctors' instructions. I'd attended workshops on the challenges of getting patients to take their prescribed drugs on schedule, but everything is different when you are the patient. I thought medication compliance was a challenge only for old people, but here I was, a highly educated executive, substituting my own judgment for that of my doctors, struggling day by day to keep my prescriptions filled and to take them on time, regardless of my resentment about my dependence on them.

Later that month, I got the opportunity to share my experience with a group of doctors. Penn Presbyterian invited me to give a talk on the "patient perspective" to their trauma staff. They probably caught me on the second day of a fentanyl patch when they asked me to do it because I jumped at the opportunity. It was a chance to contribute and do something useful outside my house.

The room was filled with about seventy-five doctors, nurses, and administrators. Other staff members had called in remotely. As I took my place at the podium, I sensed a glimmer of my old self. This was almost like being back at work again. I had done a lot of public speaking for my job, and it was satisfying to be standing before a group of professionals, wearing a pair of dress shoes (albeit low-heeled ones), a professional black dress, with my hair done and makeup on. It felt like a triumphant return. I was back—not as a patient—as the real me.

I started by saying thanks. For saving my life, of course, but also for some of the specific ways they approached their work. I thanked the doctors for sharing information with my family and letting my siblings listen in when they came on their rounds. I thanked them for meeting my siblings where they were, addressing them not only with both the professionalism and detailed information about my condition that a fellow physician deserves, but also with the compassion a distraught family member needs.

I thanked the staff for their kindness as well, especially the nurses. They held my hand, made sure my large family had enough space, and an administrator even brought me flowers from her own garden. I recounted the day Nurse Liz had my bed and all the machines moved so I could face the window. They tried to help me feel some kind of control over my own body, maintain my dignity, and keep me as comfortable as possible. I had said thank you in the hospital before, but doing it with clothes on felt far more meaningful.

Then I went on to share my recommendations. First, I talked about what a difference it made when the nurse was a familiar face. I also spoke about the need for coordination among all the many specialists. There were so many doctors and teams coming in and out of the room all the time—trauma, neurology, orthopedics, gastroenterology, urology, vascular, pulmonary, physical therapy, pain management, pharmacy, and so on. It was confusing and overwhelming, especially with the foggy state I was in. How did it all fit together? It wasn't clear who I could direct longer-term questions to or questions that didn't clearly fit within one of the specialties.

Coordination of care is a major issue in health policy. It is both deeply complicated and vital to a patient's health. When multiple specialists are involved, especially over an extended period of time that covers inpatient and outpatient care, a host of issues arise. These include how to sequence procedures and avoid medication interactions; how to ensure the necessary information is shared among the doctors, nurses, administrators, and so on; and how to offer clarity about what each person is accountable for.

I wanted one particular person who could help me understand everything that was going on and what the future would hold. Maybe that person could have given me more information about what to expect at the rehabilitation hospital and how long my recovery might take. When they were preparing me to leave the hospital, an administrator had asked me if I had a preferred rehabilitation hospital. It seemed like a ludicrous question. I had a preferred restaurant, a preferred bottle of wine…but a preferred rehabilitation hospital? That short exchange seemed to represent how, at the stage of discharge, administrative issues seemed to take center stage—where would I go, and how would I get there? Coaching about what to expect was minimal to nonexistent.

In hindsight, I believe I would have benefited tremendously from someone talking me through what would be different, what I would be expected to do, and what milestones to recovery I should expect. Until that follow-up appointment with Dr. C.S. months after the accident, no one at either hospital had offered, suggested, or educated me about the potential mental-health challenges that often accompany major trauma. Overall, I still believe that a more realistic appraisal of the challenges I was going to face would have better prepared me to face them and helped me avoid the deep disappointment in myself I felt when I missed my unrealistic recovery goals.

I shared with the staff my joy that I was off my crutches and walking, but also my frustration that I was still so tired, still taking so many medications, still unable to drive, and still unable to return to work.

I concluded my talk by thanking the hospital staff again for their extraordinary care. I truly felt grateful that, of all places, I'd been taken to Penn Presbyterian. Afterward, many staff members came up to speak with me. The two nurses I was closest to, Liz and Melanie, came over and gave me a hug.

Some of the ICU doctors and emergency-room care staff came over and spoke to me as well. They said it was rare for them to get to see patients again after they leave. I got the sense that it was gratifying for them to meet me again and see that I was doing better. They deal with acute situations, and their job is to save people's lives and then send them off. They don't usually hear what happened to patients after that—whether they got better or went back to work again. They don't often hear someone say, "Thank you for saving my life."

I now realize that reflecting on my hospital experience, sharing it with the doctors and nurses at a top hospital, and thanking my life-savers face-to-face was helpful to my recovery. It was a glimmer of my old self—giving a speech, reflecting on issues in health-care policy, and sharing my personal journey. It was the first time I felt I was doing something useful with my experience. It was empowering.

In October, the doctors removed the filter that had been implanted beneath my lungs to prevent the blood clots in both legs from traveling up to my heart or lungs. As far as I knew, it was my last surgical proce-dure for a while. I had a major hernia on my left side that would have to be repaired at some point, but I needed to heal more before I could be ready for that surgery. About the same time, I hit the sixth-month mark after the accident. With no immediate surgeries on the horizon, it was finally the right time to start weaning myself off the pain medications. I wanted to find the quickest solution possible. I was sure that at least lowering the dosages would lift my dreary haze. I would stop sleeping during the day, and my energy would come back. I could get up with my kids in the morning and finally return to work.

I met with Dr. S to discuss the process of safely getting off the pain medicines. She explained that I would have to go off each medication one at a time—first the fentanyl, lowering the dosage 25 percent, giving myself one month to adjust, and then another 25 percent, continuing the process until I was down to zero. "It's going to feel like you have a bad case of the flu for four months," she said. After that, I would move on to the OxyContin and then the oxycodone—lowering the dose of each one in turn by 25 percent, a month at a time. Then we would talk about lowering the doses of the non-narcotics, like Lyrica. As I listened to Dr. S describe the process, I slowly shook my head. Even if I cheated on the timeline, it would be at least eight months and possibly a year before I was off the pain medications.

"What about driving?" I asked. "Am I supposed to wait until I'm off all the pain meds before I start driving again?"

"As your doctor, that is what I advise you to do," she said, pushing a strand of straight brown hair behind her ear as she spoke. The laws are fuzzy surrounding this. Most states, including New Jersey, prohibit driving "under the influence"; that is, it is not illegal to drive with the drug in your system, just illegal to drive if it actually affects your driv-ing.[55] The instructions on the medications themselves only say that doctors should "warn patients not to drive unless they are tolerant to the effects of OxyContin and know how they will react to the medication."[56] As the doctor explained, many patients take these medications for back pain and drive regularly. The reality was that I was still in no shape to drive, but in the end, it wasn't that realization or the legal questions that kept me from doing so. I simply couldn't stand the thought that any slowed reaction on my part could possibly cause a tragedy and hurt someone else like I had been hurt. I resolved not to drive until I was off the medicines. The issue was how to speed up the timetable.

"Isn't there a way to quit cold turkey?" I asked Dr. S. "What if I go to a rehab facility where they can monitor me and make sure I do it safely?"

She considered this for a moment. "That's not how we typically address this sort of situation," she said. "I suppose it might be possible to find a private facility that could do that. I don't know of one, though."

I began doing my own research. I was physically dependent on strong opioids. Physical dependence means that your body will have physical symptoms when the drug is discontinued.[57] Almost anyone who takes a drug like fentanyl for six months would end up this way. Its biochemical effect on brain and body is unavoidable. What isn't inevitable, however, is addiction. The difference is important. In general, *addiction* is defined by reference to behavioral symptoms: the irresistible cravings, the urges, the compulsive need for the drug. Addiction encompasses both mental *and* physical reliance on a given substance. As explained by the National Institutes of Health, "Although everyone who takes opioids for an extended period will become dependent, only a small percentage also experience the compulsive, continuing need for the drug."[58]

Dependence and addiction are caused by changes to different parts of the brain. Physical dependence affects parts of the brain (the thalamus and brain stem) that oversee autonomic body functions, such as breathing. The reward center in the brain remains off-line, and the patient is still capable of managing impulses and making decisions in her best interest. Addiction is caused by changes to the pleasure and reward system of the brain.[59] An addict's actions are directed primarily by an overwhelming need to accommodate the brain's reward center, and the part of the brain that guides self-control and decision-making is directly impeded. Addicted patients lose the ability to effectively prioritize their well-being over the continued use of the drug. What causes some users of opioids to become addicted and others only physically dependent is poorly understood. The latest research indicates a strong role for genetic, environmental, and lifestyle factors.[60] I was lucky in this regard.

Determined to stop taking the drugs ASAP, but aware of my body's limitations, I began reading about detox facilities on the internet. Half seemed like quacks. Most included addiction counseling as a key part of their program. I tried calling a few of the places to explain my case. I didn't feel I needed addiction counseling, I just needed help to withdraw from physical dependence on the medications. I wanted help in managing the side effects, especially considering my still-fragile medical condition. I also spoke with various friends who were physicians, including a few anesthesiologists. No one had any answers for me. The system is not set up for cases like mine. Ultimately, I realized that there were no real shortcuts or specialized programs that addressed my situation.

Dr. S's method was my only choice—I had to gradually lower the doses as the pain lessened—and if it took six (or eight or twelve) months, so be it. With the benefit of hindsight, I now recognize that in many ways, this was a positive turning point for me. My disappointment and frustration at the pace of my recovery had been tearing me up ever since I had left the hospital. I still had a long distance to travel, but acceptance of the months of weaning time was my first baby step toward emotional recovery and spiritual growth. Noted theologian John Swinton writes profoundly about the importance of "becoming a friend of time" and learning to treat time as a precious gift, rather than a ruler and source of anxiety.[61] It certainly didn't happen overnight.

Medically, I was also very lucky to have Dr. S guiding me through the weaning process and insisting on a long tapering period. Even with the new laws and a focus on reducing the number of opioid prescriptions, it is still far easier to find doctors who will prescribe these medications than it is to find doctors who will help guide you through the slow agony of withdrawal.[62] It is even harder to find doctors who will integrate medical oversight of the weaning process with other therapies proven to help reduce pain for some patients, such as meditation, hypnosis, deep breathing, yoga, acupuncture, and other techniques. Those I would stumble upon myself much later.

Nine

It was a chilly, gray late-November morning when I took the first step down from the pain medication. With the curtains drawn, it felt like the middle of the night, except for the familiar morning pain. As I put my new fentanyl patch on my upper arm, I was nervous. This patch was visibly smaller than the one I usually wore. I had no idea how I would feel. Would I shiver and vomit uncontrollably? Would I feel like I was suffocating?

I stretched back on the bed and shut my eyes, waiting for my body's reaction. As the hours passed, I didn't feel the relaxing relief I used to feel on first days. I gritted my teeth and tried to distract myself with the television. As the day wore on, the pain in my ribs and hip was worse than usual, but not excruciating. Did my hip actually hurt terribly, or was I just worried that it would hurt if I moved? Could I actually not breathe deeply, or was I just too scared to do so? When the severe pangs came, could I manage without flinching sharply? I spent hours obsessing and trying to micro-analyze my pain.

I kicked and stretched my twitchy legs. It seemed like they didn't want to lie still. I shut my eyes, feeling slightly dizzy and nauseated—but not enough to be sick. My body trembled underneath the comforter; the late autumn chill set in my bones. I spent the day with the heating pad on high, tensing and relaxing my legs and arms, trying to will the time to pass.

By early evening, I settled in front of the fireplace, bundled in my bathrobe and an electric blanket. I sat there for a long time, staring at the flames, in some far-off, zoned-out place. I didn't feel like I craved the medication. It wasn't like it had ever given me any kind of high. It only made me feel functional. I guess that's why I have trouble understanding the draw of taking opioids recreationally. Perhaps my depression or the residual pain masked the euphoria that some feel when taking those drugs. I don't recall even once feeling euphoric or pain-free. The medications simply felt necessary for any kind of normal functionality. They were difficult to take and caused all sorts of unpleasant side effects, but the trade-off in my mind was a no-brainer. I can't imagine how I would have gotten through those first six months without them.

My symptoms continued like that for days. I felt nauseated, twitchy, shaky, and always cold. I spent most of my time huddled inside my bathrobe and electric blanket. By the end of the second week on the first stepped-down dose of fentanyl, I started feeling a little more normal (or at least a sweatpants, slippers, and greasy-hair version of normal). This wasn't like the worst images of drug withdrawal floating around in my mind. I started taking short walks down my street again, especially when my arms and legs were uncomfortably twitchy. When the third and fourth week came around, I had gotten gradually better.

The holidays were coming up, and Jonathan and I planned to take a family trip to Colorado to see my family for Christmas. By mid-January I would be stepping down from the fentanyl again, and I figured I would be well enough to go back to work. I told Jen T, my orthopedic surgeon friend, about my plan. She looked at me with raised eyebrows. "And how are you going to get to work?" she asked matter-of-factly. I'd conveniently ignored the fact that I still couldn't drive, and the office was an hour away. I called the company's benefits office and asked if there was any way they could provide compensation for a car service to and from the office. It didn't occur to me that if I were too drugged to drive, the company probably wouldn't want me handling sensitive legal matters, either. As I've said, patience and a realistic appreciation of my limitations are not my strong suits.

I visited the office to meet with my new boss and update him on my progress. I told him I was dealing with pain management and building up my stamina but hoped to be back to work in the new year. I also met with CEO Ken Frazier. We got into a deep conversation about my experiences of trauma and recovery. I described those moments in the ICU when I realized that I had to put all my trust in God because the only power I had in that moment was to pray. Ken leaned forward as I spoke, his deep brown eyes intense. When I was finished, he said, "Geralyn, you have a story to tell, and I hope you will tell it." He went on to say that I was a witness to the light of God, and I needed to share that. I had been so self-absorbed in my own pain; this was the first time I considered that sharing what I'd been through might help others. It was particularly heartening to hear this encouragement from Ken, who was such an inspiration himself. I realized that talking and connecting with others in this way might also be a key to breaking out of the loneliness of my pain.

Not long after my meeting with Ken, I received an invitation from the pastor at my parents' church in Breckenridge, Colorado, Father Dyer United Methodist Church. Pastor Claire heard I would be visiting in December, and she extended an invitation for me to speak at a Sunday service about my experience of the accident and recovery. I said I would be happy to. We set the date of the talk for a week after my arrival in Colorado, on the Sunday after Christmas.

I knew Pastor Claire well and felt a bond with her. We're close in age, and she, too, has three boys. While I was in the ICU, she was in daily contact with my mother, offering spiritual support and counsel. Everyone in the church community had been praying for me and sending me cards and gifts, and from the moment my parents returned home, they were held in the warm embrace of their church family. Many members of the congregation are retired and come from other parts of the country, so they contacted the churches they had attended before moving to Colorado. Those congregations also prayed for me and sent cards and gifts, like the handmade quilt that came all the way from Minnesota. It was an incredible ripple effect—through my parents' church, I was receiving love from hundreds of people, many of whom were total strangers. I took Pastor Claire's invitation as an opportunity to share my experience and also to thank the Father Dyer community.

Travel to Colorado was difficult and tiring, and Jonathan and I fought the entire way. He's an impatient and stressed traveler in the best of times, but the holiday crowds and delays made for an especially tough trip. On top of everything, we arrived at my parents' house exhausted, only to realize that we had picked up the wrong black duffel bag at baggage claim. It was pretty obvious which one of us was going to make the four-hour round trip down the mountain to Denver to return it and retrieve our own. Jonathan stormed out of the house and slammed the door, annoyed that I hadn't been able to use my frequent-flyer status to convince the airline to bring the bag to us.

I spent the first week after we arrived resting and working on my talk while Jonathan took the boys snowboarding. I had just stepped down the fentanyl another 25 percent. The first day using the new and even smaller patch, the pain was stronger, and the shaking, chills, and nausea were back. I could see this would be a pattern. I'd feel worse the first week, but throughout the month, gradually my body adjusted to the lower dosage. Then I had to step it down again. In the high altitude, breathing was even more difficult. I relied on supplemental oxygen. But of course, the trip was worth the challenges.

In December, Breckenridge, Colorado, is a picture-postcard image of Christmastime. As you walk down Main Street, every surface is buried under a heap of glistening white snow. When you look into the distance, past the quaint Victorian cottages that have been turned into shops and restaurants, you see the white peaks of the Rocky Mountains. They're so close you can make out the tiny figures of skiers and snowboarders zipping down the slopes. It feels like there are Christmas trees everywhere you look. A forest of majestic pines circles the lower parts of the mountains, each branch heavy with snow. At night, the evergreen trees in town are lit up with thousands of twinkling lights.

My mother calls their home the "cabin" because originally, it was a tiny A-frame that they built themselves on land outside of town, purchased back in 1969. My three siblings and I spent every summer and winter break taking a twenty-four-hour drive across Texas (each way) to get to the cabin. By design, the place had no telephone and no television. It is truly a retreat, and I have many fond memories of hours spent playing cards, board games, and painting model cars with my dad and brother, Kent. The place has grown as our family has grown. The 1960s vintage flame-orange shag carpeting and oh-so-cheerful orange laminate countertops have finally been replaced. My mother fondly says the cabin wraps around you like an old shoe. Inside, the place is like a family museum, with more than a hundred years of framed photos on every wall and covering every shelf and ledge. Just to walk down the hall makes me smile.

Outside, it has a peaceful atmosphere close to nature. Towering pine trees encircle the property, and in the distance is a perfect view of the mountains. Deer and a certain little fox often come into the yard, and sometimes moose and bears, too. Away from city lights, at night in the thin atmosphere of ten thousand feet above sea level, the stars are closer and brighter. There is something about the mountains that feels sacred—it's a refuge. A visit to the cabin was exactly what I needed on the first Christmas after the accident. Plus, my parents finally got Wi-Fi.

Writing the talk for my parents' church forced me to step back and reflect on the previous seven months; it felt like a healing way to celebrate the Christmas season and end of the year. I'm not someone who shares early drafts of my work, so this was a solitary activity. When I was ready, I would show the talk to Jonathan and my parents.

As I contemplated my experience, I realized that I didn't know what to say. What had I learned from the accident? It felt impossibly shallow and unsatisfying to simply chalk it up to a weird mixture of bad and good luck. But how could I make sense of it? And how could I make peace with the question of why I lived but others sitting near me in the same train car did not? I realized that I didn't have the answers. I spent days in my room with a notepad and my computer, researching, writing, and rewriting what to say and trying to decide what I actually believed.

Ultimately, I decided that my journey since May could be summed up with three words: gratitude, grief, and grace. The alliteration felt a little corny, but these three words seemed to perfectly express what I'd been through.

As I thought back, I recalled that in the very beginning, while I was in intensive care, my gratitude was much closer to the surface. I was happy that I was alive, that I wasn't paralyzed, that I didn't have a major brain injury. I was grateful to have my family and that they had me—my boys would not grow up without a mother. During those dark nights in the hospital, God felt so close, almost as if I could whisper in His ear. I felt physically embraced.

Gratitude was also a defense. A defense against pain and against loss. When I couldn't stand it, I went to my place of gratitude. Pain meant I was alive. Thank you, Lord, for this pain. Thank you that I am alive to feel it.

After I came home, and my recovery wore on, the fortress of gratitude started to crumble. No one can give thanks for pain for very long. I hurt all the time. I couldn't do anything for myself. Any momentum in my career was fading away as the weeks passed. Jonathan and I managed to irritate each other on a daily basis. At the same time, I felt guilty for being so unhappy. I was lucky to be at home with my family. I often thought about the eight people in that accident who didn't make it home. What right did I have to complain?

As I was writing my talk, however, I began to understand these feelings as grief rather than selfishness. I needed time to grieve my pain and that of my family. I could also feel simultaneous grief for those who lost their lives while being grateful that I had lived, all without guilt. Theologian John Swinton counsels that "we have to recognize that something has been lost before we can find joy in the present."[63] Ultimately, I realized that in some ways, gratitude and grief are opposite sides of the same coin. They could and should coexist. And I didn't need to feel guilty about feeling either one.

But what to say about the hand of God in my survival? I wrestled with this question over and over. I knew that the force underlying everything, the power that made sense of all I'd been through, was God's grace. I'd experienced it, but intellectually, I didn't know what that meant—what exactly was grace? The concept is conventionally defined as the unearned, undeserved, and unmerited favor of God toward man. Grace is an inexplicable gift. I would never know why I survived when others did not. I didn't believe for a moment that I was somehow more deserving. Kate Bowler, a Christian professor of divinity and young mother diagnosed with stage IV cancer, explains powerfully (and hilariously) in her book *Everything Happens for a Reason: And Other Lies I've Loved* about the human search for certainty and reasons in the face of tragedy.[64]

While I might find it comforting to think that catastrophes are actually "divine conspiracies" designed to better the world, I don't believe it. I can't believe that I survived because God had a better plan for me. I can't believe it because to believe it means I must also believe that God didn't have a plan for the promising eighteen-year-old Naval Academy midshipman who perished on the train, or the young mother of a toddler serving as CEO of a nonprofit educational organization.

I could not accept that this was His plan, but I wasn't willing chalk everything up to dumb luck, either. Luck is random.

God is not random.

I landed on grace. Grace is a gift. My survival was simply an unearned, unexpected, and undeserved gift. There is no why. There is no reason. But I can be grateful, and I can accept a gift.

I am faithful, but I have never been much of a student of the Bible. As I was writing the talk, however, I came across Psalm 40:1–3, and the words gave me chills:

> I waited patiently for the Lord to help me, and he turned to me and heard my cry. He lifted me out of the pit of despair, out of the mud and the mire. He set my feet on solid ground and steadied me as I walked along. He has given me a new song to sing, a hymn of praise to our God. Many will see what he has done and be amazed. They will put their trust in the Lord.

I have never been so moved by a Bible passage. I felt it had been written for me. Somehow, I had been lifted from the muck, steadied again on my feet, and I would stand in front of the congregation singing my new song. I would share the light.

That Sunday after Christmas, about 250 people filled the pews of Father Dyer United Methodist Church. Jonathan and the boys sat in the front row. Brad, worrying they would make me cry during my talk, whispered to his brothers, "Don't look at her!" My parents; my brother, Scott, and his wife, Sheila; and my nieces and nephews surrounded them. As I stepped up to the pulpit, I could feel the incredible warmth of everyone present. I've done a lot of public speaking for my work and I've always enjoyed it, but this was different. This time, it was personal.

In this moment, even more than during my talk at Penn, I felt happy and strong. I was standing on my own two feet. I looked healthy, my voice was clear, and I had something important to say. After months of obsessing over my own health, I was speaking out in hopes of reaching others who were struggling with pain, disease, or crises of faith. Afterward, I was ecstatic. I had completed a project—I'd accomplished something more than dragging myself out of bed in the morning. I'd made a useful contribution.

When I got home, I considered whether to share my talk with Ken Frazier. I sat at my computer, reading the talk over again and debating about what I would say in my email. Would I assume too much familiarity if I shared this with the CEO of my company? I sent it. A few days passed, and I didn't hear back. I started to fret. Had I overstepped my bounds? What if I'd created an awkward situation? Before my mind could completely run away with mortifying scenarios, a new email popped up in my inbox. Ken explained that he had not responded immediately because he wanted to go back and reread the talk several times. He thanked me for sharing it and said the talk was personally very meaningful to him. My spirits soared.

It was the start of a new year, and I was optimistic, ready to make a fresh start. At the end of my third week of stepping down the fentanyl, I decided to push myself. Dr. S said, if I wanted to, I could skip the fourth week and step down to the lower-dose patch sooner, so that's what I did. It was another accomplishment. In less than three months, I would be off the fentanyl completely and hopefully ready to start weaning off the OxyContin.

Of course, with the optimism came a dose of reality. I was not ready to sit behind a desk for eight hours a day, five days a week. I had to tell my boss that I still needed more time before I could come back to work. I wrote yet another email saying I was still dealing with stamina and pain-management issues. I didn't go into the details of what this meant—that I was still sleeping during the day and not at night, still couldn't drive, and still struggling with pain and side effects of withdrawal from the medications.

I had assumed that pain medications were causing the waves of exhaustion that would overcome me during the day and that lowering my dose of narcotics would restore my energy. But as I stepped down the medication, the grogginess didn't go away. If anything, my sleep schedule had been thrown further out of whack. When night came, my mind and body refused to wind down. It was like someone had flipped a switch inside me, and every nerve ending was buzzing with jittery, antsy energy. The pain wasn't out of control, but it was constant. Every twist, turn, sneeze, laugh, and deep breath hurt. I would try to tell myself to think about it logically—the pain wasn't objectively unbearable—I could handle it. The problem was that there was no relief. By day, the pain sometimes retreated a bit to the background, and I could occupy my mind with other things. At night, it took center stage. The house slept, but I lay awake, hurting.

I continued to have unexpected reactions to withdrawal as well. One day, after stepping down the fentanyl another notch, I was lying on the exam table in physical therapy while Brian stretched my legs. The room was filled with the quiet chatter of other therapists working with patients. Without warning, I began to feel intense pressure around my lungs. I couldn't get a breath. I began to gulp down air, and my head felt woozy. I thought I might faint. Tears rolled down my cheeks. At first, Brian thought it was the pain. He stopped stretching my legs and stooped down to eye level. "What's wrong?" he asked.

"I…can't…breathe," I gasped.

Brian had me sit up. He checked my pulse and took stock of my complexion. "Your pulse is normal, and your color is good," he said. I tried to ignore the patient at the next table. She had turned her attention away from the physical therapist treating her shoulder to blatantly stare at me. Brian spoke in a soft, calm manner, "You're okay. This is just the drugs talking—it's not you." There wasn't a whisper of condescension in his voice. I focused on the soothing tone of his voice as he instructed me to take long, slow breaths. Gradually my faintness subsided.

The winter was bitter that year, and it matched my mood. The high of Christmas and my speech at the church had long since faded as the pain wore on and progress seemed imperceptibly slow. Yes, I was taking fewer pills, but I was still spending most of my time in bed. Reynolds Price, an accomplished writer and a professor of English at Duke University, wrote a moving memoir of his struggle through cancer. He described "the poisonous weight of idle time" that bears down on the infirm.[65]

One gray, rainy afternoon in February, I sat bundled in my bathrobe, shivering in front of the fire. This had to be the worst time of year to wean yourself off painkillers. I thought about how much I wanted to be warm and how I needed to get out of my bedroom and kitchen. I began to daydream. I saw myself lying on a deck chair with the hot sun beaming down on my face. I needed sunshine. I pulled out my phone and started searching travel sites. An hour later, I told Jonathan my plan. "I want to go to Arizona."

He could have scoffed and said I couldn't manage the trip or that it was too expensive, or suggested we wait and go somewhere as a family when the kids were on spring break. To my delight, however, he replied immediately, "Go."

My eyebrows shot up.

"Really?" I wasn't sure he was serious.

"Go. You deserve it. We'll figure it out," he said definitively. We hugged for a long time, and some of the ice between us began to melt.

The next day, I booked a reservation at a spa in Tucson for four days in March. By that point, I would be completely off the fentanyl, and the warmth of Arizona would be my reward.

Ten

As I stepped out of the Phoenix airport, I could feel the dry desert heat warming me to my core. This was my first time traveling without any assistance since the accident. I was truly on my own. Even better, I was actually going to drive myself. I walked through the airport without assistance—no one to carry my luggage or meet me at the gate. I had a special brace to bind my ribs, took pain medications before takeoff, and prayed that the flight would be smooth. I had calculated that if I took the immediate-release oxycodone before takeoff, it would get me through the flight but would wear off by the time I needed to drive after landing. As the plane touched down in Phoenix, I dug through my purse, loaded up on a ridiculous number of ordinary Advil and Tylenol, and confidently picked up the rental car.

I barreled through the desert with the windows rolled down and a country music station blasting. I was on my own and in control. Having been raised in Texas and being a childhood veteran of dozens of epic car rides across the West, the sparse Arizona landscape and beating full sun felt like home. I was free!

I was also tired.

After about an hour, the euphoria of driving myself a hundred miles across the desert gave way to the reality that I was still weak. An irresistible urge to sleep swept over me. The feeling was familiar and impossible to fight. I pulled the car onto the shoulder of the dusty two-lane road, butting up against a tall cactus. It wasn't the safest place for a nap, but I had no choice.

This sudden and irresistible need to sleep during the day would attack with regularity for another two years. At night, insomnia was relentless, but when the fog descended during the day, I could sleep— whether on the shoulder of I-78 in New Jersey, tucked under a giant cactus on the shoulder of a remote highway in Arizona, leaning against a stall in the fourth-floor ladies' room at work, or curled up under my desk. I had to sleep.

Somehow, I safely arrived at the spa outside Tucson. I took in the expanse of green desert shrubs and trees in full bloom, the huge canvas of blue sky stretched out above, and the rocky peaks of the Santa Catalina Mountains in the distance. Looking at that view, I felt like my mind was at last stepping outside the cramped rooms it had been pacing for weeks. The spa had all sorts of fun activities, but most were irrelevant to me. Horseback riding? I don't think so. Zip-lining in a tight harness around my waist? Very funny. But massage and lying by the pool? Absolutely. I set my own schedule with activities like grat- itude meditation, gentle outdoor yoga, a seminar on healthy eating, massage and facial treatments, and lots of time to lie out in the sun.

When I showed up for my first massage, the spa therapist asked the obligatory questions about whether I had any recent injuries, surger- ies, or places that felt tender. "Yes," I said, pausing for a moment as I thought about how best to explain my situation. I figured I'd try for light humor. "Well, I was hit by a train, but that's about it." She looked me up and down, trying to figure out if I was kidding. "I know my body very well," I assured her. "I'll tell you exactly what you can do and what you can't." She didn't seem convinced. "Trust me, you won't hurt me." When she saw my scars, I assured her again not to be frightened. Soon she got past her initial shock, and we were both able to relax.

One of my favorite treatments was Thai massage. I would lie on a big, soft mat on the ground, fully dressed in athletic gear, and the therapist stretched my muscles from feet to neck, twisting, pulling, and pushing my limbs this way and that, as gently or firmly as I wanted. I loved gentle yoga class, too. In the past, I had dismissed yoga as being for people too weak to do real exercise, and I had considered medita- tion to be simply a weird and boring waste of time. During my first pregnancy, I had even refused to take Lamaze classes, explaining to my husband that I already knew how to breathe. I still kind of felt that way, but while I was on vacation, I was willing to try something new.

For the previous ten months, my only exercise had been physical therapy and short walks. I soon found yoga to be an invigorating change. Maybe I couldn't do the things the rest of the class could do. Maybe I did balance exercises only on my right leg. But I was there. The wonderful strangeness of it made me realize the extent to which being injured had become part of my identity. It was part of how I thought about who I was. It was refreshing, but almost disconcerting, to be in an exercise class with "normal" people. I felt compelled to explain to the instructor that I was *not* normal, that I might not be able to do the exercises on my left side, and other things I am sure did not really matter to her or need to be explained.

I found myself talking about the accident frequently with people I met. I wanted to be normal, but part of me also wanted to be recognized as having survived something extraordinary. I was facing a choice. Was I a train-wreck survivor doing something amazingly normal? Or was I a normal person doing something extraordinary, given my injuries? It might seem like a minor difference, but it indicated the internal significance I was willing to assign to the accident. I wasn't sure of the answer.

After four days of sunshine, delicious healthy food, good wine, introspection, and luxurious spa treatments, my mood was markedly improved. I left Arizona tanned and on a high of gratitude for the experience.

As soon as I returned, I was in for a reality check. Dr. M informed me that I should undergo another major surgery that spring. The surgery would reconstruct the left side of my abdominal wall, reattach the oblique muscles that had retracted up into a wad under my rib cage, address a major hernia at the site of my shattered left hip bone, and hopefully make my left side generally less deformed. The idea was to address the problems before they became an emergency. Three surgeons would be involved—my orthopedic surgeon, a general abdominal surgeon, and a plastic surgeon. It was uncharted territory because of the extent of damage to my left hip. The pieces of pelvis bone where the abdominal muscles would attach were gone; the surgeons might or might not be able to reattach the muscles. The plastic surgeon told me to expect a three-month recovery with very limited movement, and I was warned that that area of the body is full of nerves, so recovery would be painful.

My brother, Scott, and his wife, Sheila, who is a neurosurgeon, urged me to wait. Their usual advice about dealing with pain is to suck it up. This time, though, they both thought the procedure was too big and the pain too intense for me to handle. But to me, waiting felt like no progress. I wanted to be done with surgery, not to have a major operation hanging over my future. I was also eager to have my misshapen left side made more normal looking, and I was determined to make my own decisions. I'd come this far; I could handle anything.

The plastic surgeon assured me that for the first several days, I would be on an epidural, and I would be completely numb. Then I would have to go back on the full course of painkillers.

It took a few weeks to digest this news. I'd come so far. Ultimately, I decided to slow down my withdrawal from OxyContin and oxycodone, since I'd have to start the withdrawal process all over again after I recovered from the new surgery. Any thought of returning to work went back on hold, too. I called my boss. Again.

I had two months until the surgery. What would I do with the time?

I decided to focus on trying to be happy. I would do things that gave me a reason to smile. My trip to Arizona had opened me up to the idea of natural healing and gave me confidence that I could be more physically active. I wasn't quite ready to break out the tie-dye and incense—I was still skeptical of the efficacy of anything other than Western medicine—but I could see how yoga, meditation, and mindfulness had helped me feel more in control of my body and improved my mood.

For my birthday, I'd gotten a gift certificate for an at-home massage. I asked the massage therapist if she knew anyone who made yoga house calls. I still couldn't drive without careful advance planning around my medication schedule, and I didn't relish dropping into a crowded yoga class at the gym where twenty-five women were all competing to tie themselves up into a pretzel. I could, however, find gentle ways to strengthen my body and increase my flexibility. I just needed an experienced and well-trained instructor to work with me.

Gail and I spoke on the phone for more than an hour before our first appointment. To my relief, she sounded very normal and didn't veer into advice about balancing my karma or healing my aura. When she showed up at my door for our first session, I was further relieved. I guessed that she was about my age; she wore loose brown yoga pants and a simple yellow T-shirt.

I had scheduled our session for midday, giving me time to take the morning pain pills and allow them to kick in before we started. Gail began our first session in the same way she would each week. She asked how I was feeling and what I needed that day. Had I slept? Was my stomach upset? Had I stepped down my medications that week? She would modify the session based on my specific needs. Then she had me sit in a chair and roll my neck and shoulders—making very gentle movements and then holding a stretch for a few breaths.

My left side was much weaker than my right side, and even simple exercises were difficult. While I was still seated, Gail asked me to lift each knee as high as possible. In our early sessions, I could barely raise my left foot off the ground, and I could hold it up for only a second or two. It was hard not to get frustrated. I'd always been an athletic person. Growing up, I was a competitive gymnast, and in college I was a Division I springboard diver at Duke University. Seeing that I was barely able to lift my left leg felt like proof of how far I'd fallen. But as time went on, I slowly began to improve.

Gail led me in deep breathing exercises, which I found to be incredibly boring, but I had to admit I noticed the benefit almost immediately afterward. We talked about the power of breathing for pain control and as a way of relaxing at night when I couldn't sleep.

The sessions concluded with a meditation called *yoga nidra*. I would lie down flat on the yoga mat with my eyes closed, and Gail would guide me to focus my mind on each part of my body, from the tips of my toes to the crown of my head. One day, as Gail began naming the body parts on my left side—the left hip, the left hip socket, the left side of the waist—I was surprised and embarrassed when tears began to roll down my cheeks. I didn't know why I was crying—it wasn't from physical pain. Simply focusing on the part of my body that had been so mangled stirred my emotions. Afterward, I felt strangely refreshed.[66]

The trauma of the accident had made me a stranger to my body. Time and again, I'd retreated into a dissociative state to escape the pain. My work with Gail was awakening me to my physical self again and making it safe to be there. Dr. Bessel van der Kolk, a pioneer in the field of trauma, explains dissociation and the brain chemistry that creates this state: "Dissociation is the essence of trauma. The overwhelming experience is split off and fragmented, so that the emotions, sounds, images, thoughts, and physical sensations related to the trauma take on a life of their own…[T]he stress hormones that the body secretes to protect itself keep circulating, and the defensive movements and emotional responses keep getting replayed."[67] In its mildest form, dissociation manifests as a kind of spaciness.[68] It almost always involves distortion of time or perception. More technically, trauma affects the region of brain responsible for *interoception*, which means, literally, "the ability to feel yourself." It leaves a person feeling numb, disconnected, or alienated from his or her own body.[69]

During those moments in the hospital when I had willed myself to blank out because the present was intolerable, I was like a threatened animal in the wild. I was essentially playing dead. This created a rift within me—I'd lost touch with my body. The pain drugs only furthered that sense of detachment.

What I didn't know then, but appreciate now, is that pain is a phenomenon of the mind *and* the body. Physiologically, the extent to which an injury causes pain depends not just on the signaling from the nerves in the body to the brain, but also on how the brain interprets those signals, the emotional significance it attributes to them, and the extent to which it releases neurotransmitters back "down" to the body to block the pain signals. With this understanding, it makes sense that mind–body techniques like meditation, breathing exercises, yoga, and body scans are now well accepted by the medical community for their potential to relieve stress and reduce pain.[70] Their effect on brain chemistry and activity has been validated by multiple scientific studies and brain-imaging technologies, and they are commonly used at hospital-based pain clinics and recommended by mainstream healthcare providers.

There are two basic reasons these kinds of therapies can help: first, by emphasizing the connection between the mind and the body, they can help pain patients regain a sense of control over the body and its response to pain. Second, these therapies help reduce activity in the amygdala and thereby turn off the fight-or-flight response. By reducing the stress and anxiety that accompany pain, they calm revved-up muscle, metabolic, and hormonal responses.[71]

Trauma experts speak of treatment techniques that are "top-down," or cognitively based, and treatments that are "bottom-up" and incorporate the body into treatment. Dr. van der Kolk writes, "Knowing the difference between top-down and bottom-up regulation is central for understanding and treating traumatic stress. Top-down regulation involves strengthening the capacity of the watchtower to monitor your body's sensations. Bottom-up regulation involves recalibrating the autonomic nervous system…through breath, movement, or touch."[72]

My sessions with the psychologist and beginner's attempts at meditation, mindfulness, and *yoga nidra* sessions with Gail are all examples of the top-down approach. I also came to enjoy the bottom-up approach, primarily through yoga and breathing. Yoga-based approaches to trauma treatment use a series of postures and breathing techniques to build a sense of connection to the self. Yoga practitioners can cultivate the ability to remain present, to notice and tolerate inner experience, and to develop a new relationship with the body.[73]

The good thing about breathing exercises is that they can be done anywhere at any time. Deep diaphragmatic breathing, three-part breathing, alternate-nostril breathing, rapid forced breathing—I practiced them all. Don't get me wrong—to this day, I find yoga and breathing exercises boring, and I still harbor a hint of my long-held bias against them, but I do them because they help. I find myself relying on them when the pain is bad, the stress is bad, or if I'm desperate to sleep.

For Jonathan's fiftieth birthday, I planned a special surprise. At our family birthday dinner, I presented him with three hints inside little gift bags. He stuck his hand inside the first one and felt around, pulling out…a dirty gray rock. Jonathan rolled his eyes and quipped, "Turning fifty sucks." It wasn't supposed to be a gag gift. I'd loaded down the bags with rocks to make them feel more substantial. Jonathan stuck his hand back in the bag and pulled out a pair of cheap drugstore sunglasses. He gave me a puzzled look and then said with a bemused smile, "Thanks, Honey."

"It's a clue," I assured him. Jonathan put his hand inside the second bag and took out…another rock. "Keep looking!" I urged. He felt around again and this time pulled out a tube of sunscreen.

"Okay," he said with a grin. "I'm sensing a theme." He stuck his hand in the third bag, bypassed the rocks, and pulled out a folded piece of paper. He opened it, revealing the large grid of a calendar page—it was the month of April. I'd marked four large X's over the dates April 25 to 28. "So, we're going somewhere…when?" Jonathan asked.

I laughed at him and teased, "You're staring at a calendar and your question is *when?*"

"Right. Okay, smarty. Where?" he asked.

"I'm not going to tell you till we get to the airport," I smirked.

A few weeks later, we were lying in bed on a Saturday morning. I was making a mental to-do list. Without thinking, I blurted out, "We have to remember our passports for Bermuda."

"Bermuda?" Jonathan responded. I clapped my hand over my mouth. I stink at keeping secrets.

I'd picked Bermuda because it was a place neither of us had been before, it was a short plane ride away, and I knew it would be a sunny, relaxing destination. The trip would be an opportunity to have some alone time with Jonathan, celebrate his birthday, and have a real getaway before my surgery. From what my doctors told me, I was going to be spending another summer in bed or on the couch, so this was a last hurrah for a while.

In *Surviving Survival,* resilience expert Laurence Gonzales writes that "[t]ravel is a time-honored strategy for healing…it is an excellent way to fool the brain and relieve it of its horrors."[74] The theme is also frequent in literature. At the beginning of *Moby Dick,* Ishmael says, "Whenever I find myself growing grim about the mouth; whenever it is a damp, dreary November in my soul,… then, I account it high time to get to sea as soon as I can."

Bermuda was more of a paradise than I could have imagined. It was vacation, trauma-recovery–style: sleep until noon, pick at a delicious fish sandwich and French fries, and then settle my newly skinny body onto chaise lounges under one of the resort's blue-and-white-striped umbrellas. Tranquil, aquamarine waters lapped up on soft pink sand and rushed between the grooves of craggy rocks that dotted the shoreline. Add in a few spa treatments and rum drinks, and we were genuinely happy. We found ourselves discussing the future. Whole conversations would pass with no mention of the accident, pain, trains, lawsuits, drugs, surgery, or therapy.

During this idyllic interlude, my orthopedic surgeon's recent advice came back to me. At my last appointment, Dr. M had given Jonathan and me a meaningful look and assured me that my pelvis was completely stable. *Completely stable.* Ugh. I could have killed him. I knew there was no actual risk of injury, but the idea of having sex sounded awful and made me incredibly anxious. I had only just begun to feel more comfortable in my body, and I was deeply afraid of pressure or pain. It didn't sound quite so awful to Jonathan… We gave it an awkward try, and I think Jonathan appreciated the effort—but normalcy would remain out of reach for quite a while.

Bermuda did help us regain other levels of intimacy. It was meaningful to Jonathan that I'd taken the initiative and planned this trip for the two of us. We took long, meandering walks along the beach, snapped pictures of each other, and stared at the waves. We laughed more over those four days than we had in the past year. We started to remember what it felt like to be a couple and equal partners, rather than a patient and caregiver. I remember shutting my eyes, taking in the healing warmth of the sun, the salty breeze playing with my hair, the soothing murmur of the surf, and feeling deeply at peace. The one-year anniversary of the accident was around the corner. Jonathan and I had made it through. We would continue to struggle, but we were going to be okay.

Eleven

It was early May, and I was rushing home after a humiliating psychiatric evaluation by a doctor representing the State of New Jersey. I needed to change my clothes and put on some makeup before a reporter from Philly's ABC News station arrived at the house. The first anniversary of the crash was approaching, and news outlets were profiling passengers of Amtrak 188.

The evaluation was a requirement of my application for federal disability benefits, which in turn was a requirement to maintain my private disability insurance benefits. I kept thinking I would be better soon and wouldn't need the benefits for much longer. I certainly couldn't think of myself as permanently disabled. However, as recovery dragged on and I needed one surgery after another, I couldn't risk losing my insurance, so I dutifully followed the process to apply for permanent disability.

At first, it just meant more piles of forms and phone calls to deal with. I spent hours trying to track down all my medical records from the many specialists who had been treating me. I began getting calls from the State of New Jersey Office of Labor and Welfare and found myself explaining my case over and over again. It was awkward to argue for a status I didn't even want. Long-term disability? *Definitely*. Permanent disability? *No way*.

When you fill out the forms, they don't ask if or when you think you'll get better. They ask, "How many hours a day can you work? Can you drive? How far can you walk? What tasks can you do around the house?" The honest answers to those questions described a person I didn't want to recognize.

The welfare office needed more information, so they asked me to go for orthopedic evaluations with a state doctor. A letter came in the mail notifying me of the address, time, and date for the appointment. They'd scheduled it for June 1, the same day as my next surgery. I rolled my eyes. I called to request another date. The man reviewing my case hassled me. "I thought I saw in your file that you already had surgery," he said. "Why are you going for another one?" As if I was asking for a second helping of dessert.

"Have you looked at my file?" I asked pointedly. "I've had ten surgeries."

"So, why are you having another one?" he repeated, defensively. I explained that it was both abdominal and orthopedic—that they were fixing a hernia, but it involved my broken pelvis and a pretty major reconstruction of the entire left side of my abdomen and that they weren't able to do it earlier because I hadn't been healed enough until now.

"You should really try to get to the disability evaluation before the surgery," he said. "It will look better for your case if they do the exam before you have those issues fixed." Clearly this guy was used to a different kind of claimant. I wanted to get better, not successfully prove that I would never get better.

"I can't move the surgery," I said with finality, and eventually he agreed to give me a new date for the state-ordered exam.

Included in my case were the issues of pain management and post-traumatic stress disorder. A week later, I was shocked to receive another letter from the State, saying they were sending me for a psychiatric evaluation. This time, it was on the same date as the TV interview, and there was no way around it.

Mercia drove me to and from the exam. It was in a small, grim office in New Brunswick, New Jersey, with dark, thinning wall-to-wall carpeting, a drop ceiling, and fluorescent lights. Half the vinyl chairs were already filled with people waiting. Mercia and I took a seat next to an elderly man. I felt like I'd hit a surreal new low. In less than a year, I had gone from a being an accomplished executive traveling the world to being evaluated by the State to determine whether I had a permanent mental disorder.

While it was true that I often cried at random moments, felt inexplicable sadness much of the time, couldn't sleep at night, and was fearful when going around turns in a car, I didn't want to think of myself as being forever disabled by depression and PTSD. I had no interest in playing up my case to ensure I got the benefits. I would answer the doctor's questions honestly, and that would be all. I imagined a rather dry, straightforward conversation.

The psychiatrist was a young Black woman with kind eyes behind her wire-frame glasses. She didn't know anything about my case, so I started off by explaining that I'd been in a train accident. She asked about all the things I couldn't do—I was unable to sleep at night; I would wake up in a strange trance with my arms raised in the air; I cried at random times. The anniversary was just one week away, and after that, I was going in for another major surgery. My voice tightened up, and tears rolled down my cheeks. She handed me a box of tissues. I explained that I had mood swings and was taking antidepressants. I also told her that I was going to get better.

The psychiatrist leaned in, taking notes. She seemed to look at me with genuine sympathy. At the end of the conversation, she wished me well. I appreciated her kindness but was still left feeling empty. My emotional outpouring had all been for the sake of another form she would send on to the next office so they could close a file.

When Mercia and I arrived home, I tried to shake off the misery and embarrassment of the evaluation. I was about to tell my story again, in a completely different context. I made a beeline for my closet. I pulled out a dress, a button-down shirt, and a sweater set. As I tried on each outfit, I grimaced at the mirror. My eyes and nose were still red from crying. I settled on the sweater set and went to the bathroom to fix my hair as best I could and put on a little makeup.

When I sat down with the reporter, I felt awkward. It wasn't like me to share my private struggles in such a public way. I'd agreed to the interview because I wanted to speak about the reality of trauma recovery and the long-term challenges many survivors of accidental trauma face. And, more specifically with regard to the trauma caused by the Amtrak accident, it had been a full year. Families still missed their loved ones; survivors like me still hurt every single day. Yet the only legislative reaction to the crash had been to extend, by three years, the deadline for railroads around the country to install the type of Positive Train Control system that would have avoided the tragedy.

The ripple effects of trauma are poorly appreciated. It seemed important that people know the consequences of an accident like this one. I hadn't found many resources describing what it was like to recover from trauma, and maybe someone else who was going through something similar would find my story valuable. So I agreed to the interview, ever conflicted. I spent the days before and afterward worried that people would think I was seeking attention or trying to sensationalize what happened.

The reporter also spoke to Jonathan, and then the producer asked if they could get a few shots of me doing my physical therapy exercises. I felt a little silly showing off how bad I was at doing a sit-up—truthfully, I wasn't that great at them before the accident, either.

We told the boys they didn't have to be involved with the segment if they didn't want to. Jonathan and I didn't want them to feel paraded in front of the camera, but they were surprisingly eager to participate. Maybe in part, it was exciting to have a television crew in the house, but they also felt like this was their story, too. They wanted their side to be told.

A few days before the anniversary, on Sunday, May 8, a photo of Amtrak 188's decimated first car dominated the front page of the *Philadelphia Inquirer*. In giant block letters, the headline read "Surviving Car 1." The article profiled me and two other passengers who made it out. This story was much more in-depth than the television interview. I'd met with the reporter multiple times. The focus of the article was the deep impact of the accident and how the passengers continued to cope with it one year later. Seeing the story on the front page increased the momentum I'd felt building all month. The anniversary was coming up in a few days.

In late April, I received a letter with the seal of the City of Philadelphia on the envelope. It was an invitation from the mayor to attend a remembrance service at City Hall in honor of those lost in the derailment and to pay tribute to the survivors and the first responders. It became clear the day would naturally be both a celebration and a memorial. My parents flew to town to be with me. I gathered gifts and cards to give to everyone who had supported me through the past year. I sent my siblings crystal hurricane lamps with the inscription "forever grateful," and I dropped off cards in my neighbors' mailboxes, thanking them.

When the day arrived, I felt its weight from the moment I opened my eyes. I went through the motions of getting dressed like I was in a dream, saying little to anyone. I kept returning to the thought that May 12, 2015, had started out as an ordinary day for an ordinary business trip. When I had woken up one year before, my body was whole, and my family hadn't known this level of grief. I felt the stark contrast between that ordinary life and the life I was living now. It was a year later, and I was still reaching for the bottle of Oxy as soon as I opened my eyes in the morning. A year later, and I was getting ready for another surgery. A year later, and I was still unable to work. The future was precarious. What if I was out for two years? What if I never recovered?

I was haunted by thoughts of what others were going through today. What about all the families who woke up a year ago with a mother, wife, sister, or daughter who did not return that evening? I felt guilty for complaining when I thought about them. I was so lucky.

During the drive to Philly, Jonathan turned on the radio and began flipping through stations. The morning DJ chatter didn't match my mood. All I wanted to do was withdraw into my numb cocoon. I asked him to turn it off. A few minutes passed in silence, and then Jonathan started making conversation—talking about nothing in particular. My irritation grew, and I refused to respond. In hindsight, I know it was his own subconscious stress management, but in that moment, I had no emotional space left for his stress. I was just annoyed.

When we reached the city, Jonathan began to complain about traffic. A car cut him off, and he burst out with expletives. I wanted to scream, *"People are dead. Shut up about the traffic!"*

"Where are we supposed to park?" he muttered. "Is there a special place for us to park? Did they send you parking instructions?" he wondered aloud as we took a second loop around the traffic circle. "They should have reserved spaces," he continued.

I couldn't take it anymore. I knew I was on the verge of saying something that would make a difficult day even worse. I stifled myself, uttering three short words instead: "Let. Me. Out." I spoke in a whisper, but there was no mistaking my intensity. Just then, the front entrance to City Hall came into view. Jonathan pulled up to the curb.

"You go inside," he offered. "I'll figure it out and meet you in there." Wordlessly, I got out. My anger soon evaporated, but it brought home to me how differently we were experiencing this day. And it was not even 10:00 in the morning.

In the vestibule, I sent my bag through the X-ray machine and showed the security guard my ID. He gave me directions to the reception hall, where a crowd of reporters and photographers stood outside, snapping photos as people entered. The service was for invited guests only. I waited outside the view of the cameras until Jonathan caught up with me, and we entered together.

The formal décor of the hall suited the somber occasion. A high ceiling was bedecked with ornate moldings and an enormous chandelier. On every wall, above dark wood wainscoting, hung portraits of past mayors in gilded frames. Heavy satin drapes adorned towering windows. First responders—police officers, firefighters, and paramedics—in full dress uniform stood at attention against the walls, nearly circling the entire room. The crowd filled the rows of chairs, yet the room was pin-drop quiet. Many guests were looking down, some softly weeping.

Jonathan and I searched for seats together. The unoccupied chairs in the first two rows were marked off with paper signs: "Reserved for Family." We looked toward the podium and the stage where the speakers were seated. Eight wreaths of snow-white flowers had been placed at the front. Each wreath displayed a sash with the name of a passenger who died. The sight took my breath away and brought tears to my eyes. I looked from the wreaths to the families of the deceased in the front rows. The physical divide was trivial—two rows with little white paper signs—but it signified an unbridgeable chasm between their experience and the rest of ours. Theirs was one of terrible finality; ours was an uncertain future. I wanted to reach across the divide, to find the strength to convey how sorry I was for their loss, but I didn't know how. For now, I found a seat near the back, sat down, and cried. In a room smothered in sadness, I felt guilty for giving thanks that there was no wreath for me.

The ceremony began with a blessing given by a reverend of a Philadelphia church. After a city representative said a few remarks, Joseph Boardman, the president and CEO of Amtrak, spoke. Jonathan was instantly furious and offended by Boardman's presence—his intrusion. I felt differently. He should be there; he should stand up, face the families, and apologize. I don't remember much of what he said, and I suspect the actual words mattered little to most of us wrestling with emotions between white-hot anger and impenetrable sadness. I do recall that he expressed sorrow and regret and promised that he would try to make sure it never happened again.

Speeches by the deputy police commissioner and the fire commissioner honored the heroism of the first responders. A fellow passenger spoke about the eight who died. He read each of their names and told us about them, their families, and their work. The mayor gave a speech followed by the tapping of the bells. Heavy iron bells filled the room with deep, resonating, sorrowful tones. By now I was sobbing. A woman seated nearby handed me a stack of tissues, but within minutes they were wet. I can't remember ever crying so loudly and unabashedly before or since. I was powerless against the waves of tears and simply gave in to them.

A twelve-year-old Black boy with a round face and close-cut hair stepped up to the microphone. He wore a plain white dress shirt, buttoned all the way up, no tie, and dark slacks. He had been introduced as Bobby, the young man who had sung for Pope Francis during his visit to Philadelphia the previous fall. Today, he would sing "Amazing Grace" *a cappella*. As he belted out the words in an impossibly high soprano, it was as if my heart was cleansed by the sound. I listened to the verses—"Amazing grace, how sweet the sound that saved a wretch like me. I once was lost and now I'm found. Was blind and now I see"—and I felt the inspiriting power of that grace I'd spent so much time ruminating over. I recognized myself so clearly in the words; it was as if every line of that classic hymn had been written to describe my exact experience. My prayers, for those who were gone and for my own health and happiness, were being carried on those notes. I was overwhelmed and sobbed even harder.

When the service concluded, I was still weeping, with my head resting on my knees, and the woman seated behind me asked if I was okay. She told me she had been in the accident, too. I tried to gather myself, wiped my eyes, and turned to her. "Were you badly hurt?" I asked.

"I broke all my ribs," she said. "It still hurts too much to drive, because I can't twist or turn to check my blind spot." I commiserated. She patted the breast pocket of her flannel shirt. "I've got the oxycodone right here."

I smiled and shook my purse. The pills rattled in their prescription bottles made the same sound. "Don't leave home without it," I replied. The brief exchange sanded down ever so slightly the sharp splinters of my loneliness and isolation. Others were still struggling with the aftermath, too.

I approached the fire commissioner, Derrick Sawyer, knowing emergency medical services for the area reports to the Philadelphia Fire Department. I thanked him, saying that I was alive today to attend the service because of the Philadelphia emergency responders. It felt wonderful to thank him personally. I told him that Jonathan and I had been trying to find the actual team who found me, to thank them, but we hadn't been successful.

"Maybe I can help," he said. He brought me to the deputy commissioner of EMS, Jeremiah Laster. I took his hand and thanked him as well, saying his team unquestionably saved my life. I told him that I wanted to thank the individuals who pulled me out of the wreckage. "I can tell you what I was wearing, where I was found, and where I was taken," I said. He gave me his card and asked that I send him a note. I was hoping to find a bit of closure by thanking the people who found me, resuscitated me, and got me to a hospital within forty minutes of the crash.

Both EMS and the hospital made inquiries. Unfortunately, the specific people who saved me couldn't be identified. It's one of those loose ends that still nags at me to this day. I may never get to thank them.

Jonathan and I walked down the hall for the reception. Carrots, dip, and small sandwiches were laid out on the table. No one had much of an appetite. I wasn't sure I wanted to stay; I was emotionally spent. I saw the young singer, Bobby, and his mother. I told him how he had moved me. "Your mother must be proud," I said, looking to her. Bobby seemed shy now that he was offstage and humbly accepted the compliment.

A sixty-something woman in a simple black dress with pretty blonde hair that fell to her chin approached me. She was with a gentleman who had a short, white beard, maybe her husband or her brother. Her eyes were wet with tears and her expression deeply sympathetic. "Were you in the accident?" she asked.

Like Jonathan, she had also spent that night searching for her daughter, calling hospitals and Amtrak's 1-800 line, only to be told to call another number, and then another. The next morning, the phone had rung. Her eyes glistened as she recounted how the voice on the other end requested her daughter's dental records. It was clear from that moment that her daughter wasn't coming home. They had found her body under the third car. Hearing this, I wrapped my arms around the woman, and we stood there holding each other in the crowd for a long time. Her daughter had been the exact same age as me.

"This past year has been so unreal," she said. "And now that it has been a year…" She paused, choking back the tears and steadying her voice. "Now it is just the reality—no Laura." As we cried together for her loss, I felt the familiar clash between sadness and gratitude for my own reality.

I was also struck by how graceful this grieving mother was. She was resigned and filled with sadness, but she didn't appear bitter. She had lost her daughter, yet she was kind enough to ask how I was doing and to listen to Jonathan's story of his own search that night, which had ended so differently from hers, and to wish me a full recovery.

That afternoon, there was going to be a ceremony at the site of the accident where families of the deceased would lay the white wreaths. I told Jonathan I didn't want to go. I didn't think I could handle seeing the exact site of the destruction.

We were both quiet on the drive home.

When we got to the house, my parents came out to meet us. They had just arrived from Colorado. We gave each other long, lingering hugs.

I went upstairs to change my clothes and splash water on my face before joining my parents on the porch. The boys and Jonathan started up a game of volleyball, and my parents and I watched them from the outdoor sofa. I talked about the service and meeting the mother who lost her daughter.

As I recounted the day with my own mother, I began to pull back from the sadness. I gazed at the clusters of red geraniums in their pots, lined up along the white posts of the porch, and then I looked out at the lawn, where the boys and Jonathan were popping the volleyball back and forth. They called out to each other, voices filled with the joy of play. In the past, I would have been on the grass with them, and part of me wished I were. Another part of me was able to step away from that feeling of regret and loss and see the perfection of this moment. I was here with my family. It was a beautiful evening. We had been given so much. *How could I possibly be sad about this?* I thought. We stayed out until the sun reached the horizon, putting on a brilliant show of fiery oranges and pinks that grew brighter and brighter until, at last, the sun sank behind the hillside and the landscape dimmed. Dark clouds began to gather, and the wind picked up as we headed inside for dinner.

I had set the table the day before with our wedding china, crystal glasses, and seven tapered candles, plus two more candles on the credenza. After filling our plates with a simple meal and dimming the overhead lights, the kids, Jonathan, Mercia, my parents, and I took our seats at the table. Mirrored place mats reflected the dancing flames of the candles as Mercia led us in prayer. She said she was grateful that I was with them today. She gave thanks that Nana and Pop Pop were sharing the moment with us and thanks for all those who helped. She was thankful to be together on this journey with me, a journey that's still ongoing. She explained that the journey was transformative, not only for me—we were all being transformed.

I suggested we sing "Amazing Grace" because I wanted to hear that song one more time. Listening to our eight voices praising grace brought me right back to that moment during the service when I felt God's pure benevolence. The sound was so sweet.

Earlier, I had placed a gift wrapped in silver paper beside each place setting, and now I invited everyone to open them, one by one. I'd put a lot of thought into how to mark this day and how to show my gratitude to family and friends. Symbolism was important.

I'd given everyone a butterfly ornament and a crystal remembrance, most of them votive candleholders. Butterflies are deep and powerful representations of endurance, change, hope, and life. In Mandarin Chinese, the word for "butterfly" means seventy years and symbolizes long life. In Christianity, the butterfly is a powerful symbol of the resurrection. A Native American legend also tells of a grieving butterfly who is eventually filled with gratitude and joy for a new life as she unwraps her wings and begins to dance.

Candles are an even more powerful and universal symbol. In every major religion I know of, candles represent light, warmth, joy, life, and knowledge. They are lit to celebrate birth and marriage and they are lit at funerals. The symbolism is no less powerful for its familiarity. To this day, one of my favorite songs that I played during my recovery in the ICU is "Go Light Your World."

Brad opened his gift first—a three-inch candleholder that looked like a heavily faceted rock. "I chose this gift because you are such a rock," I said. "You are so solid in your courage." Austin's was a crystal baseball because the day after the accident, he had the steadiness to pitch a winning game. I gave Steven a flat, round crystal votive candleholder engraved with the words "I love you." It looked to me like the spreading ripples of a stone tossed in a pond. The ripple effects of Steven's laughter had lit up so many of my gray days. Mercia's was an angel because she had been our angel, looking after the family. For my parents, I had chosen a series of four votive holders, each engraved with a different message of love and gratitude. For Jonathan, a crystal clock engraved with an infinity symbol and the words "gratitude and love" because I was grateful for more time together. We lit every candle, and the table almost looked like an altar. As we ate, we went around in a circle, adding to Mercia's prayer, saying why we were grateful. We kept coming back to the main one—we were together.

Looking at my sons' faces above the warm glow of the flames, I said, "I chose the theme of light for this dinner because you boys have been my light." At that precise moment, a clap of thunder roared, the lights in surrounding rooms flickered, and the whole house went dark.

As we gaped at each other, stunned by the coincidence, Steven was quick to add one more reason to be grateful: "Good thing we've got all these candles!" And for the first time that day, we all erupted in genuine laughter.

Twelve

The kitchen was a mess. Opened cardboard boxes and plastic storage containers were piled on top of one another, overflowing with old clothes, toys, sports equipment, and Christmas ornaments. Meanwhile, the kids and dogs were zipping in and out, adding to the confusion. I had entered full-on nesting mode, getting ready for my upcoming surgery. Like when I was pregnant with the boys, I felt the need to prepare for the big event by going on a crazy cleaning frenzy. When I was eight and a half months pregnant, I had sat on the floor, breathing heavily as I reached my soapy rag to the back corners of the cabinet under the kitchen sink. Jonathan had assured me with a straight face that we weren't going to stash the baby back there.

In this case, getting ready for another hospital stay meant prevailing on Jonathan and the boys to drag the contents of the basement upstairs to be sorted and cleared away. I hadn't exactly stopped to think why a clean basement seemed so important for my recuperation, but the boys indulged my silly priorities with relatively good humor.

As I was tying up another trash bag to be tossed in the dumpster, Steven wandered into the kitchen and began rummaging through the boxes. "Stevie, we're trying to get rid of stuff here," I warned.

"Hey! I always wanted one of these," he said.

I glanced over. He was holding an old, cracked Magic 8-Ball. "What do you want to ask it?" I said absently.

"Will Mom live?" The question popped right out of his mouth, as if it had been sitting on a loaded spring. I swiveled around, jolted to attention.

"What?" Taking the 8-Ball from Steven's little hands, I pulled him into a hug. "Of course I will!" I exclaimed. "This surgery is going to make me stronger." Eager to set him at ease, I angled the ball away from his view, said a quick prayer, and turned it over (fully prepared to drop it and pronounce it broken if the answer was not in my favor). *Will Mom live:* "Yes, definitely," the floating purple triangle proclaimed. I showed it to him as undeniable proof.

I had hoped the fears left by the accident had faded from Steven's awareness as the year went on and I got better. But it looked like the cut ran deeper than I knew. It was hard for him to understand why I had to go back for another surgery and why I would be in the hospital again for so long. He asked pleadingly, "Why are they always taking you away from me?" The best I could do was to show him that I was not afraid. And I wasn't.

Waiting in the pre-operating room on the morning of the surgery, I felt confident—even empowered. Unlike before the other surgeries, when I would retreat into a passive, disconnected state, this time I was prepared. I was strong enough to handle the surgery, and it would be my last one—or so I thought. When this was all over, my body would look and feel more normal. While the nurse put in my IV, I chatted with Mom, Dad, and Jonathan. Mom and Dad had booked a nearby hotel room for the week. Jonathan would stay for the surgery and then head home to be with the kids.

The anesthesiologist introduced herself. She was a young woman with Southeast Asian features, narrow shoulders, and long, straight black hair. She explained that she would administer the epidural before putting me under general anesthesia and that throughout the surgery, she'd monitor my vital signs. Minutes later, the surgeons arrived, and I was rolling into the OR.

Five hours later, I woke up screaming in agony. As the anesthesia wore off, pain seared through my abdomen. Something was wrong. The anesthesiologist made some kind of adjustment, bringing me numb relief. The experience scared me. It was an ugly way to wake up. I was assured, though, that the surgery had gone well and there was nothing to be concerned about. Now it was just a matter of healing. I stared down at the neat but angry 30-centimeter incision that circled the left side of my body from the center of my belly to the center of my back, and the two tubes protruding from my hip with drains attached. I'd been through worse. I could handle this.

My parents and Jonathan met me in my hospital room. I raised the head of my bed a bit and chatted with them for a while before sending Jonathan home to be with the kids. My parents lingered until 8:30 or 9:00 p.m., when I urged them to go back to the hotel and get some rest.

At first, it was only a subtle twinge in the pit of my stomach. But the twinge quickly became a flare that took hold and stayed. I called the nurse. She said she would contact the doctor on call for pain management and swiftly left the room. The pain was growing stronger by the second. I called the nurse again. She said she was expecting to hear back from the doctor soon. By now, it felt like some awful beast had sunk its teeth into my belly and was gnashing at my insides. I called the nurse again and again. "You've got to do something," I demanded angrily. The all-consuming pain was razor-sharp, penetrating through my bones. This wasn't like anything I'd ever felt before. I started kicking with my good leg, pulling my hair, and digging my nails into my arms—struggling against the monster that was devouring me. When I felt I couldn't breathe anymore, I tried to stay motionless so I would not jostle a single screaming muscle. I pressed the call button for the nurse almost constantly. Each time she appeared, it seemed there was another reason I had to hold on a little longer. I was supposed to have an epidural and be completely numb, so why was I in agony? The nurse said there might be an issue with the epidural, but it was late at night, and to fix it, they would have to book a procedure room and call in an anesthesiologist. Instead, the pain doctor on call had prescribed more Dilaudid. He'd called the order in, but she was waiting on the pharmacy. In my agonized state, it seemed to me that the nurse was saying she'd done her job, so now I should be quiet and wait. "Screaming won't help," she chided.

"You think I'm screaming because I think it will help?" I shouted back. "I'm screaming because I can't stand it!"

At last she brought the pain medication, but it seemed to me it was too late. The beast was beyond submission now. The drugs did nothing. I continued to scream and cry, powerless against the thing raging in my side. The nurse turned out the lights in an attempt to calm me. Declaring that she had other patients who needed her, she left the room. I later found out that she had gone to the stock of medication on the floor and wondered to herself about my level of pain and the amount of drugs being pushed through my IV. Something wasn't right. On her own initiative, she opened the cabinet and grabbed a dose of Naloxone (Narcan) and put it in the pocket of her scrubs.

Alone, sobbing in the dark, I picked up my cell and called Jonathan. "Hello?" he answered.

"It hurts. So bad," I panted. "Just be with me."

"I'll call the doctor," Jonathan said.

"No," I said. "I've already told the nurse." Jonathan listened as I let out another wail. "I'm on fire!"

"Maybe your parents can come."

"No," I said again, my words strained. "It's late. Just do what I say. Just be with me and listen to me. The nurse said they are getting more pain meds."

"I can't sit here while you're in pain and not do anything," he said.

"Just be with me," I begged.

"I can't just sit here and listen to you crying in pain."

"Fine, then don't," I shouted irrationally, hanging up on him.

A short while later, my dad appeared in the doorway. Jonathan had called him. "I didn't want to wake you," I said, tears streaming down my cheeks. Truthfully, I was glad to see him.

Dad pleaded with the nurse. "Can't you do something?" he asked. She said she'd speak to the doctor again.

A few minutes later, she returned to the room. "We are adding more pain medication to the IV, and you have the button you can push for breakthrough pain."

"It's all breakthrough," I protested. Ignoring my comment, she calmly informed me that it was also time for my antidepressant. Depression seemed the least of my issues at that moment, and the little pill and Dixie cup of water she handed me struck me as ludicrous. Too exhausted and hurting too much to argue, I swallowed the pill and closed my eyes, hoping that the narcotics she had added to the IV would do their job. Dad reclined the bed again, dimmed the lights, and took my hand. I tried to will myself to relax. Merciful darkness closed in. I don't know how much time passed, but the next thing I knew, I was awake, thoroughly confused, and squinting under the blaring fluorescent lights. The head of my bed had been raised again, and someone was practically yelling in my face. It was the anesthesiologist I had met in the morning. She was holding what looked like a rubber bag above my head. Two burly men in dark nylon jackets were beside the bed, along with a red metal cart full of drawers. The room was crowded with people all watching me. "You stopped breathing!" the young doctor yelled. "You stopped breathing!"

I blinked, shook my head, and tried to understand. Just then, my dad ducked into the room with tears in his eyes—Dad, whom I had never seen cry. He pushed past the crowd of white coats around my bed, bent down, and kissed my head, whispering, "I love you" through choked-back sobs. He turned and ducked out again.

Then the pain hit. The beast had come back with an army. I thrashed and screamed. As I was writhing on the bed, the anesthesiologist tried to explain that they'd just resuscitated me.

"You overdosed!" she said. Was that an accusation? *I* overdosed? Excuse me, I just had surgery and have been lying here, crying in pain with an IV in my arm and a useless epidural. *I* didn't *do* anything. She said they'd given me Narcan to get me breathing again, but it blocks the effect of the pain medication for at least an hour. I had just undergone a five-hour surgery to rearrange my insides and reattach my abdominal muscles to my hip bone. And now I was being told I couldn't have *anything* for the pain. How was that possible?

Words are inadequate to describe the next hour.

"I can't do it!" I pleaded. "You have to help me. There must be something…"

The doctor shook her head, noting, "We don't want you to stop breathing again." *No shit.* I didn't want to stop breathing, either. But I couldn't take this. If they had asked me where I was on the pain scale from one to ten, I would have said twenty. This was profound and violent beyond anything I'd ever felt.

Dad was by my side again. He tried to hold my hand, but my whole body was shaking like crazy. There were maybe a dozen people surrounding me. They all seemed to be standing there with their clipboards, watching me writhe and scream. I was dimly aware of the doctors debating whether to bring me to the ICU. "Is a bed available?" one asked another. The answer was apparently no, but they found a place in the neurological ICU. I didn't care if it was an ICU for circus animals. I wanted to be somewhere else, a place where maybe they could fix my pain. They pulled on the four corners of the sheet, lifted, and slid me onto a gurney; impossibly, the agony shot up. I don't recall being wheeled down the hall—I believe I passed out. When we reached the ICU, I became aware they were going to move me off the gurney. I resumed screaming at the top of my lungs. I writhed and sought my father's hand. I begged him not to let them move me.

Dad was by my side, holding my hand. "I can't do this," I cried. "Let me die." Even through my pain-induced fog, I registered the seriousness of these words, and I spoke them deliberately. Never in my life had I wished I were dead. Over and again, I'd thanked God with all my heart that I was alive and had survived the accident. In this moment, however, I felt completely coherent and got the words out of my mouth with effort and intent. I only wanted one thing—to be free from the pain. *Let me die.*

After what seemed like hours, but was no doubt less, the Narcan wore off, and the opioids were flowing again. I gradually calmed down. Multiple doctors arrived with ice and needles to check whether I had any feeling in my thighs. Yes, I could feel the pinpricks. Yes, I could feel the ice sliding across my skin. And no kidding, the epidural obviously wasn't working. Finally, morning broke, I closed my eyes—well monitored and medicated in intensive care—and I slept.

Later, my dad shared his perspective. He had been sitting beside me, holding my hand, as the nurse gave me the last dose of pain medication. He had felt relieved as my cries quieted, my muscles relaxed, and he thought I had finally drifted off to sleep. When the nurse turned around after typing in her last round of notes, the room was dimly lit, and the change could have easily gone without her notice.

Notwithstanding her brusque bedside manner, I'll be forever grateful to her. She sensed something was wrong and took a closer look. I'd turned blue—my breathing had stopped. She hit a button on the wall, and within seconds, an emergency team rushed in. Another nurse pulled my dad from the room. He watched from the hallway with tears in his eyes, listening to the emergency workers yelling orders to each other as they tried to resuscitate me. He prayed and called my mom. My mom immediately called my siblings, and they sat on the phone in a miserable huddle, waiting for news. The moment I revived, Dad burst into the room to kiss me and to say he loved me before darting back out of the doctors' way. For a second time, I'd come very close to dying, and this time, I nearly slipped away as he was sitting beside me, holding my hand—unaware anything was wrong. Dad was such a tremendous comfort to me through that hellish night, but I know the memory haunts him. It haunts me, too.

My experience was rare[75] but far from unique. Unfortunately, there is a paucity of medical evidence and procedures in place to prevent it from happening to others.[76] An academic study on postsurgical patients found unresponsive during treatment for pain revealed that most such incidents happen during the twenty-four hours following surgery and are associated with high pain scores preceding the "life-threatening critical respiratory event." Furthermore, most deaths occur during the nighttime hours.[77] I now understand I had several other risk factors as well—I was "opioid-tolerant" before receiving the large doses associated with the surgery and recovery, and I had had a lengthy surgical procedure and a large abdominal incision.

After talking to doctors and nurses, hearing my father's testimony, and trying to research the phenomenon, I still can't explain why I nearly died that night. My sister-in-law, a respected neurosurgeon, has explained to me that there is some level of pain that we simply cannot control—it is why some badly injured patients are put into induced comas. Perhaps I was subject to unhealthy "dose-stacking" of the pain medications. Perhaps because of the pain medication I had been prescribed for the previous year, I was suffering from what they call "opioid-induced hyperalgesia" or abnormal sensitivity to pain.[78] It seems that when people have been on opioids for a long period, they have a more severe reaction to pain and require larger doses of painkillers, which can put them in danger of being overdosed.

I am grateful that I was resuscitated before any brain damage occurred. Psychologically, however, the incident was a tremendous setback. Strangely enough, my surgery had taken place on June 1—exactly one year after I had left Penn—and now I'd landed in intensive care again.

I was kept in the ICU for the rest of the week. I didn't really need to be there the entire time—the emergency had passed—but I didn't complain. Staying in the ICU is like flying business class; you get a lot of individual attention, which was reassuring because now I was afraid—afraid of not having enough pain relief, afraid of falling asleep and not waking up. I was seeing some of the same nurses and physician assistants who had cared for me a year earlier. One of them told me she had been there the night I was taken off the helicopter, and she was also there the night I was overdosed. She said, "No one should have to go through what you went through—not only once, but twice."

For several days, I wasn't getting out of bed, keeping the pain at bay by moving as little as possible and staying on a steady high dose of meds. When I was finally ready to get up, I was using the same type of walker I had gleefully thrown away nine months earlier. I had surgical drains pinned to my clothes again, too, and the same circulation devices wrapped around my legs. The feeling of déjà vu was inescapable and depressing.

Jonathan brought the kids to visit. With the seven of us crammed into the room, we decided to watch a movie together. Steven sat beside me in bed, being careful not to disturb my wounds. The hospital scene almost felt routine at that point.

I was sent home after nine days, and I laid low for the rest of the summer. Within a few weeks, I managed to get off the walker. After two months, I was ready to start weaning myself back down from the pain medications. I told myself I'd taken a step back, but I would take two steps forward.

In August, we visited my parents in Colorado. Pastor Claire asked if I would speak again at Father Dyer and update the congregation on how I was doing. I agreed out of gratitude to the community. That's when Pastor Claire told me the theme of the month—living with joy. *God has a sense of humor*, I thought. Did Claire really think I was the appropriate person to speak on the topic of joy? I told her I was going to need some help. Living with joy felt like a high bar. We met for lunch.

Claire explained that in the Bible, joy isn't described as jumping for joy. It's not glee, or exhilaration, or even happiness. Joy is having the continuous presence of God in your life through all its highs and lows. I smiled. This was the insight I had been missing. Since the accident, I'd become much more aware of God—whether thanking Him, crying out to Him, or asking for guidance. Maybe I did have something to say about living with joy.

Our conversation wound around to the image of a quilt. I pictured the events of my life as colorful patches. So much had happened since December. I called forth the wonderful moments: the trip to Bermuda with Jonathan, the spa in Arizona, and precious time spent with our boys. One perfect example had taken place two weeks prior. I had shuffled to the kitchen in the (late) morning and was surprised to see a basket on the counter island overflowing with Nacho Cheese Doritos. In front of the basket was a note scrawled in pencil: "Life is a Gift." Ten-year-old Steven had woken up feeling inspired and wanted to share it with the family. I would never look at a bag of Nacho Cheese Doritos the same way again. There is joy in unlikely places.

Mixed in with the pleasurable moments were daily challenges with pain and managing my medications, the intense experience of nearly losing my life, and the extreme pain after the surgery. The bittersweetness of the memorial service and the anniversary dinner brought other shades of color to my quilt. In some ways, those darker colors made the bright moments even brighter. In every instance, I felt God's protection.

As I researched joy, I found a teaching from the Bible that advises us to meditate on things that are good: *"Finally, brothers and sisters, whatever is true, whatever is noble, whatever is right, whatever is pure, whatever is lovely, whatever is admirable—if anything is excellent or praiseworthy—think about such things"* (Phil.4:8).

It struck me that this was some of the best advice I ever heard. God was with me during pivotal moments; He was also with me through all my little day-by-day decisions and the meditations of my heart and mind. God was the thread running through this quilt—the fine stitching that gave it strength and held it together. He was connecting all the instances of wonder, gratitude, beauty—*and* sorrow—making possible a full-fledged life of joy.

Thirteen

S haking the rain off my jacket and smoothing my hair, I peered into the bar. The place was nearly empty. I chose a small table near the front. A few minutes later, a man appeared in the doorway. He was a few years older than me, wearing a leather jacket over his compact frame. I approached him asking, "Michael?"

"You must be Geralyn," he said. Michael Walsh looked at me intensely and reached out to shake my hand. He apologized for being late.

"I just got here myself," I replied. "Traffic was a mess, and it wasn't easy to find this place in the pouring rain."

Our meeting spot was a random bar inside a Marriott, halfway between my office near Newark and his hometown in upstate New York. We sat down and began to get acquainted while waiting for the server to come over. I might have felt the usual awkwardness of meeting someone for the first time, but Michael was speaking freely, as if we were old friends. He had the Brooklyn accent you'd expect of a retired NYPD lieutenant, and behind his keen gaze was an easygoing, gregarious nature.

Michael was also in the first car of Amtrak 188. He too was thrown from the train, and he suffered open wounds on his head, face, hands, right ankle, and back. He fractured ten ribs and punctured a lung. There were broken bones throughout his body, a frighteningly fractured vertebra at the base of his neck, as well as a golf-ball-sized hole where his right ankle had been.

He had passed out at the scene of the accident as a cop stood over him, and he awoke in a hospital bed, covered with a white sheet, his mother by his side. He didn't feel any pain. The room's only window looked out into the hallway. As Michael saw family and friends filing past, his first thought was, *I must be dead.* He was certain his family members had come to the morgue to identify his body. As a police officer, he'd seen families in situations like this. Sadness consumed him— his life had been so short; he had so much more to do. He watched a cousin file past—he hadn't seen him in five or six years—followed by a friend and his old partner from the police department. *It was nice of them to come,* he thought. His two teenage daughters were there, too.

Later, his former partner came into the room. "I didn't make it," Michael murmured.

"No, you're okay," his partner responded.

Michael's eyes snapped open wide in disbelief. With some persistence, his friend convinced him that he was actually still alive.

As the pain took hold, it was so severe the doctors offered to put him into a medically induced coma. Michael refused. In retrospect, he might have agreed if they hadn't used the word "coma." It sounded too awful. After such a narrow escape from death, he couldn't let them knock him unconscious. He was overjoyed to be alive, and maybe the pain would serve as a further reminder that he had survived.

Michael's ankle required immediate surgery. To deal with the pain, like me, Michael tried to lie as still as possible. As he was rolled down the hall, every seam in the tile floor sent shock waves through his body. When he arrived in the pre-operating room, the space was filled with other patients, lying in beds partitioned with blue curtains. Michael suddenly felt as if he was merely a list item—an inanimate object on the factory floor. How would anyone know who he was or what surgery he needed? The doctors gathered around his bed, talking about him as if he weren't there or couldn't understand. They were deciding whether it was too late in the day to operate. Michael had no choice in the matter—he was muted and utterly powerless. The doctors decided to go ahead with the surgery.

As he headed into the operating room, Michael was relieved; going into surgery felt like progress. But when he emerged from the fog of anesthesia after the operation, he found himself back in the same busy room. Again, he looked at the rows of patients, all wearing blue hospital gowns and cap. He felt lost, gripped by the sense that he was nobody; his existence was meaningless. He asked for a phone, but he didn't know what number to call or what to tell them about where he was.

When the team of doctors came around, they informed Michael that his ankle was severely infected. He needed another operation to remove the dead tissue. Enduring such an experience again the very next day was unthinkable. But of course, there was no real choice if he wanted to keep his leg. He agreed to the surgery, only to find out that he would need a similar surgical procedure every other day for the next two weeks.

Michael was forced to come up with a way to cope. He asked his buddy to meet him before and after every surgery. His friend sat with him in the pre-operating room, and they talked casually and made jokes with the orderly—nothing profound—but seeing and being seen by a familiar face made all the difference. His ankle was placed in external fixation—the surgeons screwed rods into the bones inside his ankle and then secured them with a metal frame outside. He stayed in the hospital for two months, until it was healed. Thirteen surgeries later, he returned home. He was bedridden for four months, cared for by his mother, girlfriend, and daughters.

When we got up from the table at the end of the evening, Michael and I both took a minute to shake off the stiffness from sitting too long. We joked about our battered bodies and Amtrak having turned us into old people.

As we started to walk away, the television above the drab bar highlighted a special news report. We glanced up at the same time. By strange coincidence, it was about Positive Train Control (PTC). The National Transportation Safety Board (NTSB) had advocated for this safety measure that would automatically slow a speeding train since 1970. In 2008, all US train lines were federally mandated to install PTC, but Congress had repeatedly granted extensions. Even after Amtrak 188, Congress granted another extension, this time to December 2018. The reporter speculated that the railroads would lobby for yet another extension because they were well behind schedule to install and test the equipment. Michael and I shook our heads as we stared at the TV and remarked on the sad certainty that others would no doubt join our club as a result.

On December 18, 2017, a derailment near Olympia, Washington, killed three people and injured dozens. Dramatic photos of a brand-new train hanging off a highway overpass and crushing the cars underneath dominated the news that evening. Transportation officials had pushed to open the refurbished route before the end of the year to collect federal stimulus funds. They were just two months away from having PTC installed and operational.[79] The train had sped into a curve at more than twice the posted speed limit. Another strange coincidence: my sister-in-law, Sheila, a neurosurgeon, was one of the doctors called to the local hospital in Olympia to treat the injured passengers.

By December 2018, only four out of forty-one rail systems had met the 2018 deadline to install PTC.[80] It was only at the end of 2020 that the Federal Railroad Administration announced full implementation of the technology on those trains that were required to do so under the law. In this age of self-driving cars, it is tragic that it took 50 years, 154 preventable accidents, 6,883 injuries, and 305 lives lost before we summoned the political willpower to slow a speeding passenger train.[81]

My conversation with Michael was therapeutic, in part because we had both lived in the same bizarre world. We've gotten together multiple times since that first evening, and our families have met and shared their stories with each other as well. We've laughed over beers at how many parallels there were in our journeys. As Susan Sontag has said, "Everyone who is born holds dual citizenship, in the kingdom of the well and in the kingdom of the sick. Although we all prefer to use only the good passport, sooner or later each of us is obliged, at least for a spell, to identify ourselves as citizens of that other place."[82] Michael was my countryman from the kingdom of the sick.

Recovery does not take a straight course—it loops and weaves. In June 2016, I thought I'd had my last surgery…and then there was another, and another. In November, the doctors removed the metal plates caging my ribs. Long after the bones healed beneath the plates, I continued to feel pain each time I took a breath. It wasn't excruciating pain, but it was constant—as if someone had placed a heavy stone on my chest. The doctors said removing the plates might help and the surgery would break up the extensive scar tissue, which would likely give my chest more freedom to expand and contract when I inhaled and exhaled.

The plates were harder to remove than anticipated. The two ten-inch incisions down my back had to be reopened; the scar tissue was dense, and the screws were stripped. When the surgeon met with me afterward, he looked winded. The way he described the procedure sounded more like a construction job than surgery.

I endured another winter of recovery, pain, and weaning myself off painkillers. For the longest time, I'd heard the same plaintive refrain in my head—like a kid on a long car ride—I kept asking, *Are we there yet?* Could I finally put the accident behind me and go back to my old life?

I'd been pushing myself to get back to work because working meant I was back to being me. Aside from taking brief maternity leaves, I'd worked full-time for my entire adult life. Once I began feeling stronger, however, I realized my mistake. I hadn't worked in more than two years, but I'd been a professional patient, a walking pain barometer, and a physical therapy junkie. I needed a vacation.

There was an opportunity here that I didn't want to miss. I didn't exactly need *more* time. I needed *good* time—a shining visible experience to lay on top of all the difficult memories I'd collected over the previous two years. Furthermore, my boys were growing up—Austin was already visiting prospective colleges—so this was a chance to finish this chapter in my life on a high note. I decided to take each of my kids on a spectacular mother–son trip before I went back to the office.

Jonathan and I still worry about the residual toll the accident has taken on the boys. One day, without thinking much of it, Steven's elementary school teacher began to read a classic math problem to the class: "If train A is traveling seventy miles per hour toward Eastford, 260 miles away…"

Steven broke in, "Let's hope the train isn't Amtrak 188." The kids were puzzled, but the teacher looked stricken.

"I meant a *plane*," she stammered. "A plane! A plane was traveling east…" A concerned teacher–parent phone call followed. Jonathan and I laughed, but there was a serious concern underneath. After something awful has happened, how do you go back to feeling safe again? The pain and fear had subsided and been shallowly covered over with new memories and new confidence in my healing, but both had a disturbing tendency to break through the surface unexpectedly and remind all of us of their latent power. I needed to bury them deeper under good memories. As it turned out, taking trips with the boys was the perfect way for me to reassure them—and myself—that I wasn't so fragile anymore. I could play.

Initially, I'd planned on taking ten-year-old Steven only on a modest vacation. I thought we'd go to the beach for spring break. It would be just the two of us because his brothers were busy with high-school sports camps. When I pitched the idea of a special mother–son trip to him and asked him where he wanted to go, he said matter-of-factly and without hesitation, "Japan." I laughed out loud before quickly covering my mouth.

"What an *interesting* choice…," I stammered. I didn't want to hurt his feelings and reject his idea outright. "Let's think about that," I continued. Steven's face fell just a bit. Even a ten-year-old knows that phrase out of a mother's mouth rarely means yes.

Later that night, I told Jonathan about Steven's crazy idea, explaining how Steven had told me that they were studying World War II in school and he was really interested in the descriptions of Japanese life. I realized I was inspired by my son and his out-of-the-box thinking—inspired enough to check my frequent-flyer-miles account, the benefit of a twenty-year career of international business travel. *Why not?* Another half-hour of typing revealed the availability of two business-class seats on a discount Chinese airline through Beijing…Tokyo Disney beckoned.

Adventuresome Bradley chose Hawaii, and Austin settled on Portugal and Italy after he graduated the following year. With a completely straight face, Austin later expressed his shock and surprise that his girlfriend would be traveling to Portugal at the exact same time. What a coincidence! The memories the boys and I made on each of those trips went a very long way toward rebuilding my confidence in my body, but most importantly, my confidence that I was still me.

Steven and I laughed deliriously at the Japanese toilets that cleaned our nether-regions far more thoroughly than we were accustomed. Bradley dared and taunted me into zip-lining over a 100-foot waterfall on the Big Island of Hawaii (although I got my revenge by signing us up to swim with giant manta rays that looked like they could devour us whole). And Austin and I ate and drank our way across Portugal and Italy. Snapshots of Steven and me wearing silly animal hats in a crowd of Japanese tourists at Tokyo Disney, my pathetic attempt at surfing in Maui while Bradley confidently ripped through the waves, and eating gnarly, salty barnacles with Austin and his girlfriend in a seaside Portuguese village have all gone a long way toward countering the other searing memories that I will never forget.

Neuroscience tells us it is possible to retrain your brain. Sometimes, trying new things can help. For me, getting back on a plane and going places I'd never been, attempting crazy adventure sports, and keeping up with my yoga and meditation have all helped tamp down my anxiety and rebuild my confidence that my body is strong enough.

I have been retraining my brain on other levels, too. Throughout so much of my recovery, I was preoccupied with time. How long would I be in the hospital? How long until I could walk, drive, return to work? How long to get off the pain meds? John Swinton writes in his powerful book *Becoming Friends of Time*, "The time of the clock is linear and unrelentingly progressive, moving forward toward a goal that has no name." Recovery from major trauma is anything but linear and not easily measured with clock time. By contrast, Swinton explains, "God's time is created, gifted, slow, generous, gentle, and designed to enhance the purposes of love. God's time does not seek to burden people with schedules, deadlines, targets, and competition." This strikes me as a much better perspective on time spent in recovery, one that I've only recently come to appreciate.

In a similar vein, in a wonderful book titled *Three Mile an Hour God*, Japanese theologian Kosuke Koyama makes a resonant observation about the way in which God uses time.[83] Koyama points to the fact that the average speed at which a human being walks is three miles per hour. "Jesus walked slowly. *Love has a speed.*" Koyama's point is that real love takes time. Keeping the faith in trauma recovery—whether one's faith is in God, or medical science, or both—sometimes means accepting slowness and being attentive to the things that would otherwise pass us by. "There is a great power in slowness."[84]

Jonathan and I managed to give our love the time it needed as well. So much tension was relieved when Jonathan was able to give up the dual role of caretaker/husband and we both got out of the house again. He began a new job at a local start-up company around the same time I went back to work, and the pattern of our days seemed much more in sync. More significantly, my own irritability and volatility seemed to fade in proportion to the return of my independence and self-confidence, while Jonathan's defensiveness, anger, and self-doubt were sanded down by time and the launch of the new business that he could pour his energies into.

It was more than two years after the accident, autumn 2017, when I went back to work part-time. I still didn't have the stamina to commute every day or sit at a desk for eight hours. My body is creakier and stiffer, and I stretch daily to keep the soreness at bay. I'm still an excellent customer of my local pharmacy—I am vulnerable to infection and take antibiotics at the first sign of a fever—but unless I've had a recent surgery, I buy buckets of Advil rather than prescription painkillers. Sleep remains an issue, and I curse the fact that all the melatonin in the world seems to be no match for the aftermath of a train wreck. My company kindly agreed to put a couch in my office for emergency naps. I don't advertise its purpose, but when colleagues come in and remark on how nice it must be to get a couch, I joke that all they have to do is get hit by a train, and they could get one, too.

I have continued to give talks about my experience at church services. When I spoke at my home church, Flemington Presbyterian, I was touched that many of my friends who aren't religious or who practice different faiths came to hear me. I also visited Mercia's church and a few other Moravian churches she is connected to. Giving the talks feels like a way of pulling pieces of what was good and unbroken from a shattering loss.

One such testimony took place at a large church in Harlem. Surrounded by a sea of unfamiliar faces, I was part of an annual prayer breakfast called "Growing in Faith." I gave testimony alongside two others who had overcome trials—facing cancer and the grieving the loss of a loved one—and was warmed by the chorus of enthusiastic *Amens!* that punctuated my testimony.

The pastor gave a rousing sermon. He told an Old Testament story from Daniel 3:13-30—about boys who were thrown in the fire but came out unscathed because of faith. The reverend kept repeating the refrain, "I don't look like what I've been through. Through faith in God, I have come through the fire." The words touched me on many levels. I don't look like what I have been through. God is stronger than my trials, and I love that it is plain for the world to see.

I joke about how lucky I am not to look like a train wreck. At first glance, no one would guess that I've spent years recovering from catastrophic injuries and have massive scarring around my torso, but the truth is that the crash is a part of me, and not a day goes by that I don't think about it. When people ask whether I mind talking about the accident, I appreciate the sensitivity, but it almost seems like a bizarre question. They might as well ask whether I mind telling them the color of my eyes or my middle name. On the other hand, I don't want my life to be defined by one horrific event, and I don't want it to be the first thing on people's minds at the sight of me. I am *more* than what I've been through.

At the conclusion of that service in Harlem, a slight and stooped elderly Black woman approached me. Mercia introduced us, saying, "Sister Stephanie, meet Sister Geralyn."

I had to lean over to hear her as she reached inside a rumpled plastic bag. Sister Stephanie placed a tallit, a traditional Jewish prayer shawl, in my hands. "This is for you," she said in a soft but steely voice. This tiny Black woman who looked like she might be ninety years old had just come back from Israel. After hearing me speak, she said she knew this tallit was meant for me. As had happened so many times since the accident, I was astounded by the love and generosity of a complete stranger.

Today, one wall of my home office is a kaleidoscope of faith and blessing. On it hangs that white and blue Jewish prayer shawl from Israel via Harlem, the rich burgundy knitted shawl from the local Catholic church near my home in New Jersey, and the vivid purple and aqua quilt made at the Methodist church in Minnesota and finished at Father Dyer Methodist Church in Colorado, as well as photos of family and friends.

These shawls, and quilts, and snapshots, alongside the framed print of a butterfly taking flight, remind me daily of the good in the world. Recovery can be an alienating and lonely experience. Retreating into the loneliness is tempting, but ultimately, I believe you can't get better without the support of others. Standing before my wall of blessings, I'm reminded that I wouldn't be here today if someone hadn't reached out time and again to offer their hand.

Epilogue

I have tried—and probably failed—to ensure that this book doesn't seem self-obsessed or self-congratulatory. The truth is, I am proud. Many people have heard of survivor's guilt; fewer have heard of survivor's pride. It is real. I have no reason to be proud that I survived May 12, 2015, but I do take pride in surviving May 13, 2015, and 2016, and 2017, and that I live joyfully and meaningfully today. As author Reynolds Price noted in his memoir about suffering spinal cancer, "Any survivor of a long ordeal will know that no one makes it on pure good luck or the backs of others; and in the glare of that knowledge, either some degree of self-confidence grows or the mind disintegrates rapidly. Concealing that awareness would only be a form of deceit."[85]

Please trust me that my confidence was hard-won and that I am well aware of my continuing debt to fate and to the doctors, nurses, and my family, friends, and colleagues. But there is also room in the story for pride because survival is hard.

After pushing myself to get back to my former life, I've finally come to realize that my previous life is not my future. I may live in the same house and work at a similar job, but so many things are different. Reluctantly, over time I have come to accept that I will always have a before and an after. The only way forward is to accept this version of normal.

As I was making the final edits on this manuscript, I went to bed one night as usual but awoke in the morning with a strange stomachache. I informed my colleagues at the office that I would be working from home that day. By that evening, I was in an ambulance headed back to the hospital with a "cecal volvulus," a dangerously twisted intestine that had gotten caught on all the scar tissue in my abdomen and was threatening to burst. I would have major surgery the next morning, spend two weeks in the hospital, and take another disability leave of absence from work to recover. After that surgery, nearly four years after the accident, I awoke from anesthesia with my arms outstretched toward the ceiling. For safety.

It may come as a surprise that I continue to ride the train, and I often take the very same route on the Northeast Corridor. As I walk down the aisle, I'm not overwhelmed by flashbacks—I know where I am and what I'm doing—but the memory is stored in my bones. Goose bumps rise on my skin as the train rounds a curve, and those chilling moments before the crash noisily break through the surface of my thoughts. This is the burden of "invisible memory."[86] Healing trauma is not about remembering, it is about learning to dial down the body and mind's reaction.[87] My brain must relearn what is dangerous and what is not. I am trying to teach it. Why do I take the train? Because I don't look like what I've been through. If I give up the intensely rational and practical side of my nature, I will have ceded a part of me to Amtrak—and I won't do that. I joke with my colleagues that I must be one of the safest people to travel by train or plane with—after all, what are the chances?

In *The Pain Chronicles*, Thernstrom quotes Dr. Keltner, an expert on pain, anesthesia, and functional brain imaging and psychiatry, on the ways chronic pain changes a person:

> [C]hronic pain involves a bifurcation. There is a normal state, where you used to live, and you are conditioned to that state. Then you face a debilitating circumstance that lasts for months or years. When you're in that second state, you hold on to expectations of that first life: you mourn that first life—you want it and want it a million times over. But people have to let themselves die and lose their old expectations. If they let it die, they can rise like a phoenix from the ashes and can have a new life.[88]

Dr. Keltner's words describe my journey. Letting go of the need to return to my old self was difficult and painful; especially when the potential and limitations of my new self remained unclear. In hindsight, however, the months of depression and sadness that followed my discharge from the hospital seem like a necessary grieving period.

I think this is a critical element of resilience. When bad things happen, we have to feel the bad. There may be some role for denial and blind optimism at first, but ultimately, progress demands a steely realism. Setbacks and future challenges demand accommodation. Optimism is vital—but it has to be realistic optimism. Denying the sadness or the difficulty of the journey ahead is setting oneself up for failure. I was beyond fortunate to have not only a large loving and patient family, but also a network of friends who listened to my crying, complaints, and general craziness as I came to terms with what had happened and what must be accepted. Social support is vital for real resilience.

I'm also grateful for the stories of fellow survivors. Several months after the accident, when I recovered my ability to focus sufficiently, I began to read every trauma memoir and textbook I could find. I've quoted many of them in these pages. Reading the stories of other survivors helped me understand, face, and forgive my own weaknesses and lessened my sense of isolation.[89]

Just as important as feeling the bad—facing reality and grieving for what is lost—is to work actively to find the good. Every book on trauma recovery that I have read is unanimous on this point. Passive positivity is not enough. I would like to amend Friedrich Nietzsche's oft-quoted line, "That which does not kill us, makes us stronger." That which nearly kills us can make us dramatically weaker in body and spirit. If we work at it, though, it may change our perspective and deepen our self-awareness. It can fine-tune our ability to discern, in a heartbeat, the things that matter and the things that do not. It can inspire us to learn new things, to challenge ourselves in different ways, and to say, "I love you" a bit more often. We must decide how to use our time, our energy, and whatever resources we have. As survivors, we have choices.

I firmly believe that whether it's learning, reading, crafting, traveling, mentoring, or any of a host of different strategies, forcing something positive from a negative situation is key to healing. It doesn't come naturally. It takes deliberate effort. We must find something good in the ashes.

This doesn't mean it is all for the best. It means dealing with the hand we've been dealt and trying to make it better. They say there is no going back. Finding the good is the key to going forward and living with joy. Certainly, the accident was no gift. But my survival and the enforced slowness of two and a half years at home with my family and friends and my own reflections was indeed a gift. My continuing medical vulnerability is not something I welcome, but I try to use it as a reminder to stay centered and grounded in the things that matter. Even in a chaotic house with three teenage boys (and all their friends, who seem to live in our basement), a husband, three dogs, and a not-so-part-time job, I try to remember to be a "friend of time."

Another important way to find something good in the aftermath of trauma is to pay it forward. Helping others is one of the most therapeutic things we can do. There is power in sharing our stories and helping others who are struggling. Writing, teaching, preaching, volunteering, or just listening…there are so many ways to use the survival experience to offer others at least a tiny respite from their suffering or loneliness. In the words of Archbishop Desmond Tutu, "God uses each of us in our own way, and even if you are not the best one, you may be the one who is needed or the one who is there."[90]

Today I try to spend my time reveling in love and gratitude, finding connection with the souls who flutter in and out of my life and, most of all, sharing my heart with those dearest to me. Instead of wondering when life will return to how it was before, I choose to look around and appreciate how good it is. I didn't make it back, but I made it forward.

As my son, Steven, once reminded me with a basket of Nacho Cheese Doritos, "Life is a gift." Cherish and share it. It is grace.

Acknowledgments

This book would have never existed without the bravery and expertise of the front-line responders, medical experts, and the entire care teams that helped me survive the unthinkable. To this day, I regret that I have not been able to find or express my gratitude personally to each and every one. Thank you for what you do, day-in and day-out, and for saving my life.

As I hope is obvious in these pages, I will never be able to repay the kindness and support that I received from my family, friends, and colleagues during my recovery. You stood by me, listened to me, cried with me, and celebrated with me. You truly pulled me through and helped me to rediscover the possibility of a life of joy.

To my three sons, I must express my undying gratitude and respect. You were my North Stars and my reason to keep fighting. Too many days, you were also the only reason I could make myself get out of bed. Today, you are amazingly perceptive, empathetic, driven, and successful young men. You are my heroes, and I could not be prouder of each of you.

I also would never have made it through without my parents' selfless presence and care, as well as my husband Jonathan's no-holds-barred love and advocacy for me as a wife and patient. When I could not advocate for myself, when I needed a jolt of normalcy, you were there. I regret that this stubborn patient often did not express her gratitude at the time, but you three know me best. Thank you for your forgiveness when I snapped at you, for your steadfast support day and night, and for the example you set for our boys of what it means for families to be there for each other, no matter how long it takes.

I am also incredibly lucky to have three siblings and two siblings-in-law who are highly trained and accomplished physicians. From the day I was identified and given my own name rather than Jane Doe, my own kitchen cabinet of experts gathered from every corner of the country—to consult, translate medical-ese, and provide comfort during the crisis. For years now, my siblings and their spouses have listened to my concerns, answered my questions, and tolerated my occasional need to vent. Their patience, advice, and willingness to answer the phone at any hour continue to be invaluable.

My thanks to my family must also include my sister-in-spirit, Mercia Solomon, who has provided wise counsel, spiritual guidance, and rock-solid support for my boys for well over a decade. She put her studies and other personal goals on hold to support us during our darkest days and to keep our boys' lives as normal as possible. God has truly blessed us with her presence in our lives.

I also want to thank those who made my journey back to the professional world possible. Ken Frazier is the most inspiring servant-leader I have ever known. My mentors and supervisors at Merck & Co., Inc., the company who waited for me, who expressed confidence in me, and who accommodated my limitations when I returned, were incredible. As my professional career has evolved, I also thank my current colleagues at Organon & Co.—a new global company dedicated to women's health. Thank you for your faith in me, for your dedication to supporting women re-entering the workforce, and for your support for those with special health challenges. And thank you for demonstrating the power of the private sector to make a positive contribution to our society.

My sole goal in writing this book is that it might support others whose lives are upended in an instant on an ordinary day. Almost nothing positive came out of the wreck of Amtrak 188 on May 12, 2015. But if I can possibly share my newfound understandings with other victims of accidental trauma, then I will have salvaged some tiny sliver of good from an accident that destroyed far too many lives. I cannot undo the past, but I can make some contribution to paying forward the kindnesses, lessons, advice, and perspectives I have been blessed to receive.

Acknowledgments

It is for this reason that 100% of my profits from this book will be donated to non-profit organizations that support trauma professionals and trauma survivors. I am hopeful that anyone reading this book can find some opportunity to learn from my experience, although I am acutely aware that everyone has their own journey and suffers their own challenges. There is no one size fits all recovery plan, but if the only learning from this book is what will *not* work for you, I humbly suggest that is valuable as well.

Finally, I absolutely must thank those who played starring roles in helping me to make sure that this story found its way into print and other media. I am especially grateful to Margaret Wright, who helped me organize and articulate a massive volume of notes, discussions, rough drafts, interviews, medical records, and research. World-renouned photographer Bill Bernstein took all of the wonderful 2021 photos that appear in this book and on the back cover. Thank you to my agents Keely Boeving and Greg Johnson at WordServe Literary for taking a chance on a first-time author with something to say. And special thanks to Robert Walker and Nadia Guy at The Core Media Group, as well as Lydia Rasmussen at Smith Publicity, Inc., for believing in the value of my story to help others.

Such is the power of grace.

My warmest regards,
Geralyn Ritter

Endnotes

1. Bstan-'dzin-rgya-mtsho, Dalai Lama XIV, Desmond Tutu and Douglas Abrams. *The Book of Joy* (New York: Avery, 2016), 212.

2. Bessel van der Kolk. *The Body Keeps the Score: Brain, Mind, and Body in the Healing of Trauma* (New York: Viking, 2014), 3.

3. Jason Laughlin, "A Guy in a Hat: A Brave Man in the Ruins of Amtrak 188," *The Philadelphia Inquirer* (February 1, 2016), https://www.inquirer.com/philly/blogs/in-transit/The-story-of-a-guy-in-a-hat-whose-bravery-shone-in-the-ruins-of-the-Amtrak-derailment.html.

4. Jason Laughlin, "Surviving Car 1," *The Philadelphia Inquirer* (May 8, 2016), http://www.philly.com/philly/news/special_packages/Amtrak_Car_1_survivors_speak_about_their_recovery_a_year_later.html.

5. "Amtrak Passengers: It Was Complete Chaos." CNN (May 13, 2015), http://www.cnn.com/videos/us/2015/05/13/ctn-bts-passengers-amtrak-derailment-chaos.cnn/video/playlists/deadly-amtrak-train-derailment-in-philadelphia/.

6. Caitlin Keating, "Wife of Chef Eli Kulp, Who Was Paralyzed in Deadly Amtrak Derailment, Speaks Out: 'You Can't Prepare Yourself for This.'" *People Magazine* (December 7, 2015),

http://people.com/human-interest/chef-eli-kulp-paralyzed-in-deadly-amtrak-derailment/.

7. Matthew Shaer, "The Wreck of Amtrak 188," *The New York Times Magazine* (January 26, 2016), https://www.nytimes.com/2016/01/31/magazine/the-wreck-of-amtrak-188.html.

8. Roseanne Tabachnik, "First Responders Talk About Amtrak Derailment," NBC 10 Philadelphia (May 15, 2015). http://www.nbcphiladelphia.com/news/local/First-Responders-re-live-talk-Amtrak-Derailment-Philadelphia-303891441.html.

9. Laughlin, "Surviving Car 1," *The Philadelphia Inquirer.*

10. "Derailment of Amtrak Passenger Train 188: Executive Summary," National Transportation Safety Board (May 17, 2016), https://www.ntsb.gov/investigations/AccidentReports/Pages/RAR1602.aspx.

11. Shaer, "The Wreck of Amtrak 188," *The New York Times Magazine.*

12. A study by the US Government Accountability Office found that as many as two-thirds of the twenty-nine commuter railroads in the United States would not have installed PTC by the end of 2018. See "Positive Train Control: Many Commuter Railroads Still Have Significant Additional Implementation Work and Opportunities Exist to Provide Federal Assistance," US Government Accountability Office (March 1, 2018), https://www.gao.gov/products/GAO-18-367T.

13. According to the time stamp on the author's medical records.

14. E. Hermans, M. J. R. Edwards, J. C. Goslings, and J. Biert, "Open Pelvic Fracture: The Killing Fracture?" *Journal of Orthopaedic Surgery & Research* 13, 83 (2018).

15. Christopher Dente, David Feliciano, Grace Rozycki, Amy Wyrzylowski, Jeffrey Nicholas, Jeffrey Salomone, and Walter Ingram, "The Outcome of Open Pelvic Fractures in the Modern Era," *The National Center for Biotechnology Information* 190, no. 6 (2005): 836.

16. V. Giordano, H. A. Koch, S. Gasparini, Serrao de Souza, P. J. Labronici, and N. P. do Amaral, "Open Pelvic Fractures: Review of 30 Cases," *Open Orthopedic Journal* 10 (2016): 772–778.

17. Cameron Palmer, "Major Trauma and the Injury Severity Score," *Annual Proceedings Association of Advanced Automotive Medicine* 51 (2007): 13–29; A. Lavoie, L. Moore, and N. LeSage. "The Injury Severity Score or the New Injury Severity Score for Predicting Intensive Care Unit Admission and Hospital Length of Stay?" *The National Center for Biotechnology Information* 36 (2005): 477–483.

18. Accident ID# DCA15MR010, Document No. 151, filed Mar 9, 2016, "Injury Group Chairman's Factual Report: Attachment A, Occupant Injuries, Amtrak Derailment," *NTSB Docket* (May 2015), https://dms.ntsb.gov/pubdms/search/document.cfm?docID=437528&docketID=58167&mkey=91159.

19. van der Kolk, "Dissociation is the essence of trauma," *The Body Keeps the Score,* 66.

20. Steve Haines, *Trauma Is Really Strange* (London: Singing Dragon, 2016), 20–21.

21. Emily Dickinson and Thomas H. Johnson, ed. *The Complete Poems of Emily Dickinson* (Boston: Little Brown, 1960), 294.

22. Haines, *Pain Is Really Strange,* 5, 15.

23. Melanie Thernstrom, *The Pain Chronicles: Cures, Myths, Mysteries, Prayers, Diaries, Brain Scans, Healing, and the Science of Suffering* (New York: Picador, 2010), 148–149.

24. "Derailment of Amtrak Passenger Train 188," NTSB.

25. E. Azoulay, F. Pochard, N. Kentish-Barnes, S. Chevret, J. Aboab, C. Adrie, D. Annane, G. Bleichner, P. E. Bollaert, M. Darmon, et al., "Risk of Post-traumatic Stress Symptoms in Family Members of Intensive Care Unit Patients," *American Journal of Respiratory and Critical Care Medicine* 171 (2005): 987–94; Choi JiYeon and Judith Tate, "Risk of Post-traumatic Stress Disorder in Family Caregivers of Neuroscience Intensive

Care Unit Patients," *Journal of Emergency and Critical Care Medicine* 2, no. 75 (October 2018).

26. "Caregiver Health," Family Caregiver Alliance, www.caregiver. org/caregiver-health. *Citing* S. Zarit, "Assessment of Family Caregivers: A Research Perspective," from *Assessment: Voices and Views from the Field: Report from a National Consensus Development Conference* (Vol. II) (San Francisco: Family Caregiver Alliance, 2006), 12–37; *see also* K. J. Haines, L. Denehy, E. H. Skinner, S. Werrillow, and S. Berney. "Psychosocial Outcomes in Informal Caregivers of the Critically Ill: A Systematic Review," *Critical Care Medicine* 43 (2015): 1112–1120.

27. L. Rose, F. Muttalib, and N. Adhikari, "Psychological Consequences of Admission to the ICU: Helping Patients and Families," *Journal of the American Medical Association* 322, no. 3 (2019); Ilse van Beusekom, Ferishta Bakhshi-Raiez, Nicolette F. de Keizer, Dave A. Dongelmans, and Marike van der Schaaf, "Reported Burden on Informal Caregivers of ICU Survivors: A Literature Review," *Critical Care* 20, no. 16 (2016).

28. S. Barrow and R. Harrison, "Unsung Heroes Who Put Their Lives at Risk?" *Journal of Public Health* 27, no. 3 (2005): 292–297; W. S. Shaw, T. L. Patterson, S. J. Semple, S. Ho, M. R. Irwin, R. L. Hauger, and I. Grant, "Longitudinal Analysis of Multiple Indicators of Health Decline Among Spousal Caregivers," *Annals of Behavioral Medicine* 19 (1997): 101–109.

29. Sinha Smit, "Trauma-induced Insomnia: A Novel Model for Trauma and Sleep Research," *Sleep Medicine Reviews* 25 (2016): 74–83, http://dx.doi/10.10.16/j.smrv.2015.01.008.

30. V. Spoormaker and P. Montgomery, "Disturbed Sleep in Post-traumatic Stress Disorder: Secondary Symptom or Core Feature?" *Sleep Medicine Reviews* 12, no. 3 (2008): 169–84.

31. Vincent Mysliwiec, Matthew Brock, Jennifer Creamer, Brian O'Reilly, Anne Germain, and Bernard Roth. "Trauma Associated Sleep Disorder: A Parasomnia Induced by Trauma," *Sleep Medicine Reviews* 37 (2018): 94–104,102, 101; Smit, "Trauma-induced Insomnia," *Sleep Medicine Reviews.*

32. Robert Bolash and Michelle Drerup, "How to Beat Insomnia when You Have Chronic Pain," Cleveland Clinic (December 15, 2015), https://health.clevelandclinic.org/managing-insomnia-for-those-with-chronic-pain/.

33. Patrick Finan, Burel Goodin, and Michael Smith, "The Association of Sleep and Pain: An Update and a Path Forward," *The Journal of Pain* 14, no. 12 (2013): 1539–1552.

34. A. Krauss, "The Pain of Sleep Loss: A Brain Characterization in Humans," *Journal of Neuroscience* 39, no. 12 (2019): 2291–2300, https://doi.org/10.1523/JNEUROSCI.2408-18.2018.

35. Paul A. Boakye, Camille Olechowski, Saifudin Rashiq, Michelle J. Verrier, Bradley Kerr, Manisha Witmans, Glen Baker, Anthony Joyce, and Bruce D. Dick, "A Critical Review of Neurobiological Factors Involved in the Interactions Between Chronic Pain, Depression, and Sleep Disruption," *The Clinical Journal of Pain* 32 (2016): 327–336.

36. J. Lewis, "Is Telogen Effluvium Reversible?" *Harvard Health Publishing* (April 23, 2018), https://www.medicalnewstoday.com/articles/321590.php; R. Sinclair, "Diffuse Hair Loss," *International Journal of Dermatology* 38 (1999): 8–18, https://onlinelibrary.wiley.com/doi/pdf/10.1046/j.1365-4362.1999.00003.x; S. Malkud, "Telogen Effluvium: A Review," *Journal of Clinical Diagnostic Research* 9 (2015): 9.

37. van der Kolk, *The Body Keeps the Score*, 178–179.

38. Boakye, et al., "A Critical Review of Neurobiological Factors Involved in the Interactions Between Chronic Pain, Depression, and Sleep Disruption," *Clinical Journal of Pain*, 327–336. *See also* Michael J. Robinson, Sara E. Edwards, Smriti Iyengar, Frank Bymaster, Michael Clark, and Wayne Katon. "Depression and Pain," *Frontiers in Bioscience* 14 (2009): 5031–5051; "Pain, Anxiety and Depression," *Harvard Health Publishing* (June 5, 2019), https://www.health.harvard.edu/mind-and-mood/pain-anxiety-and-depression.

39. Bair, Matthew, Rebecca Robinson, Wayne Katon, Kurt Kroenke. "Depression and Pain Comorbidity: A Literature Review,"

Archives of Internal Medicine 163 (2003): 2433–2445.

40. Judy Foreman, *A Nation in Pain* (Oxford: 2014), 92.

41. Boakye, et al., "A Critical Review of Neurobiological Factors Involved in the Interactions Between Chronic Pain, Depression, and Sleep Disruption," 328.

42. R. Gallagher and S. Cariati, "The Pain–Depression Conundrum: Bridging the Body and Mind" (2002), https://www.medscape.org/viewarticle/441743.

43. Thernstrom, *The Pain Chronicles,* 171.

44. *See* N. J. Annotated Statues §§ 24:21-15.2 and 45:9-22.19 (2017). In 2017, New Jersey enacted one of the most aggressive acts to prevent opioid overdoses. Beginning in May 2017, the state limited the initial prescriptions of opioids to treat acute or chronic pain to a five-day supply. Subsequent prescriptions of Schedule II controlled substances must be limited to a maximum of a thirty-day supply, https://www.njleg.state.nj.us/2016/Bills/A0500/3_R1.PDF. *See also* Marilyn Bulloch, "Opioid Prescribing Limits Across the States," *Pharmacy Times*, February 5, 2019, https://www.pharmacytimes.com/contributor/marilyn-bulloch-pharmd-bcps/2019/02/opioid-prescribing-limits-across-the-states.

45. Travis Rieder, *In Pain: A Bioethicist's Personal Struggle with Opioids* (New York: HarperCollins, 2019), 183.

46. M. Serafini, "The Physicians' Quandary with Opioids: Pain Versus Addiction," *Catalyst* (April 26, 2018), https://catalyst.nejm.org/quandary-opioids-chronic-pain-addiction/.

47. Christine Vestal, "Rapid Opioid Cutoff Is Risky Too, Feds Warn," The Pew Charitable Trusts (May 21, 2019), https://www.pewtrusts.org/en/research-and-analysis/blogs/stateline/2019/05/21/rapid-opioid-cutoff-is-risky-too-feds-warn.

48. Rieder, *In Pain: A Bioethicist's Personal Struggle with Opioids,* 239.

49. "FDA Identifies Harm Reported from Sudden Discontinua-

tion of Opioid Pain Medicines and Requires Label Changes to Guide Prescribers on Gradual, Individualized Tapering," US Food and Drug Administration (April 9, 2019), https://www.fda.gov/drugs/drug-safety-and-availability/fda-identifies-harm-reported-sudden-discontinuation-opioid-pain-medicines-and-requires-label-changes; "CDC Advises Against Misapplication of the *Guideline for Prescribing Opioids for Chronic Pain*," Centers for Disease Control and Prevention (April 24, 2019), https://www.cdc.gov/media/releases/2019/s0424-advises-misapplication-guideline-prescribing-opioids.html. *See also* Claudia Wallis, "Pain Patients Get Relief from War on Opioids," *Scientific American* (April 19, 2019), https://www.scientificamerican.com/article/pain-patients-get-relief-from-war-on-opioids1; Vestal,. "Rapid Opioid Cutoff Is Risky Too, Feds Warn"; "Health Professionals Call on the CDC to Address Misapplication of its Guideline on Opioids for Chronic Pain through Public Clarification and Impact Evaluation," Health Professionals for Patients in Pain (March 6, 2019), https://healthprofessionalsforpatientsinpain.org/the-letter-1; Tamara Mathias, "Mandatory Taper Off Chronic Opioids Might Be Harmful, Experts Say," Psychiatry & Behavioral Health Learning Network (January 2, 2019), https://www.psychcongress.com/news/mandatory-taper-chronic-opioids-might-be-harmful-experts-say; "CDC Guideline for Prescribing Opioids for Chronic Pain," *Centers for Disease Control and Prevention* 65, no. 1 (March 18, 2016): 1–49, https://www.cdc.gov/mmwr/volumes/65/rr/rr6501e1.htm; Elizabeth Llorente, "As Doctors Taper or End Opioid Prescriptions, Many Patients Driven to Despair, Suicide," Fox News (December 10, 2019), https://www.foxnews.com/health/as-opioids-become-taboo-doctors-taper-down-or-abandon-pain-patients-driving-many-to-suicide.

50. The CDC Guideline states, "Clinicians should use caution when prescribing opioids at any dosage, should carefully reassess evidence of individual benefits and risks when increasing dosage to =50 morphine milligram equivalents (MME)/day, and should avoid increasing dosage to =90 MME/day or

carefully justify a decision to titrate dosage to =90 MME/day," D. Dowell, T. M. Haegerich, and R. Chou. "Guideline for Prescribing Opioids for Chronic Pain—United States, 2016," *Centers for Disease Control and Prevention* 65, no. RR-1 (2016): 1–49, http://dx.doi.org/10.15585/mmwr.rr6501e1.

51. To convert opioid dosages to MMEs, see "Calculating Total Daily Dose of Opioids for Safer Dosage," Centers for Disease Control and Prevention, https://www.cdc.gov/drugoverdose/pdf/calculating_total_daily_dose-a.pdf.

52. Laurence Gonzales, *Surviving Survival: The Art and Science of Resilience* (New York: Norton, 2012), 60.

53. "Highlights of Prescribing Information: Lyrica," US Food and Drug Administration, https://www.accessdata.fda.gov/drug-satfda_docs/label/2018/021446s035,022488s013lbl.pdf.

54. Sadiq Naveed, "Pregabalin-Associated Discontinuation Symptoms: A Case Report," *Cureus* 10, no. 10 (2018): e3425.

55. Michael J. Walsh, "A State-by-State Analysis of Laws Dealing with Driving Under the Influence of Drugs," National Highway Transportation Safety Administration (December 2009), https://www.ems.gov/pdf/811236.pdf. *See also* New Jersey Statutes Annotated Section 39: 4–50.

56. "Highlights of Prescribing Information: OxyContin," US Food and Drug Administration (October 2019), https://www.fda.gov/media/131026/download.

57. According to the CDC guideline for prescribing opioids for chronic pain, physical dependence means "Adaptation to a drug that produces symptoms of withdrawal when the drug is stopped," T. M. Haegerich and R. Chou, "Guideline for Prescribing Opioids for Chronic Pain—United States, 2016," Centers for Disease Control and Prevention 65, no. RR-1 (2016): 1–49, http://dx.doi.org/10.15585/mmwr.rr6501e1. The National Institute on Drug Abuse describes the difference between physical dependence and addiction as follows: "Addiction—or compulsive drug use despite harmful consequences—is characterized by an inability to stop using a drug; failure

to meet work, social, or family obligations; and, sometimes (depending on the drug), tolerance and withdrawal. The latter reflect physical dependence in which the body adapts to the drug, requiring more of it to achieve a certain effect (tolerance) and eliciting drug-specific physical or mental symptoms if drug use is abruptly ceased (withdrawal). Physical dependence can happen with the chronic use of many drugs—including many prescription drugs, even if taken as instructed. Thus, physical dependence in and of itself does not constitute addiction, but it often accompanies addiction. This distinction can be difficult to discern, particularly with prescribed pain medications, for which the need for increasing dosages can represent tolerance or a worsening underlying problem, as opposed to the beginning of abuse or addiction.

58. "Opioid Addiction," US National Library of Medicine (October 15, 2019), https://ghr.nlm.nih.gov/condition/opioid-addiction#definition.

59. "The Neurobiology of Drug Addiction," National Institute on Drug Abuse (January 2007), https://www.drugabuse.gov/publications/teaching-packets/neurobiology-drug-addiction/section-iii-action-heroin-morphine/8-definition-dependence; "Drugs, Brains, and Behavior: The Science of Addiction," National Institute on Drug Abuse (July 2018), https://www.drugabuse.gov/publications/drugs-brains-behavior-science-addiction.

60. "Opioid Addiction: Causes," US National Library of Medicine (October 15, 2019), https://ghr.nlm.nih.gov/condition/opioid-addiction#genes.

61. John Swinton, *Becoming Friends of Time: Disability, Timefullness, and Gentle Discipleship.* (Waco: Baylor University Press, 2016), 76.

62. Travis Rieder, "Doctors Prescribed Me Pain Meds but Couldn't Get Me Off Them," *The Washington Post* (January 22, 2017), https://www.washingtonpost.com/national/health-science/doctors-prescribed-me-pain-meds-but-offered-no-help-when-i-got-hooked/2017/01/20/d68a0f42-c171-11e6-9578-

0054287507db_story.html?noredirect=on&utm_term=.
dbc306ea1fd3.

63. Kate Bowler, "Interview with John Swinton," *The Speed of Love*, podcast audio, 2019, https://katebowler.com/podcasts/john-swinton-the-speed-of-love/.

64. Kate Bowler, *Everything Happens for a Reason: And Other Lies I've Loved* (New York: Random House, 2018), xiv–xvi.

65. Reynolds Price, *A Whole New Life* (New York: Scribner, 1982), 77.

66. "Body Scan Mindfulness Exercise of Pain," *Harvard Health Publishing*, https://www.health.harvard.edu/pain/body-scan-for-pain.

67. van der Kolk, *The Body Keeps the Score*, 72.

68. P. Levine, *Waking the Tiger: Healing Trauma* (Berkeley: North Atlantic Books, 1997), 137.

69. David Emerson, *Trauma-Sensitive Yoga in Therapy* (New York: Norton, 2015), 22–24.

70. Melissa Colbert, ed. *Pain Relief Without Drugs or Surgery* (Boston: Harvard Health Publishing, 2019), 17.

71. Ibid., 8, 17.

72. van der Kolk, *The Body Keeps the Score*, 63.

73. David Emerson and Elizabeth Hopper, *Overcoming Trauma through Yoga* (Berkeley: North Atlantic Books, 2011), 24.

74. Gonzales, *Surviving Survival,* 119.

75. M. U. Wener, L. Soholm, P. Rotboll-Nielsen, and H. Kehlet, "Does an Acute Pain Service Improve Postoperative Outcome?" *Anesthia Analgesia* 95 (2002): 1361–1372. The study found that the incidence of serious postoperative respiratory depression requiring the administration of naloxone was 0–2.2 percent, depending on the opioid used and method of administration. More recent studies suggest that "opioid-related adverse drug events" among surgical patients are more

common and as high as 13.6 percent when including nonse-
rious reactions such as itchy skin. Shahid Shafi, Ashley Col-
linsworth, Laurel Copeland, Gerald Ogola, Taoran Qiu, Maria
Kouznetsova, I-Chia Liao, Natalie Mears, George Wan, and
Andrew Lasica, "Association of Opioid-Related Adverse Drug
Events with Clinical and Cost Outcomes Among Surgical
Patients in a Large Integrated Health Care Delivery System,"
JAMA Surgery 153, no. 8 (2018): 757–763.

76. In 2018, recognizing the absence of guidelines, evidence, and
medical consensus on the prescribing of opioids in hospitalized
patients with acute noncancer pain, the Society of Hospital
Medicine sought to develop a consensus statement to guide the
practice. Shoshana Herzig, Susan Calcaterra, Hilary Mosher,
Matthew Ronan, Nicole Van Groningen, Lili Shek, Anthony
Loffredo, Michelle Keller, Anupam Jena, and Teryl Nuckols,
"Safe Opioid Prescribing for Acute Noncancer Pain in Hospitalized Adults," *Journal of Hospital Medicine* 13, no. 4 (April
2018).

77. Satya Krishna Ramachandran, Naeem Haider, Kelly Saran,
Michael Mathis, Joyce Kim, Michelle Morris, and Michael
O'Reilly, "Life-Threatening Critical Respiratory Events: A Ret-
rospective Study of Postoperative Patients Found Unresponsive
During Analgesic Therapy," *Journal of Clinical Anesthesia* 23
(2011): 207–213.

78. The condition is characterized by a paradoxical response
whereby a patient receiving opioids for the treatment of
pain could actually become more sensitive to certain painful
stimuli. "A Comprehensive Review of Opioid-Induced Hyperalgesia," *The National Center for Biotechnology Information*
14, no. 2 (March–April 2011), https://www.ncbi.nlm.nih.gov/
pubmed/21412369.

79. Mike Baker, Christine Willmsen, and Mike Lindblom, "Train
Derailment Near Olympia: Officials Pushed 'Aggressive'
Timeline Before Safety Technology Was Ready," *The Seattle
Times* (December 19, 2017), https://www.seattletimes.com/se-
attle-news/train-derailment-near-olympia-officials-pushed-ag-

gressive-timeline-before-safety-technology-was-ready/.

80. Gregory Wallace, "Most US Rail Systems Miss Safety Deadline," CNN, January 1, 2019, https://www.cnn.com/2019/01/01/politics/positive-train-control-deadline/index.html.

81. Federal Railroad Administration, *Federal Railroad Administration Announces Landmark Achievement with Full Implementation of Positive Train Control* (December 29, 2020); National Transportation Safety Board, "NTSB Closes 3 Key Positive Train Control Safety Recommendations," January 14, 2021.

82. Susan Sontag, *Illness as Metaphor* (New York: Farrar, Straus and Giroux, 1978), 3.

83. Kosuke Koyama, *Three Mile an Hour God* (Norwich: SCM Press, 2015), 7.

84. Swinton, *Becoming Friends of Time*, 69.

85. Price, *A Whole New Life*, ix.

86. Gonzales, *Surviving Survival*, 20.

87. Haines, *Trauma Is Really Strange*, 32.

88. Thernstrom, *The Pain Chronicles*, 229–230.

89. van der Kolk, *The Body Keeps the Score*, 239.

90. Bstan-'dzin-rgya-mtsho, Dalai Lama XIV, Tutu and Abrams, *The Book of Joy: Lasting Happiness in a Changing World*, 211.